This is the O.P. treatment for schizophrenia and reflects a certain type of theory to the schizophrenic population

MODERN PSYCHOANALYSIS OF
THE SCHIZOPHRENIC PATIENT

MODERN PSYCHOANALYSIS OF THE SCHIZOPHRENIC PATIENT
Theory of the Technique
Second Edition

Hyman Spotnitz, M.D., Med. Sc.D.

 **HUMAN SCIENCES PRESS,INC**.
72 FIFTH AVENUE
NEW YORK, N.Y. 10011

Printed in the United States of America
987654321

Library of Congress Cataloging in Publication Data

Spotnitz, Hyman
Modern psychoanalysis of the schizophrenic patient.
(second edition)
Bibliography: p. 308
Includes index.
1. Schizophrenia—Treatment. 2. Psychoanalysis.
I. Title. [DNLM: 1. Psychoanalytic Therapy.
2. Schizophrenia—therapy. WM 460 S765m]
RC514.S72   1985   616.89′8206   85-8257
ISBN 0-89885-250-1

CONTENTS

ACKNOWLEDGMENTS

Grateful acknowledgment is made for permission to use material contained herein to the Hogarth Press, London, publisher of The Standard Edition of the Complete Psychological Works of Sigmund Freud; *to International Universities Press, Inc., publisher of "The Widening Scope of Indications for Psychoanalysis" by Leo Stone in the* Journal of the American Psychoanalytic Association, Volume II; *and to Imago Publishing Co. Ltd., Basic Books, Inc., publishers of Paul Federn's* Ego Psychology and the Psychoses. *Appropriate bibliographic reference is to be found in the text.*

PREFACE
to the Second Edition

Since the appearance of the first edition of this book, advances in the field of modern psychoanalysis have made the issuance of this updated and expanded edition imperative. It is indeed overdue.

The introduction of the specific operational theory presented in this book (modern psychoanalysis) has opened up new perspectives for the treatment of the preoedipal disorders. In 1971 a training and research center organized to prepare candidates for the practice of modern psychoanalysis was opened in New York City. Chartered by the Board of Regents, University of the State of New York, to award certificates in psychoanalysis, the Center for Modern Psychoanalytic Studies has been followed by similar institutes established in various parts of the country. These training centers now exist in Boston, Philadelphia, in Colorado, and southeast Florida, as well as four centers that have been established in New York City and neighboring counties.

The "parent" Center for Modern Psychoanalytic Studies began publication of the scientific journal *Modern Psychoanalysis* in 1976. Its founders and faculty are making important contributions to the extension of psychoanalytic treatment to the full range of emotional disorders. For studies completed at the Center, a growing number of its graduates are being granted academic credit in the graduate-degree programs of universities in various parts of the country.

To the hundreds of students who have completed, or are now in the course of basic training at the modern psychoanalytic training institutes, the first edition of this book was required reading. The updating of the book was undertaken to meet the needs of the students now attending these institutes as well as their graduates as they embark on practice. The book is also addressed primarily to practitioners affiliated with other schools of analytic psychotherapy who work with prepsychotic and postpsychotic schizophrenic patients in mental health clinics and private practice.

My own recent experience and that of colleagues who apply the modern psychoanalytic approach in individual or group psychotherapy have led to little change in the theory of technique and working hypothesis presented in the first edition. The conceptualizations introduced there are maintained, and some are formulated in a more detailed way in this edition. An important example is the concept of narcissistic countertransference, which was not systematically elaborated until the 1970s.

In the course of that decade the clinical literature, focused increasingly on the borderline and narcissistic disorders, suggested that practitioners of the classical school have been confirming modern psychoanalytic theory. Contributors to the psychoanalytic journals who report on their work with psychotic and borderline patients agree that their primary problem is destructive action, which they defend themselves against by developing these states. Recently, too, a prominent spokesman for the classical school confirmed the teaching of modern psychoanalysis that the traditional approach "was not designed for treatment of developmental arrest, deficit, or deviation" (Harold P. Blum, 1982, p. 976).

The major new development in the field over the last 15 years has been the understanding of the emotional responsiveness of the analyst as an essential instrument in the psychological reversibility of the severe psychiatric disorders. The increasing success of the modern psychoanalytic approach, which is based on that recognition, suggests that we are on the road to a new psychoanalytic science. We are in the process of learning how to apply the specific interventions that will facilitate the therapeutic handling of the hereditary, constitutional, and environmental factors that make their presence felt in the analytic relationship and are being recognized in modern neuroscience.

The completion of this book would not have been possible without the loving cooperation of my wife, Dorothy Harten Spotnitz.

I am pleased to acknowledge the editorial collaboration of Julia Older Bazer in the preparation of the second edition.

PREFACE
to the First Edition

As a medical student in the early 1930s, I became interested in understanding schizophrenia. It was one of the important research areas at that time, and the acceptance of a victim of this disorder for psychoanalytic therapy often reflected no more than the hope of the practitioner that an "unknown something might change him to a normal being."[1] Several years later, when I entered the practice of psychiatry, the prevailing attitude was still one of therapeutic futility.

Consequently, I was surprised to discover that the schizophrenic patients I worked with responded to psychoanalytic understanding. My own experience contradicted the notion that they could not be helped through psychological means, but I was uncertain how best to go about it. There was no general theory of the application of the psychoanalytic method to schizophrenic patients, and my efforts to apply it in such cases were discouraged by the outstanding analysts with whom I trained. While conducting the treatment on a research basis, I tried to

---

[1] A.A. Brill (1929) in the *American Journal of Psychiatry.*

find out precisely why the application of Freud's concepts led to disappointment.

In attempting to account for my successful results and—even more important—my failures, I systematically reviewed the various obstacles reported in the literature and the solutions arrived at in my own cases. Eventually, it became evident that, with due allowance for the complexities of the transference phenomena in a case of schizophrenia and the role of aggression, the whole treatment process could be formulated within the framework of the basic psychoanalytic method.

The operational principles I developed have been taught to others, and applied by former students and colleagues in the office treatment of psychotic and borderline conditions. Some of the principles have been the subject of brief published reports by myself and other psychoanalytically trained practitioners, and the clinical implications of the theory were explored by me in a series of lectures (unpublished) at the Stuyvesant Polyclinic, New York, in 1962. But the theory, as it has been systematized, is presented here for the first time.

Written for both the student-analyst and the clinician richly experienced in the application of the general principles of the psychoanalytic method, the book is designed to serve as a theoretical guide to the management of ambulatory cases of schizophrenia and to facilitate understanding of their outcome. Clinical illustrations of some formulations are provided but the book is not intended as a manual of practice. My hope is that it will contribute to the development of a systematic approach to the therapy of the preoedipal disorders and to the establishment of a sound theoretical basis for extensions of the basic model technique.

A specific working hypothesis for the treatment of the schizophrenic patient is presented. He is viewed in a perspective that contributes to the resolution of the illness through fundamental change and maturation of the personality. The nuclear problem is regarded as one that can be mastered psychologically with the aid of specific emotional responses from the psychoanalyst. How these responses are generated and when and how to provide them are described. The relation between emotional interchanges and therapeutic progress is explained.

Teachers and colleagues and, particularly, my patients and students have given invaluable assistance in the development of the theory. The ideas I present have been discussed with many patients. Time and again, they have enhanced my understanding of the emotional factors that facilitated their therapeutic progress and recovery.

My wife, Miriam Berkman Spotnitz, has provided the inspiration, interest, and cooperation that made the work described in this book possible. Our sons, Dr. Henry M., Alan J., and William D., have furnished much needed criticism.

Julia Older Bazer, through her editorial collaboration, has contributed in many ways to this book.

Hyman Spotnitz
New York City

Chapter 1

INTRODUCTION

> *Errors are the greatest obstacle to the progress of science; to correct such errors is of more practical value than to achieve new knowledge.*
>
> —Eugen Bleuler (1950, p. 280)

The broad general principles for reversing the schizophrenic reaction were discovered by Freud. It is widely acknowledged that his "formulations have enabled subsequent theorists and therapists to develop a more comprehensive understanding of the etiology and treatment of this illness" (Day & Semrad, 1978, p. 200). Nevertheless, scientific errors of historic significance obscured Freud's discovery, and his early clinical experience convinced him, as he stated in 1913, that the disorder was psychologically irreversible.[1]

Rejection of the schizophrenic individual as an unsuitable

---

[1]Apparently Freud did not adhere indefinitely to this view. See the statement by A. A. Brill, cited later in this chapter, from a report published after Freud's death.

candidate for psychoanalysis reflects the continuing influence of Freud's warning (1913) that the analyst who undertakes to treat such a case "has committed a practical error; he has been responsible for wasted expenditure and has discredited his method of treatment. He cannot fulfill his promise of cure" (p. 121).

Freud did not equate "cure" with the disappearance of the pathological signs and obvious symptoms of the illness—in other words, with the attainment of "normality" in terms of mental functioning and behavior (Joseph, 1982). Nor did he equate "cure" with teaching the patient to adjust to it, or even with effecting a marked degree of improvement. Eradication of the cause of the illness, thereby producing basic change in the dynamics of the personality, was what he meant by the word. The mental life of a person who cooperates successfully with the rules and requirements of psychoanalysis is "permanently changed, is raised to a high level of development and remains protected against fresh possibilities of falling ill," according to the founder of psychoanalysis (1917, p. 451). That was the promise he withheld from schizophrenic individuals.

The belief that they were incurable—now attributed by many to the feeling of incurability they characteristically induce in the analyst—was shared by Eugen Bleuler, the Swiss psychiatrist who early in the century applied psychoanalytic understanding in studying these patients at the Burghölzli hospital near Zurich. His general approach to the condition was fundamentally different from that of Emil Kraepelin, who in 1896 attributed it to deterioration of the brain or some other irreversible organic process. In classifying it as "dementia praecox," a single disease entity, Kraepelin made use of the term, *démence précoce*, introduced in 1852–1853 in a treatise by Benedict A. Morel, a French psychiatrist, to categorize a degenerative mental disease whose victims were usually young people (Cancro, 1982a). In 1911 Bleuler conceptualized a "group" of disorders, highly variable in course and severity but all characterized by a "specific type of alteration of thinking, feeling, and relation to the external world which appears nowhere else in this particular fashion" (Bleuler, 1950, p. 9). Since this alteration betrayed a "split" in psychic function, he coined the name "schizophrenia" from the Greek *schizein* (to split) and *phren* (mind) to designate these related disorders. Despite evidence of their modifiability through psychological and other therapies employed at Burghölzli, Bleuler believed that schizophrenia did not permit a full *restitutio ad integrum*. "We do not speak of cure," he reported, "but of far-reaching improvements" (p. 9).

The voluminous literature on the illness, which includes an estimated 100,000 papers published between 1912 and 1978 (M. Bleuler, 1979), indicates that the search for one specific etiology has thus far been inconclusive. The disorder appears to be overdetermined. In the words of Roy R. Grinker, Sr. (1969), "The problems associated with schizophrenia demonstrate clearly that there is no single cause and that multiple factors enter into every aspect of cause, course, and outcome" (p. 22). Manfred Bleuler (1979) has stated that there is now every reason to be certain that hereditary and environmental influences are interwoven, in an individual way, in the schizophrenic psychoses.

As far as we know, no one is born schizophrenic; the hereditary factor appears to be a biologically inherited disposition for the disorder—a *predisposition* of some importance, combined with experiential and constitutional factors. Cases that appear to have been primarily determined by life experience are regarded as the easiest to reverse. Regardless of etiology, however, there is no evidence that the condition is not completely reversible. The view that it might be a functional disease of the nervous system has been supported by the many spontaneous remissions reported, as well as by the rapid reversibility of psychotic states associated with severe cases of the illness through shock therapy, especially insulin shock, and—since midcentury—through the antipsychotic drugs.

The therapeutic negativism that surrounded the diagnosis at the beginning of the century has somewhat waned from generation to generation. In 1912, for example, M. Culpin, a British analyst, reported that he had cured a few cases in which the diagnosis seemed merely probable. Revisions made by Karl Menninger in the third edition of *The Human Mind* (1945) reflect the slowly rising curve of optimism. Less apologetically than in the first edition, published 15 years earlier, Menninger points out: "But while it is true that most cases of schizophrenia do not recover, it is also true that many cases *do* recover. . . . I am glad to be able to say that it is now well recognized that this dread disease is by no means hopeless, granted the availability of prompt and skillful treatment" (p. 103).

A judgment representative of the present decade is that of Robert Cancro, Professor and Chairman of the Department of Psychiatry, New York University Medical Center. In a recent article on the current role of psychotherapy in the treatment of chronic schizophrenic patients, Dr. Cancro stated (1983):

> Clinical experience has repeatedly shown that some individuals who are called schizophrenic can develop a close relationship with another person and that relationship appears to make a difference in the patient's subsequent adjustment. . . . Individual psychotherapy can only be evaluated as to its effectiveness within the context of an appropriate specification of the goals of the intervention. By and large these goals involve intrapsychic and interpersonal change. The change in the patient's personality ideally would lead to better adaptation and, therefore, to diminished risk for future relapse. (p. 496)

This and similar judgments that might be cited do not mean that practitioners who work with these patients do not, at one time or another in the relationship, begin to harbor feelings of hopelessness about the outcome. Those transient feelings are elements of the narcissistic countertransference, the often confusing and disagreeable psychotic or near-psychotic emotional state that the schizophrenic patient induces in the therapist. As more and more therapists are able to tolerate the induced feelings and utilize them as a source of therapeutic leverage, the prognosis of the schizophrenic patient will steadily brighten. The use of the analyst's emotions as a propulsive force in resolving preoedipal resistance patterns opens up a relatively unexplored area.

The influence of the analytic practitioner's personal qualities and technical skills on the outcome of treatment is occasionally cited in the literature. The need for a "caring" therapist used to be stressed or implicitly illustrated in the reports of such pioneer figures in the field as Federn, Schwing, and Sechehaye. A current notion is that "gifted" therapists are able to produce cures.

Also contributing to the note of cautious optimism was the gradual outmoding of the label "dementia praecox." For the countless practitioners to whom it conveyed a "meaning of disaster," that term served to prejudice the therapy (Will, 1965, p. 32). After lingering for some time in such formulations as "dementia praecox (schizophrenia)," Kraepelin's label was superseded by Adolf Meyer's more dynamic term, "schizophrenic reaction." The first edition of the American Psychiatric Association's *Diagnostic and Statistical Manual of Mental Disorders* (DSM-I, 1952) classifies nine types of schizophrenic reactions among "disorders of psychogenic origin without clearly defined physical cause or structural change in the brain" (p. 5). (Subsequent changes in terminology are discussed in the section on diagnosis.)

In recent decades, the disorder has been tackled in various ways. Somatic and psychological methods of treatment have been applied, singly or in combination in individual cases, and often supplemented by environmental manipulation. The general orientation of the therapist and his preconception of the problem have probably influenced his approach as much as practical considerations and local conditions. Practitioners who accept the notion that the patient suffers from a basic personality defect that cannot be corrected try to reduce its handicapping effects through some remedy or by teaching him to "live with it" (Hoffer & Osmond, 1966). At the other extreme are those who, in the belief that the nuclear defect can be eliminated, explore the method which they consider most likely to accomplish this aim.

As a resident psychiatrist and research worker at the New York State Psychiatric Institute from 1938 to 1950, I studied the range of therapies employed at that time with hospitalized schizophrenics. Insulin shock was widely used. I saw many patients suddenly recover from an acute psychotic episode after undergoing this treatment. Even more impressive was their response to nondamaging injections of insulin. Given daily in subcoma doses, it kept them free of psychotic manifestations (Polatin & Spotnitz, 1943).

But the succession of chemical and physical methods employed to restore these people quickly to the world of reality, or to "tranquilize" them sufficiently to keep them there, has failed to enhance our knowledge of the schizophrenic process. Nor do these methods offer the possibility of effecting lasting structural changes in the personality.

I also investigated the various systems of psychological treatment employed in these cases. The psychoanalytic theory of personality development gave me more understanding of severely disturbed people than other approaches. The use of whatever psychoanalytic knowledge I had acquired inspired the greatest hope of sharing that understanding with them in a therapeutic way.

Training in the psychoanalytic method made it possible for me to test out the responsiveness of schizophrenic patients to the customary analytic procedures and ascertain what modifications were indicated to work most effectively with them (Spotnitz, 1976a; Spotnitz & Nagelberg, 1960). Subsequent clinical experience has strengthened my impression that Freud's views about the inaccessibility of these patients to psychological influence led to an unjustifiable constriction of the whole field of psychoanalytic therapy.

A reversal of this trend has been under way since midcentury. Over the last 2 decades, psychoanalytically trained psychotherapists, as well as practitioners of other schools of psychotherapy, have devoted themselves fruitfully to the treatment of the severe emotional disturbances. Their pioneering efforts, in addition to bringing eventual recognition to the emotions of the therapist as an important limiting factor in the psychotherapy of the schizophrenic patient, have brought to light errors in the early application of the psychoanalytic method to such patients.

FREUD'S EARLY IMPRESSIONS

The obstacles that Freud encountered in treating schizophrenics led him to conclusions that are now refutable on a theoretical basis. The weight of clinical evidence in recent decades enables one to appreciate the reservations he expressed and to reconcile them with our present understanding.

The theory of psychoanalytic technique pivots on the investigation of transference and resistance. Freud discussed these conceptual guides in his *Introductory Lectures*, from which the brief quotations that follow are drawn (1917, 26th–28th lectures). Because of the tendency of a patient to transfer emotions derived from the crucial relationships of early life to the analyst, the treatment partnership serves as a matrix in which "new editions of the old conflicts" (p. 454) can be produced, investigated, and resolved. Transference therefore provides the necessary "battlefield on which all the mutually struggling forces should meet one another" (p. 454). Resistance embraces the various obstacles to the analytic process, chief among them being the patient's inner resistance to the basic rule of free association. The essential achievement of the treatment is to raise the mental life of the patient to a "high level of development" through the "overcoming" of these resistances (p. 451). In that task, Freud relied primarily on the technique of interpretation, through which the meaning of the patient's communications were explained to him.

Freud regarded this method of treatment as a causal therapy for the various forms of psychoneurosis, such as hysterias and compulsions. These were designated as "transference neuroses" because patients with these relatively mild conditions reacted to the classical analytic situation by developing a transference neurosis, which made them responsive to psychological influence.

On the other hand, it appeared to Freud that persons with the more severe disorders—the "narcissistic neuroses," including schizophrenia—"have no capacity for transference or only insufficient residues of it" (p. 447). The working concepts of transference and resistance could not be profitably applied in their cases, he reported, because "they manifest no transference" (p. 447) and "the resistance is unconquerable" (p. 423).

There is now general agreement that Freud's early impressions were incorrect,[2] but they are easy to explain in the same frame of reference. The psychoanalytic method as Freud conceptualized and applied it was effective with patients capable of developing transference to the analyst as a separate object. What he had in mind when he wrote of transference was the only kind recognized at the time—*object* transference. He believed that the stone wall of narcissism doomed a case to failure because such resistance could not be resolved through one mode of communication.

Amend the statements just quoted to read, "they manifest insufficient object transference" and "their resistance does not yield to the technique of interpretation" and most analytic psychotherapists who treat pathologically narcissistic patients today would agree with him.

In other words, on the basis of successful clinical experience with patients on a higher level of emotional development, Freud postulated the need for a *certain type* of transference and recommended a *specific technique* for overcoming resistance. This is what led him astray.

All schizophrenic individuals are capable of some degree of object transference, but to develop it sufficiently to make them responsive to interpretation, in the technical sense of the word, is the crucial problem in their treatment. Implicated in the illness are pre-feelings or early ego states experienced in the first months of life before the infant differentiates self from non-self (Mahler, Pine, & Bergman, 1975). In some cases these undifferentiated feelings foreclose the transfer of feelings that developed for significant objects a few years later; one then

[2]According to A. A. Brill, Freud initially advised against analysis in such cases, reasoning that "as the dementia praecox process was in itself a sort of adjustment, albeit morbid, if it were destroyed the patient would be left without any support whatever. But when I discussed this problem with him later, I was pleased to learn that he no longer entertained this view. On the contrary, he felt that in time we would develop a psychoanalytic therapy for the psychoses" (1944, p. 97).

observes what Freud (1917) referred to as the "wall which brings us to a stop" (p. 423). The phenomenon is now referred to as "narcissistic" transference (also as "preoedipal" or "selfobject" transference). Freud and his contemporaries did not recognize the presence of narcissistic transference as such, and they did not know how to utilize it for therapeutic purposes.

Since their day it has been repeatedly demonstrated that the narcissistic transference is therapeutically useful. To facilitate its development, the analyst treating a patient in the narcissistic state functions as a narcissistic or ego-syntonic object; narcissistic transference unfolds and is eventually superseded by the usual object transference. And the patterns of resistance that cannot safely be overcome through objective interpretation can be resolved through other modes of communication. Furthermore, if these communications are oriented to the ultimate goal of helping the patient to emotional maturity, the operational concepts of transference and resistance control the entire process of clearing away the obstacles the patient encounters each step of the way.

These discoveries are helping to dispel the notion that a person afflicted with schizophrenia is inaccessible to analytic cure. We now recognize and know how to exploit narcissistic transference phenomena to revive symbolically very early clusters of experience implicated in the illness and to exercise a more powerful influence. Therefore there is no justification for excluding the relevant working hypotheses from the theory of psychoanalytic technique. Now that we recognize, too, that resistance may be a definite and primitive form of communication—clearly and consistently so, in my experience—the theory of the treatment can be based on the other clinical cornerstone of the psychoanalytic method.

Resistance is frequently conceptualized as a force in opposition to making the unconscious conscious. In the effective treatment of a person suffering from schizophrenia, one encounters obstacles that are usually more formidable; indeed, the patient may be conscious of the intrapsychic interferences and demonstrate a more compelling need for emotional unlearning and new learning than for insight. Broadened to cover whatever obstacles to personality growth become manifest in the treatment relationship, the concept of resistance provides a clearer guide to the therapeutic task in each case.

Interpretation alone does not resolve these various forms of resistance. The combined influence of many modes of communication, nonverbal as well as verbal, is required to produce psychological change and understanding. As Anna Freud (1926) has pointed out, "In the technique of the analysis of adults, we find *vestiges* of all the expedients which prove necessary with children. The extent to which we use them will depend upon how far the adult patient with whom we are dealing is still an immature and dependent being, approximating in this respect to a child" (p. 17). A recodification of permissible responses to resistance liberates the practitioner from undue reliance on the one type of verbal communication specified in the basic theory of the technique. Considerable progress has been made in that area; more and more types of interventions that are effective with the schizophrenic patient are being reported in the literature (e.g. Marshall, 1982).

Of particular importance in the psychoanalytic treatment of schizophrenic patients is the expansion of the concept of countertransference to include the therapeutically useful aspects of the patient's influence on the analyst's impulses and feelings. Concentration on the danger of utilizing the patient as a source of emotional gratification has tended to obscure the distinction between the resistance potential of these countertransference manifestations and the feelings realistically induced in the analyst by the patient's behavior and communications. Derivatives of the relationship, uncontaminated by the practitioner's own emotional concerns, are an essential source of therapeutic leverage.

Issues of Terminology

The theoretical framework in which the working concepts just discussed are applied is referred to as "modern psychoanalysis." This is also employed by some authors to designate the incorporation of new concepts in the classical method. But some degree of semantic confusion is unavoidable in view of the disparate contemporary usages of this and other terms in the field. I hold no brief for the name; "modern indirect psychotherapy" or "resistance analysis" might be equally appropriate. But I believe that "modern psychoanalysis" best indicates that the theory of treatment presented in this book is basically Freud's theory and Freud's method of therapy, reformulated on the basis of subsequent psychoanalytic investigation.

Among other alternatives considered, some were rejected for specific reasons. Reports of treatment referred to as "modified psychoanalysis" or "psychoanalytically oriented therapy" suggest that it is often conducted without firm adherence to the task of investigating and resolving resistance, and may be oriented to relatively limited goals. To qualify in the same way an approach that adheres to the structure of the classical method and is similarly oriented to analytic cure seems inappropriate.

To refer to treatment based on the principles formulated in this book as "psychoanalysis with parameters" also seems out of order. Dr. K. R. Eissler, who introduced this hypothesis (1953), has made stipulations regarding the use of parameters that are incompatible with my approach. He specifies, for example, that these modifications "must never transgress the unavoidable minimum" and that the "final phase of the treatment must always proceed with a parameter of zero" (p. 111). Whether or not the technical innovations I suggest meet these stipulations, the concept of parameters—though useful in training the practitioner—drops out when any technique employed to deal with resistance is regarded as permissible.

Freud's own definition of psychoanalysis covers "any line of investigation" which recognizes transference and resistance and "takes them as the starting-point of its work" (1914, p. 16). Over the years, however, some representatives of the classical school have claimed a vested interest of sorts in the term, arguing that it should be applied exclusively to the basic model of psychoanalytic technique. While attempting to reserve the term "psychoanalysis proper" for the approach enshrining interpretation as the chief technique, they suggest that terms like "psychoanalytic psychotherapy," "expressive psychotherapy" and "supportive" psychotherapy be used for other approaches (e.g., Kernberg, 1982, p. 516).

But despite objections to the linkage of "psychoanalysis" with departures from the classical method, I believe that term will be applied in the future to all treatment conducted within the scientific framework of Freud's method to meet the changing patterns of mental illness. Psychoanalysis appears to be in the process of transition from a "philosophy and technique of treating certain kinds of patients in a certain way," to cite Karl Menninger's neat description (1958, p. 16), to a broad psychotherapeutic science applicable to all cases of psychologically reversible illness, including psychosomatic conditions. This evolutionary process is suggested by "modern psychoanalysis."

There is another reason why that term seems appropriate. Competent medical practitioners of today, rather than committing themselves to any one method of treating a physical illness, draw upon their knowledge of the various methods available to apply the most effective treatment for the case at hand. Analysts who address themselves to the same purpose, giving no quarter to orthodoxy for the sake of orthodoxy, exemplify the modern approach to psychoanalysis.

Some psychoanalysts who treat schizophrenic patients today adhere substantially to the classical technique, defending its suitability for such cases, and deviating from it to a very limited extent (McLaughlin, 1982). At the other extreme are practitioners who appear to have abandoned the general framework of the psychoanalytic method, and operate more or less by happenstance in each case. Although the classical technique does not, in my experience, resolve the basic problem in these cases, I believe that a purely intuitive approach is undesirable. Satisfactory as well as very disappointing results may be achieved when one does not operate on the basis of a general plan for the case; but whatever the outcome it is difficult to account for it and learn from it.

An aura of mystery and magic surrounds many reports of successfully treated cases that did not adhere to a rational system. The authors are generous in sharing their clinical impressions and personal insights but chary in conveying the structure, movement, and goals for the case. They fail to make clear what they were trying to accomplish or to identify the essential curative factors.

Objective formulations are of great scientific significance. They enhance knowledge of the psychodynamics of schizophrenia and suggest effective treatment procedures. (Such information is best kept to oneself, however, until late in the treatment; then it may be communicated to the patient).

To be of maximum value to pathologically narcissistic patients, psychoanalytic investigations have to be conducted empirically and with all the technical skills at the therapist's command. However, a theory of the treatment that the therapist can learn as a student and apply in these cases is, in my view, indispensable. Unless the practitioner has some way of taking readings of progress at each stage of the case, it is impossible to determine the degree of reversal of the schizophrenic reaction that has been secured and, later, whether the patient has been properly immunized against its return. If the analyst fails to achieve the goal in a case, it is important for him to understand *why the failure*; from our therapeutic failures we sometimes learn more than from our successes. One value of adhering to an operational theory is that it helps the practitioner take these readings and answer these questions.

THE CONTEMPORARY LITERATURE

Diagnosis

The catchall character of definitions of schizophrenia has given rise to dissatisfaction and uncertainty. Jaynes (1976) refers to a "rather vague panorama of dispute as to what schizophrenia is, whether it is one disease or many, or the final common path of multiple etiologies, whether there exist two basic patterns variously called process and reactive, or acute and chronic, or quick-onset and slow-onset schizophrenia" (p. 407). Conflicting views have interfered with the formulation of definitions that would serve as guides to effective treatment and facilitate a reliable prediction of outcome. As Fenichel (1945) pointed out, "the label 'schizophrenia' is applied to so many different things that it is not even of value for the purpose of prognosis" (p. 442). Another representative complaint, voiced by Cancro several decades later, is that the heterogeneity of persons diagnosed as schizophrenic "makes the question of the 'correct' or even the preferred treatment utterly meaningless" (1979, p. 50).

Successive editions of the *Diagnostic and Statistical Manual of Mental Disorders* (American Psychiatric Association, 1952, 1968, 1980) reflect concerted efforts to reduce the confusion by differentiating with greater specificity the disturbances that give rise to severe degrees of psychic dysfunction. DSM-I, as mentioned above, classifies nine types of schizophrenic reactions "characterized by fundamental disturbances in reality relationships and concept formations, with associated affective, behavioral, and intellectual disturbances, marked by a tendency to retreat from reality, by regressive trends, by bizarre behavior, by disturbances in stream of thought, and by formation of delusions and hallucinations" (1952, p. 12).

Although these reactions are descriptively classified as psychotic, the 1952 manual categorizes one of the reaction types as "chronic, undifferentiated" and another as "residual." These two types embrace the so-called latent, incipient, prepsychotic, and postpsychotic illnesses now treated in office practice.

DSM-II (1968) does not sustain Adolf Meyer's psychobiological concept of schizophrenic reactions. These are supplanted by "schizophrenia"; in addition to the nine types identified as "reactions" in DSM-I, two additional types are recognized—"latent schizophrenia" and "other [and unspecified] types" (p. 8).

The designation "latent schizophrenia" is applied to individuals displaying clear symptoms of schizophrenia who have no history of a psychotic schizophrenic episode; it encompasses disorders that are "sometimes designated as incipient, pre-psychotic, pseudoneurotic, pseudo-psychopathic, or borderline schizophrenia" (p. 34). The term "residual" is applied to individuals who have experienced such an episode but are no longer psychotic. The type of disorder in which schizophrenic symptoms are mixed with strong affects is designated as "schizo-affective" and subdivided into "excited" and "depressed" types. Whereas mental status in the schizophrenic disorders is "attributable primarily to a *thought* disorder," the major affective psychoses are "dominated by a *mood* disorder" (p. 33).

DSM-II, in the opinion of Cancro, stresses the clinical picture in schizophrenia, conceptualizing the various types as a group of similar end-states. The manual does not, however, facilitate understanding of the schizophrenic process as a "particular and ongoing adaptational effort by an individual to his environment. . . . the need for further increasing diagnostic reliability becomes more manifest" (Cancro, 1974, pp. 4–5).

On the other hand, since the various types of schizophrenia are forms of adaptation, the clinical manifestations will undergo changes depending on whether the individual patient is in a favorable or unfavorable environment. The great capacity of the schizophrenic patient to regress makes a reliable clinical picture rarely available. The presenting syndrome will in large measure depend on whether the patient is becoming more regressed or is recovering from a period of severe regression.

DSM-III (1980) ushers in profound changes. Five schizophrenic disorders are classified: disorganized, catatonic, paranoid, undifferentiated, and residual. The current manual also classifies four related psychotic disorders: schizophreniform and schizoaffective disorders, brief reactive psychosis, and atypical psychosis.

The essential features of the five types of schizophrenic disorders are identified as follows: "the presence of certain psychotic features during the active phase of the illness, characteristic symptoms involving multiple psychological processes, deterioration from a previous level of functioning, onset before age 45, and a *duration of at least six months.* . . . At some phase of the illness Schizophrenia always involves delusions, hallucinations, or certain disturbances in the form of thought" (emphasis added; p. 181). As conceptualized in DSM-III, schizophrenia is not limited to illnesses with a deteriorating course but a minimal duration is specified because "the accumulated evidence suggests that illnesses of briefer duration (here called Schizophreniform Disorder) are likely to have different external correlates, such as family history and likelihood of recurrence" (p. 181).

Schizophreniform Disorder, except for the specification on duration (less than 6 months but more than 2 weeks), is defined by the same diagnostic criteria as schizophrenia. DSM-III differentiates it from the schizophrenic disorders "because evidence suggests a greater likelihood of emotional turmoil and confusion, a tendency toward acute onset and resolution, more likely recovery to premorbid levels of functioning, and the absence of an increase in the prevalence of Schizophrenia among family members compared with the general population" (p. 199).

Cases that were previously referred to as latent, borderline, or simple schizophrenia, without overt psychotic features, are identified in DSM-III as cases of personality disorder, such as schizotypal personality disorder. Excluded cases with onset after mid-adult life may be classified as atypical psychosis. Moreover, the diagnosis of schizophrenia is not applied to individuals who develop a "depressive or manic syndrome for an extended period relative to the duration of certain psychotic features or before the psychotic features appear"; these individuals are classified as having an affective or schizoaffective disorder (p. 181).

In short, DSM-III classifies the various clinical pictures of schizophreniclike reactions on the basis of duration of the illness and severity of the symptoms. The length of time necessary to reverse a condition does generally depend on its duration and the severity of its symptoms. But the question uppermost in the mind of the therapeutically oriented psychoanalyst is whether these different clinical syndromes are a significant source of information on the degree of psychological reversibility of the illness, and on the time required to reverse it completely and to immunize the patient against its return. The battle between regressive and progressive forces in the patient leads to rapid changes in clinical syndromes—from day to day, even from hour to hour.

To the extent to which specific clinical syndromes indicate the types of interventions necessary to reverse them and the

amount of time entailed in that task, they become of considerable importance to the clinician.

Drug Therapy

The psychiatric literature of the last 2 decades makes it
abundantly clear that the "whole armamentarium of psycho-
pharmacology has been turned loose on schizophrenia" (Zubin,
1974, p. viii). It is equally clear that many contributors to the
recent literature regard the introduction of the new antipsychotic drugs as the most important innovation in the history of
psychiatry since midcentury (Karasu, 1982). For practical reasons, such drugs will probably continue to serve as therapy for
the vast majority of hospitalized schizophrenic patients, often the
only type of therapy available to them.

Nevertheless, eventual recognition of serious and, in some
cases, possibly irreversible side effects from long-term and indiscriminate use of antipsychotic drugs has prompted a reas-
sessment of the risks and values of the biochemical approach,
along with suggestions for reducing the toxicity of the drugs.
For example, Davis recommends that maintenance drug therapy in the hospitals should be limited to the "lowest effective
use." Inasmuch as patients can receive psychotherapy and drug
therapy jointly, he adds, it is a "false dichotomy to think of one
versus the other" (Davis, 1975, p. 1244; Davis et al., 1982).

The either-or attitude, which has tended to put some psychotherapists on the defensive, has derived superficial encouragement from comparative studies that appear to pit one
method against the other. This is illustrated by an interesting
report on critical flaws in research studies on the outcome of
treatment in schizophrenia. The authors of the report, issuing
from the Maryland Psychiatric Research Center, attribute the
widespread use of antipsychotic drugs as "sole and continuous
treatment" to studies that demonstrated their effectiveness in
reducing florid psychotic symptoms, whereas research has
"failed to show benefits of psychotherapy on these symptoms
when applied within a limited framework to questionably suited

populations." If, on the other hand, the experimental studies had centered on interpersonal functioning over a long term and on the complex of deficit symptoms characteristic of the disorder, the antipsychotic drugs "might have been summarily dismissed as worthless" (Carpenter, Henrichs, & Hanlon, 1981, p. 466).

Other factors enter into consideration of the use of drugs as an adjunct to psychotherapy conducted on an outpatient basis. Some of these issues have been commented on by Arieti and Cancro. Although drug therapy had served as a useful adjunct in many of Arieti's cases, he obtained the best results with patients who had not received it. "Whereas drug therapy relieves only the symptoms, psychotherapy aims at changing the patient's self-image and his attitude toward himself, others and life in general" (1974, p. 248). Cancro found that a group of patients who had experienced spontaneous remissions "showed a depth of affect and a warmth in their object relations that I have not seen achieved on medication. . . . That certain of our patients are clearly adverse to taking medication but nonetheless have it forced upon them should give us pause. It is not impossible that the judgment of this subgroup of patients is superior to our own" (Cancro, Fox, & Shapiro, 1974, p. 9).

In my view, in office practice the chief justification for placing patients on drug therapy is to keep them out of the hospital and working psychotherapeutically on their problems. Drugs often serve as an acceptable substitute for hospitalization, but they should be administered in minimal doses and discontinued as soon as possible. When indicated for ambulatory patients, I refer them to a practitioner who specializes in pharmacotherapy. For analytic psychotherapists to give the drugs themselves tends to interfere with the transference situation, reducing the chances of clinical success.

The introduction of antipsychotic drugs has led to dramatic improvements in the hospital environment and facilitated the management of large patient populations. In a sense, however, administering drug therapy to individuals with schizophrenia is analogous to administering insulin to diabetics. Neither therapy is curative. The main value of pharmacotherapy is as an alternative to hospitalization; it increases the number of patients accessible to psychological treatment on an outpatient basis. The ambulatory state makes it possible for such patients to come to the office of a modern analyst, where they can be treated on a long-term basis—as is usually necessary for a successful outcome. The combination of analytic psychotherapy and drugs, judiciously administered by a cooperative psychiatrist, leads to the most favorable conditions for successful outcome (Davis et al., 1982, pp. 215–228; Gochfeld, 1978).

Prognosis

Early in the century there was universal agreement that schizophrenia was an incurable condition leading to mental deterioration. A quality of grimness continues to surround the disorder, according to Otto Will (1974), but it is "no longer necessarily equated with hopelessness" (p. 18). As yet there is no general consensus that the prognosis has improved, but one can point to a slowly rising curve of optimism.

More and more psychotherapists who work with schizophrenic patients find the outlook for their cure to be better. From study to study, percentages vary, but recent data indicate that about one-third of patients diagnosed as schizophrenic "recover completely" and that a "significant number of patients may improve or recover even after a period of severe illness that has lasted 15 years or more" (Strauss, 1982, p. 88; M. Bleuler, 1979). In the long run, schizophrenic patients "do tend to recover" (Cancro, 1982, p. 154).

Contributing to a more optimistic outlook is the recent finding that the genetic factor implicated in the etiology of schizophrenia is one of "enormous plasticity" rather than dooming the bearer to an inevitable outcome (Cancro, 1982, p. 92). This genetic factor, as already indicated, does not operate to transmit the disorder itself. Rather, it transmits a predisposition or vulnerability that "allows the individual to develop the syndrome in the face of certain environmental triggers," the environment being viewed as a sort of "biochemical bath in which the gene sits" (Cancro, 1982, pp. 96, 97). The environment is influenced, through physiological pathways, by social and psychological experiences although the precise manner in which these experiences are translated into physiologic events has yet to be determined. One may conclude that "no single gene or environment will inevitably produce a schizophrenic disorder" (Cancro, 1982, pp. 96–97).

Another recent finding, of particular interest to those who engage in psychotherapy with schizophrenic individuals, challenges the common assumption that treatment should be defined by etiology. The etiological factor itself is a complex one, involving the interaction of multiple elements; some of these are genetic and biological, others are psychological and environmental (Strauss & Carpenter, 1981). There is increasing appreciation of the fact that "even conditions involving organic factors can be significantly altered by psychologic and environmental means" (Heinrichs & Carpenter, 1982, p. 155).

For the treatment of patients in prepsychotic or postpsychotic states, psychotherapy appears to be the more effective approach. Psychopharmacological techniques tend to reverse the psychotic reactions more rapidly than psychotherapy alone. When the antipsychotic drugs are discontinued, however, the patient tends to regress again. Psychotherapeutic intervention is thus required to help the patient deal with regressive tendencies without recourse to medication. Moreover, as I have already pointed out, minimal use of these drugs is recommended because of their negative side effects.

Therapy that is oriented to a *restitutio quo ante* is not a desirable objective in the treatment of psychotic conditions, as Arieti has stated (1974), because the so-called premorbid state was already morbid, in a different way. Returning the patient to that prepsychotic state would equate with settling for the retention of both a biological and a psychological vulnerability— persistence of the potentiality for psychosis. On the other hand, many patients who undergo intensive and prolonged psychotherapy achieve levels of integration and self-fulfillment far superior to the levels at which they operated before becoming psychotic. Many successfully treated schizophrenic patients function in accordance with contemporary psychoanalytic concepts of normality (Joseph, 1982).

It is important to bear in mind that the prognosis of an

emotional disorder is significantly influenced by the capacity of those concerned with its treatment to treat it successfully (Braceland, 1978; Giovacchini, 1979; Karon and Vandenbos, 1981). As this capacity develops, the prognosis improves.

Analytic psychotherapists undergoing training at centers of modern psychoanalysis have been working with schizophrenic patients since the midseventies. Many are postpsychotic patients beginning analytic treatment after being discharged from a psychiatric institution. The trainees do not cure all of their patients, but among them are scores of individuals previously classified as schizophrenic who are no longer schizophrenic.

To work productively with schizophrenic patients, the analyst has to have the ability to get them to cooperate; the more uncooperative the patient, the more difficult it is to treat him successfully. The outcome of the treatment is very much influenced by whether the patient is unconsciously oriented to get well and also, in the instance of a child or adolescent, whether the parents behave in a way to facilitate the patient's recovery. Meanwhile, therapists are becoming more skilled in dealing with uncooperative egos; some are cooperating out of spite (Kesten, 1955). Often these patients feel hopeless, and strive mightily to nullify the analyst's efforts on their behalf, to prove that they are incurable. But they become curable to the extent that the analyst is not taken in by the feelings these patients induce that nothing can be done for them (narcissistic countertransference).

The prognosis of a large number of schizophrenic outpatients undergoing treatment with competent analytic psychotherapists has not been reported. The majority of controlled studies reported in the literature in which psychotherapy is included in the treatment program are short-term ventures conducted by inexperienced therapists, usually psychiatric interns or residents in large psychiatric hospitals (Mosher & Keith, 1979).

Most optimistic about outcome are practitioners who work with schizophrenic patients psychologically and have the most sustained contact with them. I anticipate that studies will be forthcoming in the future from these practitioners, among them people who are applying the techniques of modern psycho-analysis.

Borderline and Narcissistic Disorders

Ongoing progress in the psychotherapeutic treatment of the borderline and narcissistic disorders promises, in my view, to contribute significantly to more effective treatment of the schizophrenic disorders (Spotnitz, 1979b).

The differences among these three groups of patients impress me as purely quantitative. This impression is supported by a comparative study focused on the similarities and differences in borderline and schizophrenic patients. In reporting on this study, John Gunderson and his associates stated that "despite markedly different admitting symptoms, the borderline and schizophrenic patients had remarkably similar prognostic and outcome characteristics" (Gunderson, Carpenter, & Strauss, 1975, p. 1263).

To specify a few of the quantitative differences just referred to, the schizophrenic patient induces more intense narcissistic countertransference reactions than the borderline patient; the danger of chaotic regression is greater in a case of schizophrenia; and the course of treatment is more time-consuming. Despite these differences, the schizophrenic patient responds to the same types of interventions (employed more persistently) as the borderline patient.

Experience in working comfortably and in a goal-oriented way with borderline individuals prepares the analyst to provide schizophrenic patients with the kind of object relationship that they need, and to sustain the more turbulent emotions they induce. As these psychotic feelings (narcissistic countertransference) become more tolerable and the analyst gets to recognize that they are induced by the schizophrenic patient's feelings of hopelessness and helplessness, the analyst will be able to work effectively with schizophrenic patients.

In other words, accumulated experience in the successful treatment of borderline patients will, I anticipate, appreciably accelerate the process of achieving more consistently favorable results in the treatment of schizophrenia.

Principles of Modern Psychoanalysis

The specific operational theory that I refer to as "modern psychoanalysis" is a unitary approach that has evolved out of my own experience and that of colleagues who focus on meeting the therapeutic needs of persons suffering from the severe preoedipal disorders. The goal of modern psychoanalysis is to discover the forces that have driven a patient into emotional illness and to help the patient manage those forces so as to achieve emotional health and maturity.

The operational theory is empirically applied to take account of the initial unresponsiveness of the preverbal personality to interpretive procedures and to the patient's oscillating transference states. Post-Freudian findings on the role of aggressive forces in the early development of the mind (Rudolph, 1981) are reflected in the theory. Safeguards against chaotic regression figure prominently in the clinical approach of the modern psychoanalyst; the therapeutic alliance is permitted to evolve at a pace the patient is able to tolerate.

Viewing this approach in historical perspective, one may say that modern psychoanalysis begins where Freud left off, in the sense that it adheres to the basic Freudian framework of recognizing and investigating transference and resistance phenomena. While conducted within that framework to resolve the patient's nuclear problem, modern psychoanalysis amplifies the basic theory of psychoanalytic technique. The main departure from the classical method, as suggested above, is the extensive range of interventions sanctioned—ego-reinforcing, emotional, and symbolic.

The reader should bear in mind that the clinical procedures, working concepts, and interventions discussed in this book were formulated specifically for the treatment of individuals suffering from schizophrenia. The types and timing of interventions that are desirable when working with them may not be therapeutically effective for other patients. In treating a severely depressed person, for example, the analyst would delay mobilizing aggression because of the threat of suicide. To give another example: With a patient suffering from a psychosomatic condition (Brody, 1976), the danger to life that its further progress would constitute influences the choice and timing of interventions; thus, as with someone afflicted with a rapidly growing cancer, the analyst may have to intervene very actively. From patient to patient, moreover, regardless of the nature of the disorder, *the types of interventions employed are empirically determined by individual responsiveness.*

The operational principles discussed in this book apply specifically to schizophrenic patients who can initially control their behavior sufficiently to undergo treatment on an ambulatory basis but need help in maintaining that control. The principles also apply to the outpatient whose psychotic eruptions can be controlled through chemotherapy. But because the antipsychotic drugs have potentially serious side effects and also retard the response to psychotherapy, it is desirable to free the patient from dependency on the drugs as soon as the danger of psychotic outbreaks has been minimized (Davis et al., 1982).

These principles would be of no value in cases of schizophrenia that are not reversible through psychological means, applied exclusively or in combination with other therapies. There may be such cases, but during my four decades of studying and treating the condition, I have not encountered any schizophrenic patients who were not curable *in principle*. Success in each instance hinges, however, on the emotional sacrifice the practitioner is willing to make to deal with that patient's resistance. If the environmental realities are too unfavorable and the personal demands too great, it may be impossible to treat that patient successfully in office practice.

But the notion that a diagnosis of schizophrenia is disproved if patients respond to treatment, or confirmed if they fail to respond, is no longer tenable. Failure to respond indicates—not that the patient did not possess the capacity for recovery—but either that the therapy was inadequate or that external circumstances militated against therapeutic progress (Zimmerman, 1982).

Among factors implicated in analytic cure, in the first edition of this book (Spotnitz, 1969) I cited the need for an object capable of providing the patient with a "setting conducive to emotional reactiveness and the right kind of retraining" and for a "reasonably favorable life situation" (p. 12). I now single out, as a third essential ingredient, a real desire for analytic cure. In those who do not initially experience a strong urge to work for change and improvement—notably young people who enter treatment under parental pressure and support—or who do not develop it through changing circumstances of life, *the desire for personality maturation* needs to be created as an aspect of the treatment relationship.

The pioneering stage in the analytic psychotherapy of schizophrenia is over. In my opinion, schizophrenia is a completely reversible condition. Learning how to reverse it more consistently is the task ahead.

Chapter 2

CONCEPTUALIZATION OF THE ILLNESS

Countless observations, hypotheses, and findings have emerged from psychoanalytic investigations of schizophrenia. Their clinical value is limited, however, unless the practitioner possesses a conceptual framework in which to examine them and determine their pertinence for the case at hand. In my experience, the treatment cannot be formulated on the basis of symptom complexes; it has to be *individualized for each patient.* Virtually indispensable for this purpose are *general principles* which can be applied *empirically* in each case.

The working hypothesis presented in this chapter is broad enough to accommodate the total picture—that is, the various syndromes of the illness—but focuses psychodynamically on the nuclear problem. I have found this conceptualization of the illness of great therapeutic value when applied to meet the patient's specific need for communication and to prevent severe regression. Colleagues and trainees who have tested out the validity of the hypothesis in a wide range of ambulatory cases have found it to be therapeutically effective when they had the capacity to manage the disruptive affects aroused in the patients and themselves.

Rather than being original, the hypothesis integrates the partial theories, clinical observations, and assumptions of many investigators whose ideas make sense to me and have been corroborated by my own experience in treating schizophrenic patients. Some of the sources of this cumulative concept are traced, but what follows is not a comprehensive review of psychoanalytic formulations on the disorder.

ELABORATION OF THE CONCEPT

Early Views on Phenomenology

Freud's clinical studies before the turn of the century brought him into the full swing of therapeutically rewarding discoveries that strongly influenced his views on schizophrenia. His explorations of hysteria (Breuer & Freud, 1893-1895) led him to the theory that an unbearable idea repulsed from consciousness and memory thus became pathogenic, its affective activity in the unconscious being manifested in morbid symptoms. In case after case he was able to demonstrate that *overcoming the repelling force* was the key to recovery (Freud, 1917). Great mental effort was required to help even a strongly motivated, intelligent, and attentive person overcome this resistance, but in a harmonious relationship with an analyst for whom he developed feelings of affection, the patient could be induced to do so.

The psychological reversibility of the more severe disorders of patients in whom clinical psychiatrists had found no evidence of organic changes was then a moot question. It was hoped that psychoanalytic formulations about psychoneurosis would also be productive in treating these people. Freud called attention to the significance of defense mechanisms in psychotic conditions, conceptualizing chronic paranoia as a defense psychosis in which the repression of intolerable ideas connected with sexual experience in childhood is effected by projecting them into others (1894). If repression also figured significantly in schizophrenia, and if one was justified in assuming that it was connected with the organization of sexual impulses at a much earlier period than that associated with symptom formation in psychoneurosis, the theory of psychosexual or libidinal development might be pertinently applied.

But this approach brought disappointment. Psychological processes were found to operate in schizophrenic patients that eluded the grasp of the early formulations. These people did not appear to suffer from repression; some of them could tell their analyst more about their unconscious than the analyst could tell them. Sudden relapses into psychotic states after several years of treatment were also reported. The fact that explanations of their problems seemed to make no impression on these patients was particularly troublesome to Freud. *Why did they remain out of contact?*

While every case of psychoneurosis had obscure elements, the patient's behavior usually made it possible to clarify them one after another, and eventually to assemble the whole puzzle. "I get great satisfaction from the work on neuroses in my practice," Freud wrote Wilhelm Fliess in 1895. "Nearly everything is confirmed daily, new pieces are added, and it is a fine thing to feel certain that the core of the matter is within one's grasp" (1954, p. 120).

The failure of schizophrenic patients to cooperate in these investigations and to reward understanding with improvement baffled Freud. Exasperated by their ability to thwart his therapeutic efforts, he once remarked, "Psychotics are a nuisance to psychoanalysis" (Federn, 1952, p. 136).

One explanation Freud advanced for their indifference was that they did not possess enough mobile libido to form an analytic relationship (Nunberg & Federn, 1962, 7th meeting). The tenor of Freud's views on the problem was that the only way to solve the riddle of their inaccessibility[1] was to assume a pathological factor that was unresponsive to psychological influence.

---

[1]The solution, eventually discovered, was not that these patients were inaccessible or nonanalyzable but that the therapist was unable to create the kind of relationship with them that would have made them accessible. In some instances, nonanalyzable means *nonanalyzable by the therapist at hand* (Zimmerman, 1982).

The earliest formulation of the psychoanalytic theory of schizophrenia was presented to the First International Psychoanalytic Congress, in 1908, by Karl Abraham (1953, chapter 2). A clinical psychiatrist and former member of Bleuler's staff at Burghölzli, Dr. Abraham prepared his paper following talks with Freud, who referred to it later as the basis of his own position on psychotic illness.

Differences in the emotional life of hospitalized schizophrenics, ranging from those in the most advanced state of the severest form of the illness to persons without marked symptoms, are only a matter of degree, according to Abraham. The factor common to all forms of the illness is its destruction of the "capacity for sexual transference, i.e., for object love" (p. 69). In fact, these people "never had a proper capacity for transferring their libido to the outside world" (p. 71). Today the question is not viewed as one of libido but of the capacity of these people to relate to objects outside themselves; they seem to be more attached to objects in the mind that are part of their early ego states—selfobjects, as Kohut calls them.

To an extent determined by the degree of the illness, the schizophrenic individual boycotts the world, reacting to it abnormally or not at all. Although many symptoms of the illness resemble those associated with hysteria, schizophrenics demonstrate a morbid tendency not observed in hysteria—a blocking of feelings, which suggest that they have never "completely overcome" (p. 77) infantile autoerotism. Abraham attributed this anomaly to an inhibition in development at this early stage.

Jung had already expressed the view that feelings are probably not extinguished but only "peculiarly transposed and blocked" in schizophrenia (1936, p. 66). Abraham agreed; in 1908 he noted that "remissions may take place at any time, and even go so far that hardly any suspicion of a mental defect is left." Nevertheless, psychoanalysis as a therapeutic procedure "hardly comes into consideration" because of the absence of transference (Abraham, 1953, pp. 76, 71). Abraham was referring to *object* transference.

More significant than his formulations on schizophrenia was Abraham's statement (1911) that, like severe obsessional neurotics, people suffering from psychotic depressions greatly diminish their capacity for transferring love through their strongly hostile attitudes toward the world. The process of repressing hatred weakens and deprives them of energy. Melancholic depressions, he consistently observed, "proceeded from an *attitude of hate which was paralyzing the patient's capacity to love*" (emphasis added; 1953, p. 143). The correctness of those ideas for schizophrenia too was subsequently established.

What happens to the libido that is withdrawn from objects? Freud hypothesized that it is "taken back into the ego" (1917, p. 416). The existence of ego-libido has to be reckoned with because "the hypothesis that object-libido can be transformed into ego-libido . . . seems to us the only one which is able to resolve the enigma of what are termed the narcissistic neuroses—dementia praecox, for instance—and to account for the resemblances and dissimilarities between them and hysteria or obsessions" (1917, p. 420).

The term "narcissism" was applied to this reversion of libido. The general level of regression was traced back to the period of primary narcissism between the stage of body-ego formation and more advanced stages of object formation (Glover, 1949, p. 230).

Disappointing results in the psychoanalytic treatment of schizophrenics were comprehensible and the policy of excluding them from such treatment seemed justifiable if the withdrawal of interest from the outside world to the ego was the pathogenic mechanism in their condition. This notion also tallied with Bleuler's observations of the autistic behavior and infantile preoccupations of hospitalized patients (1950).

The impression that they turn their backs on society to love themselves and indulge their delusions of grandeur inspired innumerable descriptive formulations. Their inner experiences and mental productions attracted much speculation early in the century. Their words were carefully weighed, their thoughts and fantasies likened to those of children and primitive peoples. Attention was drawn to Jung's statement: "Let the dreamer walk about and act like one awakened and we have the clinical picture of dementia praecox" (1936, p. 79).

Symptoms were explored and elaborately classified. Some characteristic mechanisms were related to specific phases of the move backward from normal or neurotic functioning to the narcissistic state. The beginning of the withdrawal, Freud postulated in his paper on narcissism (1914a), gives rise to residual phenomena. The morbid process itself is marked by a second group of manifestations. These are followed by so-called restitutional symptoms, reflecting the ego's attempts to regain contact with objects outside the mind.

Manifestations of these three phases, which the clinician usually observes simultaneously, were subsequently described in greater detail. The first phase, as a rule, is well under way when the patient seeks help. Symptoms of hypochondria, depersonalization, delusions, megalomania, and feelings of emptiness may intensify, suggesting the reorganization within the ego of libido withdrawn from external objects. The strange sounds and mannerisms of catatonic patients have been identified with the "mimetic stages of infantile development . . . just before permanent object attachment develops" (Glover, 1949, p. 229). The discharge-directed behavior and low frustration-tolerance of severely regressed patients have suggested similar resemblances. To Otto Fenichel, the restitutional symptoms signified sudden moves in the other direction, giving the impression that schizophrenics, "leaving the narcissistic state and attempting to regain contact with the objective world, succeed in doing so only in abrupt spurts and for brief periods of time" (1945, p. 418).

The ingenious, often profound interpretations of the phenomenology of the condition would fill many volumes, but the forces that generated it are rarely discussed in these studies. This is not surprising. To reconstruct an ego by examining the products of its splitting or eventual disintegration is analogous to reassembling a plane from the debris scattered by its explosion. But scientific understanding of the original structure before it incurred the damage was lacking; detailed studies of the various phases of ego formation were not yet under way. One question that it was especially difficult to answer was this: Granted that many people in psychotic states of schizophrenia seemed to be all wrapped up in themselves, why had they withdrawn their interest from the environment in the first place?

One explanation of the abandonment of objects sustains Freud's early hope of finding the "libidinal factor in mental life as universally guilty of the causation of mental illness" (1917, p. 429). Maurits Katan postulates that the break with reality is the outcome of an intense bisexual conflict associated with extreme and pervasive anxiety (1950).

After dominating the literature on schizophrenia for many years, however, theories relating these disorders to libidinal factors have, by and large, dropped out of the picture. Investigators shifted their attention from "libido," "self-love," and "anxiety" to the affective derivatives of aggression, focusing first on the idea of an "aggressive drive" and moving gradually to the current emphasis on "psychotic rage" and "narcissistic rage," terms that came into prominence in the 1970s.

Early Views on Aggression

Psychoanalytic formulations on schizophrenia were significantly influenced by the revision of the libido theory in the 1920s to allow for the existence of an aggressive drive and the mitigation of destructive tendencies through the fusion of aggressive energy with that of the erotic drive. Actually, many of our current ideas on aggression were tossed about even earlier in the century. One finds them in the minutes of the "Psychological Wednesday Evenings" held in Freud's apartment prior to the formation of the Vienna Psychoanalytic Society in 1908. In one of these informal discussions, in 1907, for example, Freud stated that "every act of hate issues from erotic tendencies" (Nunberg & Federn, 1962, 19th meeting, p. 164). The protocols also disclose that Alfred Adler made several references to the existence of an aggressive drive.

Adler advanced the idea that where there is no love there can be no hate (12th meeting), thereby implying that the withholding of love from an object is a way of protecting it from the hatred of the ego. He also expressed the view that a child becomes aggressive when its various ways of obtaining pleasure are frustrated (53rd meeting), and called attention to a tendency of the aggressive drive to turn against the subject (50th meeting). The minutes contain the interesting notation, "Freud agrees with most of Adler's points, for a definite reason: what Adler calls aggressive drive is our libido" (53rd meeting, p. 408). Had

Adler systemically developed his views on aggression, he might have made a major contribution to the concept of schizophrenia. Some of the ideas he expressed in 1907 and 1908 were accepted by Freud later and are incorporated in the revised libido theory.

The combined influence of theoretical advances and clinical observations brought important changes in the psychoanalytic approach to schizophrenic patients. Their withdrawal, negativism, and hostile outbursts, which were originally viewed in terms of the erotic drive or were believed to indicate that these patients were uneducable, in the sense that their treatment would lead up a blind alley, were initially connected with the aggressive drive (and are now associated with destructive aggression).

Freud himself did not make this connection or extend his basic theory to account for the abandonment of object relations in schizophrenia. His formulations on pathological mechanisms in obsessional neurosis in *The Ego and the Id* (1923) are close to subsequently published views on schizophrenia. His reference to psychosis as the outcome of a disturbance "in the relations between the ego and the external world" (1924, p. 149) is also pertinent. Freud did not, however, explore these ideas in the specific context of schizophrenia.

An instinctual drive must have an aim. That of the erotic drive is to bring people together, to unite them in their mutual interests, and for the preservation of the human race. It is the drive that first operates to bring objects into the mind of the infant. The aim of the aggressive drive, on the other hand, is the destruction of object representations or their precipitates, which contribute to the formation of the infantile ego. The aggressive drive, free from control, operates to destroy and disunite, to fragment the personality, and sever the ties between people (Freud, 1940 [1938]).

The qualifying clause *free from control* suggests much of the difference between destructive aggression and constructive aggression. Spitz points out that, rather than being limited to hostility, "by far the largest and most important part of the aggressive drive serves as the motor of every movement, of all activity, big and small, and ultimately of life itself" (1965, p. 106).

Rudolph (1981) discusses the ego-energizing role of the aggressive drive and presents a clinical illustration of the conversion of "the most malignant rage . . . into constructive aggression" (p. 578).

Implicit in the early formulations on schizophrenia was the implausible notion that the withdrawal from objects is motivated by excessive love of the self and thus gratifies the erotic drive. The flight from objects can be linked more logically with the affective derivatives of aggressive impulses—hatred and the allied emotions. Indulgence in self-love, to a pathological degree, then becomes comprehensible as an attempt to obtain erotic gratification in the presence of a hated object or situation. Clinical findings support the belief that the erotic drive performs a primarily defensive role in schizophrenic withdrawal, as described by Abraham (1911) for depression.

Striking evidence to that effect emerges from the second of Herman Nunberg's two classic studies of a young man in a state of catatonic psychosis. The case, reported in 1921, was approached as one of libidinal conflict, emphasis being placed on its homosexual aspects. In a state of narcissistic identification in which there was "no longer a 'boundary' between us" (1948, p. 31), the patient experienced aggressive (cannibalistic) impulses and fantasies of sacrifice.

> He wanted to fight with me . . . finally, he wanted to kill me. These impulses, however, were at first warded off by the delusional idea of eternal life. . . . The delusional idea . . . was thus used in the service of *a defensive tendency to ward off the aggressive impulses against me.* This apparently was based on the correct endopsychic perception, that *by killing me he would lose the only object of the external world remaining to him.* (Emphasis added; 1948, p. 27)

In a similar situation, the patient said, "It seems to me that I am to hit somebody, to tear out somebody's hair." Thereupon *he struck his own head with his fist* and started to pull out his hair. "Here the defense against aggressive impulses was enacted by the instinct turning against his own person and changing into its opposite. . . . Nevertheless, the aggressive tendency continued to exist besides the passive tendency and even increased in violence" (1948, p. 30).

In other words, while Nunberg concentrated on the libidinal aspects of the case and explained it in these terms, the patient's words shed a contrary light on his fundamental problem as it was reactivated in the analytic relationship. He presented evidence for the theory that destructive impulses toward his primary object were a crucial factor in his illness. He was saying, in effect: My desire to preserve you protects you and defends me against my wish to destroy you.

An early illustration of the schizophrenic tendency to direct aggressive impulses against the self was provided by Theodor Reik in 1927 (cf. Rosenfeld, 1947). One of his patients, in a state of depersonalization, told him: "Instead of knowing you want to kill someone else, you wipe yourself out"—in other words, eliminate your own ego.

Dr. Herbert Rosenfeld calls attention to the same mechanism. Reporting (1947) on the treatment of a schizophrenic woman, he made the following observation: "Instead of attacking and destroying the analyst, the destructive impulses had turned against her desire to live, her libido, which left her half dead, as it were, and so in a state of depersonalization" (pp. 136-137).

Inferences drawn by Melanie Klein from the psychoanalysis of young children, which have influenced the approach to psychopathology in adult schizophrenia, encompass what appears to have been the earliest attempt to explain the withdrawal from objects. She attributed it to the ego's "excessive and premature defense against sadism" (1930, p. 39), beginning in the first few months of life. The turning of destructive impulses against the object, which takes the expression of fantasied oral-sadistic attacks on the mother's breast, and later on her whole body, leads to the development of mechanisms regarded as of great importance for the development of the disorder. The excessive sadism, in her view, gives rise to anxiety too severe for the infantile ego to master. The earliest modes of defense are set in motion against two sources of danger: the sadism itself and the object, from which "similar retaliatory attacks" are feared (1930, p. 25).

Melanie Klein also discussed hatred. In psychotic disorders, identification of objects with hated parts of the self intensifies hatred for other people, she observed in a paper on schizoid mechanisms (1946). Pointing out that a "kind of detached hostility" pervades the analytic relationship with adult schizophrenics, she reported an abrupt change in mood when she told a patient that he "wanted to destroy" her. The interpretation made this danger "very real" to him, and the immediate consequence was the "fear of losing me" (pp. 313-314). Klein continues:

> The patient split off those parts of himself, *i.e.,* of his ego, which he felt to be dangerous and hostile toward the analyst. He turned his destructive impulses from his object *towards his ego*, with the result that parts of his ego temporarily went out of existence. . . . If he could build up again the good breast inside himself, he would strengthen and integrate his ego, would be less afraid of his destructive impulses; in fact he could then preserve himself and the analyst. (p. 314)

Dr. Gregory Zilboorg (1931), reporting on the analysis of a young woman suffering from paranoid schizophrenia, identified the nucleus of her psychosis as an "early infantile conversion which is quite a normal finding" in the illness (p. 508). She had displaced hatred for her parents to herself. Severe frustration experienced at the age of five had "dammed up an enormous mass of instinctual energy which produced or activated her hostile impulses to the utmost degree" (p. 499). It was Zilboorg's impression that these impulses were permitted to "break through" only when she was in a state of psychosis (p. 499).

The additional element of defense of the object is emphasized by Dr. Ives Hendrick. His account (1931) of the psychoanalysis of a schizophrenic young woman on the verge of psychosis is an outstanding study of an "immature ego endangered by aggressive impulses" (p. 317). Hendrick attributes the inability of the ego to repress infantile sexual impulses to the fact that all available energy was "mobilized in the service of another function, *namely, the control of enormous impulses of aggres-*

sion" (emphasis added; p. 299).The young woman's transference to him was dominated by hatred, which stimulated retaliation anxiety. It was only when she raised "stalwart defenses" (p. 315) against this hatred that her reactions resembled those associated with regression in schizophrenia. The most "constant and decisive" of this patient's problems was her lifelong conviction that she was unloved (p. 315). The emergence of her hate was a reaction to this conviction. Hendrick viewed the social isolation of the schizophrenic as being determined "not merely by his love of self (narcissism), but by his primordial hate of others, of his potential enemies, of his parents and mankind" (p. 318).

The theory that instinctual energy undergoes a process of neutralization, whereby it is modified (de-aggressivized or de-sexualized) and is available to the ego for its defense against the instinctual drives has been applied by some analysts to schizophrenia. Citing symptoms as evidence, Heinz Hartmann (1953) has suggested that the individual's capacity for neutralizing aggressive energy is impaired. More specifically, according to Robert Bak (1954), "the sudden inability of the ego to neutralize aggression (which inherently means the loss of the object in varying degree) turns the entire aggressive drive loose, and this develops increasing impetus and destroys the self that has become its object" (p. 130). The ego regresses, in some cases, to its undifferentiated phase, or employs other defenses, such as projection or withdrawal, to "avoid the destruction of the objects" (p. 133).

Ego Formation and Frustration

Victor Tausk's 1919 report on his treatment of a schizophrenic woman describes her delusions of being influenced by a machine. This classic study in the early literature on psychosis introduces the now familiar notion of the absence (or loss) of ego boundaries. Tausk recognized the complicated "influencing machine" as a projection of the patient's own body. In the infant's prestructural experience, Tausk remarks, even thoughts are "regarded at first as coming from the outer world before they are accounted among the functions of the ego" (Tausk,

1933, p. 546). The somatic self is identified as the infant's first object (Grotstein, 1980).

Paul Federn, who began to treat schizophrenic patients, some of them referred to him by Freud during the first decade of the century, disagreed with some of Freud's formulations at that time on ego processes, in particular with his idea that in schizophrenia the ego is richly invested with libido withdrawn from objects. Indeed Federn (1952) associated the disorder with a deficiency of ego cathexis. He viewed the basic disturbance as defective ego boundaries (using that term in a sense somewhat different from Tausk's). Consequently there is a blurring of distinctions between ego and outer world, and the ego has difficulty discriminating between false impressions and realities.

Ego boundaries are the objective aspect of what Federn referred to as "ego feeling," an ever-present awareness of self which he described as disturbed in schizophrenia. These related concepts of weak ego boundaries and loss of ego feeling have enjoyed wide currency, and have been formulated more clearly by some who focus on them as the core problem. For example, Thomas Freeman, John L. Cameron, and Andrew McGhie have expressed the idea that schizophrenics experience internal and external sensations as a continuum because of their inability to "differentiate the self from the environment" (1958, p. 51).

In the normally endowed and developing human being, definite awareness of one's separateness seems to develop about the fifteenth month of life. Awareness of emotional separateness from the mother slowly increases during the next six months of life—the rapprochement phase of the separation-individuation process (Mahler, Pine & Bergman, 1975). Among the mechanisms of self-boundary formation, Mahler and McDevitt stress the "importance of libidinization of the baby's body by the earliest contact perceptual ministrations of the mother." When these are not perceived, "as in infantile psychosis, . . . boundary sensations and the sense of 'being alive' appear to be missing" (1982, p. 833).

How do the ego boundaries get damaged? Through some failure in development, through regression, or could they have been shattered by explosive emotions, such as rage, that were being checked? Speculations today might take the directions just mentioned. Federn, however, did not answer this question, perhaps because he shared Freud's view that there is, in schizophrenia, a factor of malignity that cannot be reversed by psychological methods, and that one cannot go beyond strengthening the personality and avoiding "additional emotional strains on the individual who is balanced so precariously" (1952, p. 174).

And yet it appears from his writings that Federn was groping toward the answer. In his posthumously published paper (1952) on the ego's response to pain, one finds the following statement: "Repeated frustration in childhood can result in an impairment, or even the loss, of all object libido or in the discontinuance of entire components of sexuality. Through intense instinctual frustrations, the whole character is changed and the sexual development ceases. By identifications, or with the entrance of more mature components of sexuality, it may make another start later. When no such repair is made—spontaneously, by helpful environment or by psychoanalysis—coldness and dullness in all object relations is established for life" (p. 266).

Any kind of frustration trauma to which the individual reacts with abnormal readiness can initiate schizophrenic regression, according to Edward Glover (1949). The disorder, in his view, performs a defensive function which is threefold: "To ward off the dangers of reality stimulation, to discharge dangerous id excitations and to escape the oppression of superego control" (p. 229). In the sense that traumata were suffered during the early stages of ego formation and severe frustration "both real and imaginary" was experienced from familial objects, Glover regards the illness as a "true traumatic psychosis" (p. 231).

A close relationship between schizophrenia and acute traumatic neurosis, most prevalent in wartime, has been pointed out by other investigators. Abram Kardiner (1959), for example, regards both conditions as defensive inhibitions, similar in their psychodynamics and the "ultimate withdrawal" from the environment they set in motion (p. 256).

Dr. Richard L. Jenkins (1950) views the illness as a "potentially progressive maladaptation produced by frustration beyond the capacity of the patient to sustain" (p. 252). He distinguishes between schizophrenia as a reaction and as a process, and refers to the difference between them as simply a matter of degree. The process, which sets in when the threshold of frustration tolerance is passed, is marked by the "replacement of adaptive behavior by frozen, stereotyped 'frustration behavior' " (p. 261). If this results in further frustration, the disorganization of the personality, and its reorganization in some form of psychosis takes place.

"Relief of frustrations by symbolic realization" is the subtitle of a book by Marguerite Sechehaye (1956) on psychotherapy in schizophrenia. She regarded the cure of her now well-known young patient Renée as "almost experimental proof" (p. 58) of her frustration hypothesis. Through the absence of contact, which Mme. Sechehaye believed to be the core of the intrinsic disorder, schizophrenics defend themselves against "penetration by someone else" and also against an "eruption of affective and emotional life" (p. 51). Unsatisfied oral needs led to the patterning of the defense in the primary relationship, and psychosis represents both the individual's "renewed effort to relive the initial trauma in order to overcome it and a determined flight into the world of the subjective which alone requites him for the frustrations endured" (p. 4). She reported finding in schizophrenic patients "all the intermediate phases between a highly compensated frustration and a total incapacity to find a single mitigating one; in this latter case the ego is overwhelmed by self-destructive aggressive drives" (p. 59).

In infancy, Sechehaye pointed out, the "more vital and relevant to the instinct of preservation is the need, the more is the individual obliged to inhibit his hostile reactions springing from its unappeasement. If he seeks a measure of relief, he is forced to restrain his aggression against the person on whom he depends altogether, usually his mother" (p. 164). The aggression (or rage, as we view it today) may first be transmuted to weakness, indifference, and melancholy, but eventually the infant turns it on himself. The mother's refusal to appease the need is made the infant's own refusal "since at this stage the source of all his affects resides in the mother" (p. 66).

Highlighting the theme of ego sacrifice, Lewis B. Hill pointed out (1955) that a breast that is "precariously kept, so easily lost, gets to be overvalued" (p. 141). Sensing instability in the mother, the infant interdicts his anger and the "processes are not established and the techniques are not organized whereby anger and aggression can be directed outward" (p. 143). Consequently, the schizophrenic psyche contains an "amount of destructiveness which is a very great threat to the integrity of the ego. . . . In addition to great anger there is fear. The combination amounts to lasting hate of which the patient is profoundly unaware" (p. 152). Hill viewed the break with reality as a "defense in depth against having to react to the actions of persons in the environment" (p. 88). He observed too that the schizophrenic, never having fully separated himself from his mother, experiences a "persistent craving to return to the preobjective, and certainly preverbal mother-child relationship" (p. 116).

Characteristically, though not unanimously, theorists stressing exogenous factors have drawn up a bill of indictment against the patient's mother. In his first book, John N. Rosen (1953), who has consistently demonstrated the psychological reversibility of schizophrenic psychosis, characterized the mother as a person suffering from a "perversion of the maternal instinct" (p. 97). Modifying that view, he later (1963) pointed out that the mother herself is influenced by others participating in the "mothering process, whether malevolent or benevolent," by situational stress, and whatever else impinges on the infant, a totality of experience that Rosen conceptualizes as the "early maternal environment" (pp. 7-8). The pull of "unfinished business" (p. 40) ties the immature individual to that environment, and it is re-experienced in psychosis. Psychosis serves the basic function, according to Rosen, of keeping the individual from "recognizing, consciously, the latent sources of the terror which . . . he experienced with the early maternal environment as he construed it" (p. 19). Not mentioned here, but now emphasized, is the rage connected with the terror.

A neuropsychological formulation also stresses the frustration factor. Benno Schlesinger (1962) distinguishes between a psychogenic form of schizophrenia, in which a biochemical deficit remains latent except under conditions of stress, and a physiogenic form, which can develop in the absence of an external precipitant. Neither form, in his view, can be fully accounted for by experiential factors. He submits that "the common denominator of psychologically stressful situations is frustration and that a substandard frustration-gratification ratio precipitates the disease, given a certain heredo-constitutional predisposition" (p. 193). Schlesinger thus depicts a capacity for tremendous rage.

Narcissistic Rage

Aggressive manifestations in the service of growth commence *in utero*, thus antedating libidinal manifestations, according to Margaret Mahler (1981). At the beginning of extrauterine life, aggressive activity is aimed primarily at maintaining or restoring homeostatic balance within the organism, especially physiological homeostasis. The neonate or young infant achieves this by primitive discharge activity, "which, in turn, unintentionally serves as messages for the mother" (p. 626). Should she not function to help restore the infant's homeostatic equilibrium, however, the only resource at the infant's disposal is to dissolve in what Mahler referred to decades ago as "affecto-motor storm-rage reactions" (p. 626).

A closely related, if not identical phenomenon is that of narcissistic rage. Kohut identifies it (1972) as a specific manifestation of aggression that arises when the self or the object do not live up to the expectations directed at their function. Long recognized as characteristic of schizophrenic patients, narcissistic rage is frequently discussed today as a clinical problem of borderline patients (e.g., Kernberg, 1975, p. 267). Kernberg links the "apparently simple activation" of narcissistic rage to "primitive internalized relations of the unconscious past" and states that long-term benefits may ensue from tolerating it in the transference (1982, pp. 517).

Kohut (1977) expresses similar views. Narcissistic rage tends to erupt in the patient when a "specific genetically important traumatic situation" from his early life has been repeated in the analytic situation . . . . [leading to a revival of] the precariously established self of the child" (pp. 90–91). The mobilization of narcissistic rage is regarded as a "sign of the loosening of a rigid personality structure and thus of analytic progress" (1972, p. 387). The rage is gradually replaced by mature aggression, under the control of the ego, through the "gradual transformation of the narcissistic matrix from which the rage arises" (p. 392).

David Beres (1981) describes a situation in which a patient responded to an adverse comment by turning his narcissistic rage on himself. This resulted "in a loss of self-esteem and depression, a sign of 'negative narcissism' which Karl Abraham referred to in 1924" (p. 532).

THE SCHIZOPHRENIC NUCLEUS

The formulations and observations just reviewed cover successive stages in the development of psychoanalytic understanding of schizophrenia and touch on many aspects of the total clinical picture. Some of the psychic mechanisms mentioned have to be dealt with in specific cases or are of secondary significance.

Three other factors are primary: aggression, object protection, and sacrifice of the self. These are the elements that combine to produce the schizophrenic nucleus of the personality. The operational concept follows: *Schizophrenia is an organized mental situation, an intricately structured but psychologically unsuccessful defense against destructive behavior. Both aggressive and libidinal impulses figure in this organized situation; aggressive urges provide the explosive force while libidinal urges play an inhibiting role. The operation of the defense protects the object from the release of volcanic aggression (narcissistic rage) but entails (or threatens) the disruption of the psychic apparatus. Obliteration of the object field of the mind and fragmentation of the ego are among the secondary consequences of the defense.*

This situation appears to be organized during the undifferentiated phase of development. The only object that the infant can protect is the object in his mind, but in this phase he is incapable of distinguishing between psychic reality and material reality. Moreover, what is conceptualized as protection of the object may well be protection of the self, for these representations overlap at the early developmental level antedating the emergence of the ego field of the mind. Thus, the term "object field" encompasses the earliest self-representations. In other words, the ego is seen as object because the boundary between object and ego is indistinct and fluctuates.

At the Trauma Level

In *The Interpretation of Dreams* (1900), Freud linked the earliest thought activity in life with the functioning of a primitive mental apparatus (chapter 7, C). The apparatus is pictured as a reflex arc with a sensory receiver at one end, where the perceptual and memory systems are located, and systems governing motility at the other end. He assumed that the apparatus initially strives to keep itself as free from stimuli as possible by discharging excitations in movement. Freud illustrates such functioning by describing the behavior of the hungry baby.

Excitations produced by the need for nourishment seek discharge in movement, referred to as an "internal change" or "expression of emotion." The change cannot take place without outside help; the baby must be fed to achieve an "experience of satisfaction," putting an end to the internal stimulus. A vital component of that experience is a "particular perception . . . the mnemic image of which remains associated thenceforward with the memory trace of the excitation produced by the need." Consequently, whenever the baby gets hungry, a psychic impulse or wish emerges. In a state of tension, he seeks to "recathect the mnemic image . . . to reestablish the situation of the original satisfaction." The shortest path to the fulfillment of the wish leads directly from the excitation to a complete cathexis of the perception. What Freud referred to as a "perceptual identity" is a repetition of the perception of nourishment linked with the satisfaction of the need. The aim of the first psychical activity is to secure some reduction in tension by producing a perceptual identity (1900, pp. 565–566).

What goes on in the psychic apparatus if this need is frustrated? Wailing and thrashing about somewhat alleviate tension in the hungry infant, but the need persists. He is unable to achieve the experience of satisfaction while denied nourishment. The excitations aroused by hunger pangs then flow backward—regress—toward the sensory end of the psychic apparatus. The baby tries to establish, through memory, the gratification that is being withheld by the external object.

However, the evoking of the memory of the previous feeding fails to produce the perceptual identity that is desired. Even though a mild reduction in tension may ensue, the most vivid fantasies of the breast trickling milk into the infant's mouth are never as satisfying as the actual experience.

It is reasonable to assume that the frustration mobilizes rage in the hungry infant. The gratification of getting the milk is denied him, but revenge is also gratifying. To vent rage physically on the depriving object in the outside world is beyond the infant's power, but he can destroy the object in mind—in other words, the part of the mind that is identified with the object (Steiner, 1982). The infant wipes it out psychically by falling asleep, consumed with rage. Sleep is satisfying, and not only because it is an objectless state; it also anesthetizes hunger pains and dissipates the craving for the object. In short, sleep obliterates tension.

In waking states, when the desire for the object remains great, positive object cathexis persists and, in the absence of the real object, may be expended in clinging to the psychological object. This occurs, Freud (1900) points out, "in hallucinatory psychoses and hunger phantasies, which exhaust their whole psychical activity in clinging to the object of their wish" (p. 566).

The schizophrenic psyche clings to the object with libidinal cathexis and obliterates it with aggressive cathexis. These are the basic patterns. After they are formed, the ego sets up the control of motility so that it operates in the service of object protection. Libidinal energy is used for that purpose when, in the absence of tension-reducing gratification from the object, the obliteration pattern becomes charged with aggressive cathexis.

The integrity of the psyche and the fate of the external object are the stakes in the battle between aggressive object cathexis fighting for the control of motility and *libidinal cathexis checking motility to prevent destructive action.* In these high tension states, libidinal energy is adequate to inhibit hostile behavior, but is overwhelmed as the organizing force of the mental apparatus. It is on this front that the battle is decided in favor of the more powerful adversary. The patterning of the schizophrenic reaction reduces the tension sufficiently to protect the object, but disorganizes the mental apparatus and eventually leads to psychosis.

Evidence of this manner of reconciling the conflicting claims of love and hate is observed in psychotic states. If the disruption of the mind fails to appease the hatred withheld from objects, the defense may entail self-mutilation or suicide (Menninger, 1938). If the defense fails, what is observed is the homicidal maniac in action. If homicidal behavior is thwarted by hospitalization, frenzied attempts at suicide become manifest.

The Clinical Situation

Clinically, in latent cases of schizophrenia, the defense reveals itself in many different reactions. Aggressive impulses are compulsively inactivated; libidinal impulses are utilized in countless ways to spin a web around the aggression.

A young woman's disclosures about her feelings and behavior during a meeting with an acquaintance illustrate the infantile pattern. She said,

> I felt like a monster with Betty. I was frightened that I hated her so much. The more I hated her, the more I hated myself. I felt dull and inhibited, so I smoked more and more. I hated her because she was the way I was. Well, not exactly; she has more nerve than I ever had. She upset me, and made me feel out of things.

She communicated this unconscious message: Betty is much more aggressive than I am. Her behavior mobilizes hostile feelings in me. I want to attack her. This makes me feel like a monster, so I become frightened and withdraw. Feeling dull and "out of things," I try to control myself by smoking incessantly. The oral gratification charges my ego with libidinal cathexis. Then I don't have to express my hostility. This makes it "safe" for me to talk with Betty and makes the situation "safer" for her.

The affective nucleus to be dealt with is the undischarged aggressive reactions. The problem is traced back to a specific type of damaging failure in the early stage of maturation. In consequence, the child characteristically responded to excessive frustration, excessive gratification, or both, by piling up intense negative emotions in his mental apparatus instead of discharging these to objects.

The primitive ego, taught by an object regarded as extremely valuable that the release of rage was undesirable, operated as consistently as possible to bottle it up. When this proved impossible, the rage was discharged in a way that would not be harmful to the greatly needed real object; instead, it was directed to object and egotized object representations in the mind, giving rise to the problem of intense affects blocked from discharge, notably *constipated rage*. Growth processes were interrupted or reversed by this pathological response to undischarged aggression. Its accumulation in a stagnant psychic apparatus provides the optimal condition for development of the schizophrenic reaction.

To clarify the unconscious operation, I emphasize the idea that the patient continually experiences the pressure of a strong urge to kill and defends himself against it by putting his mental apparatus, with its high potential for destructive action, out of commission (Bloch, 1965, 1976, 1978). Knocking out the potentially destructive self to forestall dangerous action against others is akin to smashing a gun to bits to prevent oneself from pulling the trigger. The notion that psychological murder of the object and psychological suicide are ways of fighting against the lifting of the barriers to actual murder and suicide helps to make the patient's behavior and the disorder itself comprehensible.

SUPPLEMENTARY OBSERVATIONS

The scientific discoveries and observations of many psychoanalysts, as I have pointed out, contributed to the formulation of the working hypothesis just presented, and to some extent they shared this understanding of schizophrenia. In this conceptual framework, it is possible to account for their clinical findings and to appreciate some of the therapeutic failures that have been reported in the treatment of the condition.

Freud's conceptualizations are the foundation of our knowledge of the phenomenology of the illness, and his understanding of its consequential effects was profound. He recognized that its symptoms are meaningful, that erotic impulses figure in the schizophrenic defense, that regression occurs with attempts at restitution, and that the ego allows itself to be overwhelmed by the id under the impact of frustration. Retrospectively, one recognizes that the development of a therapeutic concept was retarded by his early inability clearly to separate love and hate impulses and by his failure to recognize schizophrenia as a defense against destroying the object. Under the sway of Freud's formulations of narcissism, some of his contemporaries became preoccupied with phenomenology and abstract formulas on self-love and sexual interests instead of studying each case in terms of interpersonal relationships and implementing their own observations accordingly.

Federn did not recognize that regression to the undifferentiated state of psychological functioning is forced by destructive impulses, or that ego boundaries can be obliterated by the corrosive effects of undischarged rage. Nevertheless, his descriptive formulations greatly enhanced our understanding of the subjective experience in schizophrenia and provide a valuable tool for working with narcissistic transference.

Nunberg, Hendrick, Klein, and others observed a strong aggressive cathexis for the object in the schizophrenic psyche. Their reports on clinical phenomena related to aggressive impulses appeared at a time when almost undivided attention was given to the fate of libidinal impulses.

Frustration of the need to express aggression was emphasized by Sechehaye and abundantly illustrated in her outstanding case material. She did not develop sufficiently the idea that aggression is turned back on the psychic apparatus out of regard for the object, and did not recognize that ever-present impulses to destroy it might have motivated her patient's "camouflage operations." The application of her theory is complicated because it is not focused on personality dynamics. She conceptualized the therapeutic process as one of meeting the need for discharge of impulses but did not distinguish between erotic and aggressive impulses or address herself to the defense against impulse discharge. If her treatment schema had been presented in terms of transference and resistance, it would have been more readily assimilated by therapists who have mastered the basic principles of psychoanalytic therapy.

I do not challenge the theory of neutralization per se, but its application in schizophrenia would be detrimental for treatment. The erotic drive is adequate to deal with a normal quantity of aggression. The problem is not faulty neutralization but the presence of more aggressive energy than could ever be successfully neutralized. The reason that it is so excessive, which is highly specific, has to be investigated; it has some bearing on the speed of recovery and subsequent personality maturation.

To suggest briefly the psychodynamics of the situation: both drives were attached to the primary object; in other words, it was both hated and loved. And when the infant somehow developed the attitude that the relationship would be totally destroyed if he expressed hatred, his love was strong enough to motivate him to protect the object by bottling up aggressive impulses. One might say that the infant had to suffer from constipated rage. As more and more pressure built up for the release of the aggressive impulses, the libidinal impulses became relatively weaker. Eventually, the mounting force of the hatred appeared to threaten the physical destruction of the object and was countered by its symbolic destruction. To prevent himself from acting on feelings in some way that would eliminate the object as a potential source of love, the child committed himself to eliminating the feelings.

The emotional logic of that compulsive operation is obscure unless one bears in mind its infantile nature. Negative feelings do not cancel out positive ones in persons functioning at the oedipal level. Psychoneurotics are able to feel and express both. They neutralize their hatred and retain their feelings of love for the object. But for the schizophrenic individual, whose aggressive impulses are more powerful, it may be "safer" not to have any feelings for an object when too much undischarged aggression is present. However, the schizophrenic pattern of *destroying feelings to prevent action* which the ego is afraid of does not justify the assumption that it lacks the capacity for neutralizing impulses.

In fact, schizophrenia itself might be characterized as a pathological way of neutralizing aggression in the absence of adequate insulation against action impulses (Spotnitz, 1962). Ogden (1982) states that the schizophrenic individual "unconsciously attacks his thoughts, feelings, and perceptions, which are felt to be an endless source of unmanageable pain and irresolvable conflict. . . . I am referring to the fact that a person can unconsciously prevent himself from directing attention to stimuli (internal and external), prohibit himself from organizing his perceptions, and prevent the attribution of feelings and meanings to sensory registrations" (pp. 166–167).

Individuals may go to the extreme of destroying their perceptions of the object and the ego, but this is not inevitable. If they succeed in releasing aggressive impulses without damaging these perceptions, their interest in the outside world reasserts itself. Sudden improvements and the appearance of restitutional symptoms suggest that the quantity of aggression has diminished so that it can be neutralized to the extent necessary to resume contact with objects.

In any event, to communicate the idea that patients should be less aggressive is a good way to make them more schizophrenic. The aggressive impulses have to be expressed. In a sense, their expression does neutralize them somewhat; but the analytic task is to remove the *obstacles* to the discharge of mobilized rage-aggression, the primary goal being discharge in language rather than action. As Glauber (1982) points out, "Speech lends itself as the vehicle for expression of all the instinctual drives, and, inasmuch as, in the unconscious, to express a wish by means of thoughts and words is equivalent to a literal living out of such a wish, thoughts and speech are highly cathected with libidinal and aggressive energy in their various forms of expression" (p. 32).

When the obstacles to verbal discharge are resolved, the psychotic symptoms disappear and the patient is in a position to master more healthful ways of dealing with negative emotions.

CURRENT VIEWS ON SCHIZOPHRENIA

Clinical Functioning in Schizophrenia and Borderline States

In one of his rare references to schizophrenia, Kohut (1971) equates the disorder with "potential permanent loss of the self" (p. 5). The narcissistic personality disturbances, which are described as "analyzable" (p. 1) are contrasted with schizophrenias, depressions, and borderline states. In the contemporary literature on the borderline and narcissistic disorders, the terms "analyzable" and "reversible" are often employed to differentiate them from the schizophrenic disorders.

Kernberg (1975) points to a "pathological fusion between self- and object images" (p. 162) in psychotic patients, whereas sufficient differentiation has taken place in borderline patients for integrated ego boundaries to be established. He views a defensive refusion of primitive, all good self-images and object-images as "protection against excessive frustration and rage." It is also "the prototype of what constitutes, if prolonged beyond the early infantile stages of development, a psychotic identification" (p. 163).

Kernberg calls attention to differences in the functioning of borderline and psychotic patients undergoing intensive treatment. Whereas the former responds positively to the systematic probing of primitive defensive operations, such probing brings about further "regression into manifest psychotic symptomatology" in the psychotic patient (1975, pp. 171–172).

Kernberg points out both similarities and differences in the transference psychosis that these two groups of patients develop in the course of treatment. The psychotic transference of the schizophrenic patient differs particularly from that of the borderline when the schizophrenic develops an "intensive emotional relationship to the therapist" (1975, p. 177). This is marked by experiences of fusion that reflects their regression to a "more primitive stage of symbiotic self-object fusion" (p. 177). The schizophrenic patient "requires a tolerance, on the therapist's part" of the powerful countertransference reactions triggered off by the patient's "fusion experiences in the transference" (p. 174).

Stress-Diathesis Model

In the recently introduced stress-diathesis or interactional model of schizophrenia (Zubin & Spring, 1977; Marsella & Snyder, 1981) the "onset, continuance, exacerbation, relapse, remission, and adaptation of schizophrenic symptoms and behaviors are presumed to be in some kind of homeostatic balance with biological, social, and environmental events" (p. 98). Thus, these symptoms and behaviors, although identified as pathognomic in psychiatric texts and diagnostic manuals, are viewed as fluctuating and inconsequential barometers of "interacting determinants which themselves stem from underlying biological and external social processes" (Liberman, 1982, p. 98).

Under the stress-diathesis model, any event that requires adaptation, whether positively or negatively perceived and valued, is identified as a stressor. Recent studies suggest that schizophrenic individuals, owing to their perceptual and cognitive impairments, as well as their psychological vulnerability, may be stressed by events that would not be stressful to others. In an important study in England (Birley & Brown, 1970), during a period of 3 months preceding a psychotic episode that led to hospitalization, abrupt changes in their social environments were experienced by 60 percent of the schizophrenic patients under study, compared to 14 percent of the normal controls.

What characteristically trigger the stress-diathesis situation or special vulnerabilities are, in my view, the factors of inadequate care combined with the accumulation of frustration-aggression in the mental apparatus during infancy.

The stress-diathesis model is quite close to the working hypothesis introduced in the first edition of this book, and reprinted with minor editorial revisions in the present chapter. The clinical implications of the stress-diathesis model, however, are not indicated.

Studies conducted in the United States and several other countries suggest that family factors significantly influence the course of the disorder. According to Liberman (1982), studies conducted in London identify interpersonal processes within the family as "the most powerful predictors of relapse in a person having an established schizophrenic illness" (p. 103). Over a period of 15 years, it was found that patients who return to families that are "high on expressing criticism and emotional overinvolvement relapse four times as often as patients returning to families that are low in these categories of expressed emotion (EE)" (p. 103). These results have been duplicated in several studies conducted in the United States.

Although cultural factors seem to determine the proportion of families that are high on EE, "once present, high EE predisposes toward schizophrenic relapse regardless of culture" (p. 104).

Conflict and Deficit Models

Contrasting views on the nuclear difficulties of the schizophrenic patient and the implications of these theoretical models for psychotherapy have been extensively discussed in the psychoanalytic literature since the early 1970s.

Theorists who support the so-called deficit model (also referred to as the specific theory of schizophrenia) view important aspects of classical analytic technique as antitherapeutic for the patient (Wexler, 1971; London, 1973; Grotstein, 1977, 1980). They point to ego deficiency as the central problem and favor supportive psychosocial therapies oriented to repairing the ego deficits and restoring internal object representations.

The conflict-defense school (also known as the unitary theorists), on the other hand, regard psychoanalysis as the treatment of choice. They stress purely supportive therapy as harmful, inasmuch as it militates against potential ego growth and prevents the resolution of psychological conflicts. The ego deformation and loss of mental representations are associated with an active defensive operation, its purpose being to "ward off intolerable affects, threatening impulses, and painful reality" (Gunderson, 1974, p. 185). Conflict theorists include most practitioners who treat schizophrenics psychoanalytically (e.g., Boyer & Giovacchini, 1967).

My own point of view is that the schizophrenic patient's conflict about the release of aggressive impulses is a product of the patient's ego defects. These defects have to be dealt with in some way because they make the patient inadequate to cope with the aggression; this is what makes him potentially psychotic.

In the modern psychoanalytic approach, the ego defects are characteristically dealt with by emotional communication and analytic group therapy. A purely supportive, rather than analytic approach, impresses me as representing a defense against dealing with the patient's aggression.

In summary, the schizophrenic individual possesses an inordinate potential for aggressive impulsivity and deals with it in a particular way out of regard for an object viewed as more important than the self. The potential may be a hereditary or constitutional endowment, or may be associated with life experience. In many cases, the condition seems to be overdetermined. To the extent to which it is related to environmental factors, the aggression is mobilized by frustration. Clinically, it appears as frustration-aggression—potentially psychotic rage—even though the frustration may have been minor, because of the pattern that was set up for dealing with it.

It is unnecessary to postulate that a particular type of relationship produced the infantile pattern. It may be in part innate and in part learned. Even in cases where it was taught by the mother, her attitude may not have been pathological; there may simply have been disequilibrium between her emotional training and the infant's impulsivity. The dynamics of the mother-child relationship are not uniform in these cases. More significant than whether the parent actually loved, hated, or was indifferent to her infant is the fact that the *totality of his environment failed to meet his specific maturational needs*; the infant experienced it as a very frustrating object, especially in view of his specific vulnerability to stress. In some cases aggression seems to have been mobilized by too much sensory deprivation, in other cases by undue excitation (Calne, 1984), whether endogenous or exogenous in origin. In either event, more aggression was mobilized than the infantile ego could cope with healthfully.

The damage incurred by the structures of the mind often confronts the clinical observer with a scrambled picture. But eventually it can be understood, and the damaged structures can be provided with opportunities to heal themselves, if one recognizes that *the primary forces that scramble the personality in schizophrenia are impulses to destroy the object.*

Chapter 3

AMPLIFICATION OF THE BASIC THEORY OF TECHNIQUE

Psychoanalysis as a causal therapy rests on Freud's discovery that psychoneurosis is rooted in a conflict between libidinal impulses at the oedipal level of development. Love affects are of minor significance in schizophrenia. A powerful negative emotional charge, in large measure the product of unfavorable maturational factors connected with preoedipal development, has been identified as the nuclear problem. Its implications for methodology, which to my knowledge have not been systematically investigated, are far-reaching.

Focusing on the consequential changes, this chapter first scans in a rudimentary way the basic principles of psychoanalytic therapy in psychoneurotic conditions. In that frame of reference, the fundamentals of the psychoanalytic approach to the schizophrenic patient are outlined to illuminate the amplification of these principles and to account for the special emotional demands that treatment, when oriented to the resolution of the nuclear problem, makes on the practitioner. Special applications of the major working concepts, explored in later chapters, are introduced. A schema reflecting the evolution of a case of schizophrenia is presented.

APPLICATION IN PSYCHONEUROSIS

A diagnosis of "pure" psychoneurosis conveys the understanding that the patient's disturbance is rooted in the repression of painful sexual ideas. It is anticipated, since the significant impulses to be liberated are libidinal, that the patient will develop a basically positive attachment to the analyst. As these impulses are reactivated in the course of the relationship, the primarily loving attitudes that the patient developed for the parents early in life are transferred to the analyst.

As long as "transference love" motivates the patient to cooperate, it is not called to his attention. When it serves to impede the flow of his communications, the analyst, applying the working concept of resistance to obstacles to the verbalization of positive feelings, focuses on removing the interference. Hostile feelings that block communication are dealt with in a similar manner. The transference resistance of the psychoneurotic yields to appropriate verbal communications from the analyst. These give the patient feelings of being understood and loved, which stimulate verbal release, change, and emotional growth. Consequently, he does not require other forms of communication.

The patient's attitudes exert an influence on the analyst. Feelings of affection, for example, tend to induce similar feelings. These the practitioner was originally taught to suppress. Countertransference reactions are regarded as obstacles to understanding the patient's conflict and as the source of inappropriate interpretations of resistance. For a person who responds appropriately to verbal communication, what the analyst tries to achieve is intellectual rather than affective identification.

The basic theory of psychoanalytic technique developed out of such experience in treating the psychoneurotic patient. The major psychological events overlap to some extent, of course, but by and large they occur in the following sequence:

1. Transference is evoked and transference resistance is studied.
2. Countertransference resistance is recognized and analyzed.

3. Transference resistance is interpreted.
4. Resistance patterns are worked through.
5. Resistance to termination is resolved.

APPLICATION IN SCHIZOPHRENIA

When the same therapeutic principles are applied in a case of schizophrenia, the patient's behavior appears to indicate that he is not amenable to psychoanalytic influence. The most formidable obstacle is the essentially different way he relates to the analyst. When the schizophrenic patient is helped to develop a transference, it is permeated with hostility, which may be overlaid with obliviousness, indifference, or even apparent sweetness. Eventually, the patient is negative to the analyst and opposes his influence. That is the patient's conscious attitude; unconsciously the patient comes to hate the analyst.

This development baffled the first generation of analysts. Some of them equated it with the absence of transference; indeed, Abraham, in 1908, referred to the negativism as the "most complete antithesis to transference" (1953, p. 71). If it is true, as Freud believed (1912b), that corrective influence evaporates if a hostile transference gains the upper hand, the re-education of a person dominated by cravings to destroy the human instrument of his treatment is an impossible feat—and, too, an undertaking that few practitioners would care to attempt.

Perhaps, it should be made clear that it is the symbolic object, not the analyst as a real person, whose destruction is craved. Needless to say, Freud recognized that fact, but it seems that he was hypersensitive to the emotion of hate in himself or anyone else. Hostility directed toward himself was particularly difficult for him to tolerate (Sulloway, 1979; Schur, 1972).

Some of Freud's reservations about the efficacy of the psychoanalytic method support that impression, but stronger evidence emerges from his prognosis in a case that he discontinued after 4 years of analysis. The former patient, a woman, then applied for admission to the clinic of Dr. Ludwig Binswanger. A request from Binswanger for information about her was answered by Freud, in 1915, in a letter containing this passage: "She pretends that she still depends on me, but actually has been running away from me, since I was able to tell her the real secret of her illness (revengeful and murderous impulses against her husband). *Analytically unfit for anyone.* [Emphasis added.] . . . she is naturally *waiting* for his death but will never admit it" (Binswanger, 1957, p. 62).[1]

In the light of our present understanding, it is likely that we would put a different construction on the behavior that Freud described. It would appear that he had made much more progress in this woman's treatment than he recognized. Her pattern of "running away" might have been motivated by an unconscious need to protect her transference object against destructive impulses pressing for discharge, which suggests that the attachment to Freud—both negative and positive—was strong. The impression that she was "analytically unfit for anyone" could have been fostered by the incorrect ideas originally applied, in particular the belief that it is impossible to influence a patient except in a state of positive transference. But the characterization illustrates Freud's objection to being exposed to strongly negative affects.

It is now recognized that hatred can be a therapeutic force. Many analysts have reported this discovery (e.g., Pao, 1965). Hatred binds schizophrenic patients to their transference object even more firmly than love. They are willing to work *as long as necessary* to master their aggressive impulses *provided* that the danger that they will act on them destructively is kept to a minimum. Indeed, patients often experience a strong need for protection against the risk of harming themselves or others.

One danger the analyst bears in mind is that of stimulating iatrogenic narcissistic regression through an inflexible attitude; the hallucinations and delusions to which it may give rise in the schizophrenic patient are very difficult to deal with. What needs to be avoided is what Stone (1981b) has characterized as a "neoclassical" attitude—one of "robotlike anonymity" and an extreme routinization of technique (pp. 650-651).

---

[1]Dr. Binswanger subsequently accepted her in his clinic, where she was successfully treated.

Safeguards against Explosive Behavior

With the development of negative transference, the removal of obstacles to the verbal discharge of destructive impulsivity becomes the primary focus of treatment. In the process of converting the "most malignant narcissistic rage . . . into constructive aggression" (Rudolph, 1981, p. 578), the necessary safeguards against explosive behavior are created in three ways:

1. The degree of tension to which the patient is exposed is judiciously controlled.
2. To liberate the patient from pressure to act on aggressive impulses, a treatment climate in which the patient will feel and verbalize them is maintained.
3. The patient is helped to resolve the immediate obstacles to the verbal discharge of these impulses.[2]

Since it usually requires a great deal of time for the analytic team to resolve each obstacle to verbal communication, the application of these "safety measures" slows down the tempo at which the transference develops. Thus, its hostile manifestations become more manageable.

When the negative transference is established and inhibits *verbal* communication, the analyst proceeds to resolve this resistance. He reinforces the patient's opposition to *acting on* aggressive impulses in the session. Such opposition is needed, and impulsive behavior is consistently discouraged through the analyst's attitudes. In other words, the patient is encouraged to remain on the couch and talk (Stern, 1978).

The patterns of transference resistance to communication that are characteristic of the schizophrenic patient at the beginning of treatment are joined or psychologically reflected. By presenting himself as an object like the ego, emotionally as well as intellectually, the analyst helps the patient deal with the earliest pathological object representations. When a transference resistance is effectively joined, the patient responds with a tor-

[2]Specific techniques through which these safeguards are created, notably contact functioning and object-oriented questioning, are discussed in Chapter 10.

rent of threats, insults, and verbal abuse—a release of potentially psychotic rage. In other words, the constipated affects that the patient had been directing into self-attack are now freely verbalized toward the analyst.

The attitude of the analyst under this bombardment conveys the message: Words do not damage me; they are acceptable. When the analyst presents himself consistently as a willing target for verbal hostility, the patient gets to recognize that the foulest explosions of feelings and words are in order. The patient experiences such discharge, when accepted by the analyst, as tension-relieving and mildly satisfying. The patient is helped to verbalize hostility for therapeutic purposes but not for sadistic gratification. This is, admittedly, a fine distinction, but it may be necessary to make it clear to the patient repeatedly. The analyst is not to be abused!

This approach is consonant with the hypothesis that the patient's hostile impulses were originally mobilized at a time when the boundaries between the ego and object fields of the mind were indistinct and fluid—that is, in Kohut's terms, when the selfobject dominated psychic activities. When these impulses are reactivated in the analytic relationship and the resistance to verbalizing them is repeatedly reflected, the transference object is readily identified with the self. Schizophrenic patients tend to feel that the analyst is just like them—a reassuring notion. In the presence of a person like themselves, patients feel liked, understood, and thus free to proclaim hostility and rage. By direction and example, they are taught to communicate it in emotional language.

With the resolution of negative-transference resistance and the verbalization of hostility, positive transference is free to develop. The patient becomes increasingly aware of affectionate feelings for the analyst as well as a growing sense of security in the relationship. As a function of awareness of these feelings, the patient becomes more and more capable of verbalizing negative feelings. There is thus a continuing oscillation between positive feelings and the verbalization of negative feelings—a state conducive to emotional growth and to the development of auto-immune mechanisms (Wyatt et al., 1982).

Eventually the patient's feelings become oedipal in nature, and one may intervene with the more familiar interpretations.

Positive transference, in turn, is not dealt with until it becomes a resistance.

As the conceptual tools of transference and resistance are wielded in the sequence just indicated to resolve the special resistances to communication in schizophrenia, exposure to the patient's hostility induces anxiety, fear, and hatred. The analyst will become aware, not only of empathy, but of a strong negative countertransference that gives rise to resistance. He will want to attack the patient verbally, discharge the patient as unsuitable for analysis, or find some other way to terminate the relationship. However, if the practitioner can prevent himself from acting on these induced feelings and is able to analyze them, they will help him understand how the patient's hostile impulses were organized. There are many pitfalls in the hate countertransference and its derivatives; but they represent an important source of therapeutic leverage (Chapter 9).

Sequence of Events

When the schizophrenic patient is effectively treated in accordance with the therapeutic principles just described, the psychodynamics of the process of recovery differ from those that are implicitly expressed in the basic theory of analytic technique. What is commonly regarded as the middle phase of an analysis does not begin to develop until the narcissistic transference has evolved and object transference has been established. Although the approaches enjoyed earlier in the case are still required at times, the treatment is essentially similar to that of the psychoneurotic patient after the object transference has been stabilized. The sequence of events that occur in the course of the case are expressed in the schema that follows:

1. Narcissistic[3] transference develops and is analyzed silently.

[3]Used here synonymously with "preoedipal" and "selfobject" and relating to the first 2 years of life, the developmental phase in which the separation between the object and the self is indistinct. Emotional differentiation between the two tends to be initiated in the third year, the beginning of the oedipal period, and is normally completed by the age of thirteen.

2. The patient's attempts to get in contact with the analyst are studied to determine their origin and history, and responded to as necessary to control the intensity of resistance.

3. Narcissistic countertransference resistance is recognized and analyzed.

4. Narcissistic transference resistance is effectively influenced through the joining of the patient's resistive attempts to establish contact.

5. Narcissistic transference resistance is worked through.

6. Object (oedipal-type) transference develops and is studied.

7. Countertransference resistance is recognized and analyzed silently.

8. Object transference resistance is interpreted.

9. Object transference resistance is worked through.

10. Resistance to termination is resolved.[4]

Obviously, a case of this nature is no light undertaking. The narcissistic defense (Spotnitz, 1961b) holds in check forces that can be as explosive as dynamite when inexpertly handled, forces that have to be detonated in the relationship without causing undue suffering to either party. The task is predicated on an understanding of the role played by aggressive impulses in the organization of the patient's personality, their influence on his here-and-now functioning in the treatment sessions, and the emotional resiliency of the analyst in the therapeutic situation.

[4]For examples of the application of the schema, see Spotnitz, 1977 and 1979b.

Chapter 4

A NEUROBIOLOGICAL APPROACH
TO COMMUNICATION

Nature seems to move inexorably from event to event, presumably through cause and effect. People move tentatively when they try to test that relationship, particularly if they do so by the indirect method. The essence of that method is lucidly conveyed in the Notebooks of Leonardo da Vinci:

> Although nature starts from reason and ends with experience, it is necessary for us to proceed the other way around—that is . . . begin with experience and with its help seek the reason. Experience never errs; what alone may err is our judgment, which predicts effects that cannot be produced in our experiments. Given a cause, what follows will of necessity be its true effect, unless some external obstacle intervenes.

The gist of the last sentence is conveyed more succinctly in the diagrammatic language employed in scientific research:

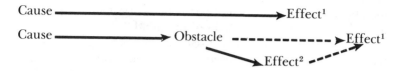

These diagrams suggest that the investigator was trying to restore a cause to its "true" effect (Effect[1]), which was known, by focusing on the unknown obstacle and eventually nullifying it. To ascertain the nature of an obstacle and remove it to produce Effect[1] instead of Effect[2] is to engage in an indirect method of research.

To physical scientists, Effect[1] might signify the direction taken by a wave of excitation in the absence of outside interference, and Effect[2] the deflection produced by an intervening force. Should they wish to restore the flow of energy to the original course, rather than trying to change Effect[2] directly, they would address themselves to the unknown obstruction. After discovering what it is and why it operates in that instance, they would attempt to remove it. If they succeed in transforming Effect[2] into Effect[1] they would assume that their understanding of the obstacle is correct and that they have neutralized it.

Freud adapted the indirect method to clinical studies of mental processes. Through its systematic application in investigations of psychopathology, general knowledge of personality development has been acquired, obstacles to healthful mental functioning have been discovered, and psychological techniques for removing them have been developed. Knowledge obtained through the method is thus converted into therapeutic power.

Clinical concepts and terminology reflect other resemblances between the scientist's approach to phenomena in the external world and the psychoanalyst's approach to events inside the mind. We generally refer to the world of sensory data, as perceived by most observers, as the objective world. The world of subjective data, available only through introspection and verbal reporting, is generally referred to as the world of the mind. The phenomena in both worlds are observed and remembered by the mind, and inevitably their data are organized in similar fashion—the fashion of the mind.

For example, the physical scientist refers to waves of excitation as "pulsations of energy" and to the obstructions these encounter in the physical domain as "resistance"; the analyst talks of psychological impulses and of resistances to their discharge in actions and words. The tendency of the scientifically trained mind to assign the same kind of structure to physical and mental data may account for many such parallelisms; but they encourage the notion that similar forces operate in both spheres and that a different organization, component, or expression of these forces is observed by each group of investigators.

Total understanding of a phenomenon frequently entails the pooling of observational data and theories based on studies of different aspects of functioning.

Nevertheless, total explanations are not always required in clinical work. Purely psychological explanations often equip the psychotherapist with sufficient comprehension of one of the milder disturbances to deal with it satisfactorily. Although Freud repeatedly called attention to possible organic involvement in the neuroses, he explained: "Our analytic experience that they can be extensively influenced, if the historical precipitating causes and accidental auxiliary factors of the illness can be dealt with, has led us to neglect the constitutional factor in our therapeutic practice" (1933, pp. 153-154).

The constitutional factor appears to be more significant in schizophrenia. The more primitive the level at which the patient operates, the greater the need to understand the nature and function of the analyst's communications to the patient. Evidence is conclusive today that communication is a function of the central nervous system—cell-to-cell communication in terms of physicochemical processes—and that communication influences chemistry and chemistry influences communication. In other words, psychoanalysis influences the functioning of the central nervous system, and changes in the central nervous system influence verbal communication. Words from the analyst are highly specific psychological medicine, and *tools for producing changes in the nervous system.*

Contemporary studies in neurobiology, molecular biology, neurophysiology, and other branches of neuroscience have produced some clues to the biodynamics of schizophrenia. Findings in these areas suggest that the curative process entails, in neuroscientific terms, the reversible deactivation of certain neuronal pathways and the activation of new pathways. Reversible deactivation is in order so that the old pathways, after being deactivated for a period of time, may be reactivated again when appropriate. For example, a dependency pattern that has operated since infancy in a severely disturbed patient may fall into disuse as he forms a pattern of taking care of himself; however, a situation may arise in which the temporary reactivation of the dependency pattern and temporary deactivation of the pattern of independence are desirable, as in a physical illness. Future research will determine the specific systems that are to be deactivated and those that are to be temporarily reactivated.

These deactivation and activation processes can be accomplished through either psychological or chemical measures, or through a combination of both. We now appear to be going in the direction of describing precisely how to influence physiological and chemical processes through psychology and how to influence psychological processes through physiological and chemical changes.

Cerebral physiologists and other investigators in the neurosciences have reported hypotheses and observations that are relevant for the treatment of the schizophrenic individual and, indeed, are generally applicable in psychoanalytic therapy. Specific implications for the therapist's communications are discussed in this chapter in the framework of a neuroscientific formulation.

DYNAMICS OF PERSONALITY DEVELOPMENT

The indirect method of investigation rests on the assumption that the relationship between cause and effect is constant unless, to repeat da Vinci's words, "some external obstacle intervenes." The specific assumption that is corroborated by modern-day neuroscience is that stimulus-and-response operates in the nervous system unless some inhibitory factor intervenes.

To the investigator of vital phenomena, this assumption may mean that a healthy fertilized ovum evolves in a succession of favorable environments until it reaches the peak of growth and development as a healthy adult. To focus on one aspect of this unimpeded movement, it is assumed that, in the absence of significantly adverse external influences, the personality continues to unfold until it reaches full term—emotional maturity.

| (Personality in infancy) | (Meeting of maturational needs) ⟶ | (Mature Personality) |

The meeting of maturational needs[1] is the favorable outcome of the series of interchanges with environmental forces—physicochemical and biological as well as psychological—in which the organism engages from conception onward. The placenta and amniotic sack and its contents, essential for maturation of the fetus, are lost at birth. Their replacement by other types of maturational agents is essential for the infant's survival. The interchanges that follow constitute different kinds of teamwork, each of which makes a specific contribution to the long-range enterprise of meeting the child's changing emotional needs.

The first environmental agent with whom the infant teams up is the mother, or the maternal environment. The early sensoriperceptive interchange between mother and infant seems to be a *sine qua non* of the infant's "earliest sense of the body self as entity. . . . the condition on which the feeling of 'being alive' rests" (Mahler & McDevitt, 1982, p. 833). There is overwhelming evidence of the crucial importance of their collaborative functioning for personality patterning. Research studies cited at the first Symposium on Infant Psychiatry (Proceedings, 1981) indicate that basic homeostatic mechanisms and reciprocal in-

---

[1]Developmental or growth needs, which are distinguished from gratification needs.

teractions are established within the first months of life through a harmonious relationship between infant and mother; foundations for the ability to love and the ability to learn are rooted in the first 18 months. The maturational experience during the oedipal period of development is more specifically with the family. Later on, the teamwork encompasses an expanding circle of adults and peers (Oakes, 1982).

The environmental transactions of the growing child bring psychic energy into play and condition the child to utilize it constructively. At birth the organism is a bundle of bodily and nervous energy, equipped with reflexes that automatically relieve the pressure of many kinds of excitation on the nervous system. By and large, however, psychic or mental energy appears to develop later, and its discharge has to be organized. The nervous system has been described as a "multi-layered hierarchical organization in which the same general principles are utilized at each layer and . . . all layers function simultaneously and in harmony" (Cotman & McGaugh, 1980, p. 489). The regulatory principles of mental functioning as a hierarchical system have been formulated by Gedo and Goldberg (1973).

The timing and quantity of the stimulation to which the child is exposed help to determine the kinds of patterns the mind organizes for the distribution of psychic energy. Stimuli appropriate to each maturational sequence and in balance with the child's own impulsivity facilitate the flow of this energy and its pleasurable discharge in emotions, words, and actions. An efficient energy-distribution system, an attribute of the well-integrated personality, is an essential requirement for the improved functioning of the schizophrenic patient.

If the personality fails to realize its growth potential, it is reasonable to assume that the individual was deflected from a natural course because the environment either lacked essential growth ingredients or exposed him to forces that militated against his behaving as the growth impulses dictated. In some cases both factors appear to be incriminated. Interferences serious enough to cause painful or disabling symptoms suggest that some damage sustained in early transactions with the environment prevent the individual from dealing comfortably with the immediate realities of life.

Highly specific reactions to maturational failure have been classified. They form a spectrum of functional disorders, ranging from mild forms of psychoneurosis to psychotic conditions and organic illnesses. Arrayed between these extremes are impulse disorders, character disorders, and some psychosomatic disturbances. The position of each component on the spectrum suggests, in inverse order, the stage at which the maturational process was thrown out of gear. The earlier this occurred, the more damaging its impact on the organism.

Psychosis is connected with disruptions of the maturational sequences that unfold during the first two years of life. During the first 15 months of this preoedipal period, the infant usually acquires a sense of self. But when, as in infantile psychosis, the mother's libidinal ministrations are not perceived, boundary sensations and feelings of being alive seem to be missing (Mahler & McDevitt, 1982). The relatively uneventful completion of the earliest sequences is implied from the classification of a disorder elsewhere in the series. Vicissitudes encountered at the later maturational levels are associated with borderline and narcissistic personality disorders, and eventually with the psychoneuroses and the relatively minor disturbances experienced by the "normal" person in emotionally stressful circumstances.

Unlike those disorders that lead to permanent damage of the central nervous system, among them some organic conditions, such as cerebral atrophy and brain tumors, there is no evidence that the functional disorders are irreversible. The psychoanalyst deals with them on the assumption that they are psychologically reversible, and by indirect means. In the role of a therapeutic object, he provides a supplementary series of interchanges—verbal interchanges—for a person whose maturational needs were improperly or inadequately met in the interchanges with natural objects. The treatment relationship is designed to help the patient reach, as quickly as possible, the high level of development characteristic of the emotionally mature individual.

One of the earliest references in psychoanalytic literature to the situation graphically depicted here was made by August Aichhorn (1936), a pioneer in the treatment of delinquents, who discussed the role of narcissistic transference in the undoing process. In a later communication to Anna Freud, cited in her

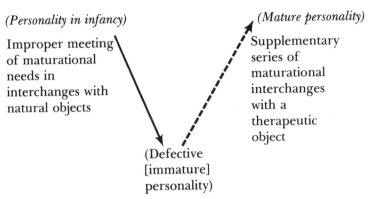

(Personality in infancy)

Improper meeting
of maturational
needs in
interchanges with
natural objects

(Defective
[immature]
personality)

(Mature personality)

Supplementary
series of
maturational
interchanges
with a
therapeutic
object

obituary of Aichhorn, he states that undergoing experiences that undo anomalies and make up for deficiencies in early libidinal development make it possible for the delinquent to "complete the structure of his personality, which was arrested at a primitive level" (A. Freud, 1951, p. 54).

In a person under psychoanalytic study, one generally recognizes two distinctly different types of interferences with personality growth: (1) The person suffers to some degree from the effects of failures, or memories of failures in the meeting of maturational needs that led to deviations in emotional growth. (2) In attempts to cope with these deviations, the individual compounds those failures with certain repetitive patterns of behavior that drain off energy into circuitous processes. These defensive patterns, to the extent to which they persist and prevent effective assimilation of experience that would serve to reduce the person's needs, become maladaptations. Their operation hinders the development of subsequent maturational sequences (as shown in Figure 1).

Specifically implicated in schizophrenia is a situation combining minimal gratification and excessive frustration that was connected with early maturational sequences and was subjectively experienced as intense and prolonged (Liegner, 1980). The situation, moreover, mobilized an inordinate amount of aggressive energy, and its expression to the object has undergone an extreme degree of repression and suppression. As a consequence of repressed frustration experienced by the infant at the breast, the aggressive drive comes to the fore at the age of three months (Almansi, 1960).

Various aspects of the psychodynamic situation outlined in Figure 1 are reflected in the literature. Angry reactions occur not only as a response to limits imposed by the mother; they are also viewed as an expression of the infant's "oral sadism and aggressive endowment" (Blum, 1982, p. 971). Assuming the existence of a primitive destructive part of the self in all individuals, how it is dealt with by the remaining parts of the personality, Steiner suggests, will be a major determinant of the outcome. He adds, "In psychotic patients, this destructive part of the self dominates the personality, destroying and immobilizing the healthy parts" (Steiner, 1982, p. 242). Mahler and McDevitt (1982) observed psychotic children compensating for their failure to develop a firm sense of self through "aggressivization of their skin and skull" (p. 833). To the extent that the sense of self develops in the context of the infant's dependence on the mother, it "will bear the imprint of her care-giving" (p. 837).

A psychodynamic formulation of the interrelationships of the various interferences with personality development mentioned above is presented in Figure 1. Molina (1982), refers to charts or diagrams of the intrapsychic, biological, and social factors implicated in pathological behavior as psychobiosocial maps, and discusses their value in therapy and clinical training.

The treatment relationship reactivates both types of interfering factors: the deficiency states created by the improper meeting of maturational needs as well as the patterns of maladaptation that eventually resulted from attempts to cope with these states. For various reasons, obstacles of the first type, though they are mollified in the treatment, are not brought into focus. To address treatment to the appeasement of maturational needs would be as pointless as gorging oneself at twenty to eradicate the memory of bouts with hunger in early childhood. The long-term impact of the memory is assuaged to a certain extent in so-called supportive psychotherapy, but the consequences of the original frustration or deprivation experience are not erased. The analyst concentrates, therefore, on interferences of the second type. Dissolution of the patterns of maladaptation that imprison energy required for further personality growth is the primary concern.

Psychological Interferences with Personality Maturation

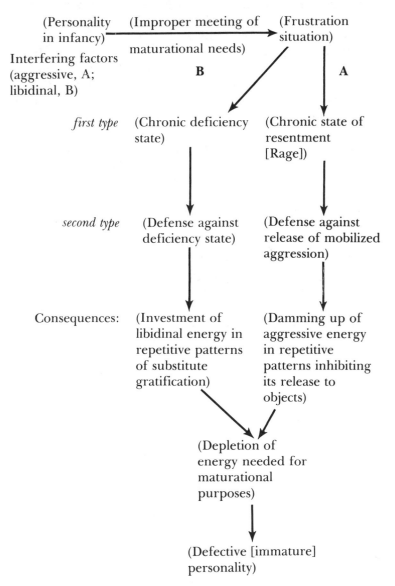

Figure 1

In other words, the analyst operates *indirectly* as a maturational agent, *primarily addressing the blockages rather than attempting to meet the needs directly*. Coincidentally some psychological growth needs that were not met early in life, such as the need for affection, may be gratified symbolically (Sechehaye, 1956) in the process of dissolving the blockages. The ultimate goal of the treatment, however, is to *resolve the behavioral tendencies* that have prevented the patient from reducing these needs. With the dissolution of the troublesome patterns, the mental energy that was concentrated on a lower level of functioning becomes available for more mature functioning and future emotional growth. Further reduction of the unmet maturational needs can then be secured by the patient in relations with other people.

The mind or psychic apparatus, with which the analyst is concerned, appears to be the product of a specific neural organization. An integration of contemporary knowledge of this "machinery" with psychoanalytic theory enhances understanding of the precise kind of psychotherapeutic influence to which the schizophrenic individual responds, and of the concomitant modifications in modes of neural functioning—an objectively identifiable factor of change. The neuropsychological approach offers an *additional guideline for communication*, one aspect of which can be quantified with sufficient precision to meet the needs of the clinician.

Explanations of the significance of neural processes for behavior are of a much lower order of complexity than descriptions of the processes. Without delving into the intricacies of neuroanatomy, neurochemistry, or electrophysiology, neurophysiological observations and ideas about the activity of the nervous system can be brought into harmony with the multidisciplinary hypothesis just presented.

The concomitants of the psychic patterns that operate as obstacles to personality maturation are patterns laid down by early learning in the organ of the mind. The analyst having some understanding of the interdependence of the mental and physical structures is better able to influence both. Recognition of the changes in neural functioning that are associated with psychological changes helps to meet the need for concrete explanations of the effects of analytic procedures.

R. W. Gerard (1960), an eloquent interpreter of recent findings on the neural mechanisms of behavior, suggests the physical imprints of what I have conceptualized as maturational interchanges:

> The raw experience of the infant is progressively categorized and differentiated to the highly discriminative perceptions and conceptions of the adult by *successive steps of patterning* in his nervous system. . . . Constant or regularly repeated *constellations of sensory inputs* generate the entities of our universe of experience, initially the material objects. . . . The *traces left by experience are real and specific patterns in the nervous system*, with morphological locus and physiological properties. (Emphasis added; p. 1945)

This statement stands unchallenged, and knowledge about the nature of the patterns has burgeoned in the last few decades. These patterns are the product of communications among the nerve cells or neurons—interneuronal communications via hormonal chemistry. Interneuronal communication, it is now clear, is not only a physical process but significantly a chemical one as well.

Computing, integrating, and recording signals in the form of action potentials is the activity of every neuron. "Integration at the level of the single cell is a microstruggle, a tiny battle of excitation and inhibition that takes place against the modulating background of the slow-acting inputs" (Cotman & McGaugh, 1980, p. 248).

FREUD'S SCIENTIFIC PSYCHOLOGY

Freud laid down a foundation for the neuropsychological approach in 1895, the year which saw the publication of the *Studies on Hysteria*. From one with his knowledge of cerebral physiology, experience in treating diseases of the nervous system, and intense interest in puzzling out both normal and abnormal mental processes, an attempt to derive a psychology from neurophysiology would be expected. Embarking on what he projected as a psychology for neurologists, in their language, he crystallized knowledge of the time about brain functioning, and drew on his introspective knowledge and clinical experience with psychiatric patients to codify psychic processes that had not been explained. He knew, for example, that the mind functioned differently in waking and dream states; but he had no objective evidence that this was also true of the central nervous system.

Within a matter of months, however, Freud abandoned the work, deciding that it was impossible to account for all psychic activity in neurophysiological terms. His uncompleted manuscript, rescued from oblivion, was posthumously published in 1950 (English edition, 1954) under the title *Project for a Scientific Psychology*.

Having failed to describe psychic activity satisfactorily in terms of the brain, Freud cast aside the unfinished work with the intention of "localizing" psychological discoveries thereafter in the mind—in other words, viewing psychic activity introspectively. Nevertheless, as he observed that one or another psychic process consistently tallied with one of the neurological formulations of 1895, it was integrated into the body of psychoanalytic theory, usually with some revision. Views derived from his neurological background were thus transplanted into the new science piecemeal, and so unobtrusively that Sulloway (1979), in an intellectual biography entitled *Freud, Biologist of the Mind*, characterizes Freud as "a crypto-, or covert biologist" and refers to the "hidden biological roots of Freudian psychoanalytic thought" (p. 3). Consequently, psychoanalytic theory has the virtue of being tied to *psychological reality as observed introspectively* and to *physiological reality as observed objectively*.

Publication of *The Project* has made it possible to separate the "pure mind" aspects of the theory—ideas derived wholly from psychological observations—from the neurophysiological postulates or, in Sulloway's words, from "fundamental conceptions [that] were biological by inspiration as well as by implication" (p. 5). For more than half a century, ignorance of Freud's precise use of these postulates made it virtually impossible to check the validity of his working hypotheses, as I personally discovered during the 1930s when I tried to track down some of the assumptions on which they were based. Clear evidence on their origin permits his inferences on mind-body relationships to be tested with the experimental techniques and tools of this era. In contemporary dream studies especially, notable progress has been made in the cross-checking of physical and mental functioning, biological phenomena being accounted for in psychological terms and vice versa.

Some of Freud's theories have been confirmed; others were incorrect. To understand where he erred, one has to study the neurophysiology of his day and compare it with modern neurophysiology. But that is another story (Cotman & McGaugh, 1980; Crick, 1979; Fincher, 1981; Hart, 1975; Jaynes, 1976; Kety, 1979, 1981; Lishman, 1983; Penfield & Perot, 1963).

Remarkable similarities have been observed between formulations in *The Project* and those of the modern neurosciences. Some of its correlations of psychologically observed processes with neural functions that could be grasped only through a priori reasoning coincide in essence with contemporary knowledge of the activity of the central nervous system. However, the general approach and the terminology in which this action is now conceptualized are much less mechanistic than Freud's general schema for linking mental and physical events, which reflects the spirit of late nineteenth century neurology. A comprehensive review of the schema would therefore have little value for the clinician, but I shall mention a few pertinent formulations.

Psychic processes are conceptualized in *The Project* as the "quantitatively determined states" of the structural units of the nervous system—nerve cells or neurons, which are assumed to be "specifiable material particles" (1954, pp. 355–356). The idea of "viewing neuronic excitation as quantities in a condition of flow" (p. 356) was suggested to Freud by the "excessively intense ideas" (p. 356) of patients with hysteria and obsessional neurosis and the necessity of describing conversion, discharge, and other mechanisms associated with these disorders.

The then prevailing theory of neuronic inertia is reflected in Freud's assertion that neurons "tend to divest themselves of quantity" (p. 356) (the sum of excitation). Their division into two classes—sensory and motor neurons—serves as a "contrivance for counteracting the reception of quantity" (p. 357). By employing it "only in order to get rid of it through the connecting path leading to the muscular mechanism," a primary neuronic system "keeps itself free from stimulus. *This process of discharge is the primary function of neuronic systems*" (emphasis added; p. 357). The primacy of this process is reflected in the fundamental rule of psychoanalytic therapy. In "saying everything," the patient engages in discharge and operates to produce the deactivation of certain nervous system patterns and the activation and discharge of new patterns.

The nervous system performs the second of its two general functions, according to Freud, when there is some interference with the trend toward inertia, of keeping the tension level close to zero. The preferred methods of discharge entail flight from stimuli, but the organism is exposed at times to stimulation from which it cannot withdraw. Notably, stimuli issuing from the body itself (endogenous) continue to operate until discharged by a "specific action" (p. 357) initiated by an outside force; for example, hunger pains persist until the need for nourishment is met. Since the "exigencies of life" may prevent such action, the nervous system "must learn to tolerate a store of quantity . . . sufficient to meet the demands for specific action. In so far as it does so, however, the same trend still persists in the modified form of a tendency to keep the quantity down, at least, so far as possible and avoid any increase in it (that is, to keep its level of tension constant)" (p. 358). In the analytic situation, the command to "say everything" sometimes facilitates this process.

In addition to the two peripheral systems of sensory and motor neurons which receive and discharge sensory input, Freud assumes the existence of a "*third* system of neurons . . . whose states of excitation give rise to the different qualities—are, that is to say, conscious sensations. . . . It is to be suspected . . . that that system consists in contrivances for changing external *quantity* into *quality*" (p. 370). In another reference to the system which carries the behavior patterns to be modified in treatment, Freud states: "We know from anatomy that there is a . . . superimposed system (the gray matter of the brain) which has no direct peripheral contacts but which is responsible for the development of the neuronic system and for the psychical functions" (p. 364).

The basic ideas Freud advanced in *The Project* to make psychic processes "plain and void of contradictions" (p. 355), as well as his focus on the neuron as a "model" of the nervous system, and his formulations about the interrelated functioning of three major groups of neurons are in the stream of contemporary knowledge. The neuron is recognized as the integrating unit of the nervous system, with each neuron computing, integrating, and recording signals into a pattern of action potentials (Cotman & McGaugh, 1980). The nervous system's fundamental activity is connected with these potentials or electrical changes, which are produced by the neurons as they conduct impulses and transmit excitation or inhibition across their connecting fibers (synapses), thus transmitting messages that appear to be related to highly complex physiological processes. *The Project* foresaw the rapprochement between psychology and neurophysiology at the level of neurons and groups of neurons.

MODERN NEUROPSYCHOLOGICAL THEORY

Structure

The energic processes which figure in psychoanalytic constructs on personality and behavior are associated with the functioning in the brain of from 10 to 100 billion neurons, with an infinite number of connections between them. Illustrating the magnitude and complexity of activity going on in the brain, it is said to be bombarded every second by 100 million messages carrying information from the sense organs (Fincher, 1981).

The neurons form three interconnected systems, with tributaries throughout the body. Stimulation emanating from the external environment (exogenous input) and from somatic processes (endogenous input) excites the sensory neurons in the receptor system. Along its "wires," the afferent impulses produced by the excitation travel to the interneurons. This group of nerve cells, often called the switchboard of the brain, integrates, records, and reorganizes the sensory input, transforming the afferent impulses into internal change or transmitting them to the effector group of neurons. This third system discharges energy—efferent impulses—into muscles and glands, actions, and speech.

With the introduction of new methods of studying brain activity, some hypotheses that were widely entertained for many years have recently required considerable revision. It used to be thought, for example, that the sole factor governing the function of neurons was their location in the nervous system. It is now known that, in addition to different locations, neurons possess different sensitivities and secrete different chemicals. Particular physiological and behavioral functions are carried on by discrete brain systems; normal operation of these systems is associated with the proper execution of certain types of behavior (Cotman & McGaugh, 1980).

Emergence of a chemical factor in brain functioning represents a notable advance. Recognition that transmission across the synapse is mediated by a variety of chemical neurotransmitters and modulators of synaptic activity is regarded as one of the most important contributions to neurobiology and knowledge of mental states in this century (Kety, 1981).

Neurotransmitters

Of the more than 50 different chemical substances that are now identified as neurotransmitters, at least seven are known to play a role in the control of behavior. The proper performance of certain behaviors appears to depend on their operating normally. The likely implication of several neurotransmitter systems in psychoses and affective states has been the subject of many recent investigations; attention is currently focused on the role of dopamine and its relation to schizophrenia.

It is hypothesized that there is a functional excess of central dopamine activity or, on the other hand, an increase in dopamine receptors (Wyatt et al., 1982; Greenberg, 1978). It is important to know that such hypotheses are being investigated, but thus far none of them has been proven. Findings on dopamine that were originally thought to be specific for schizophrenia are now associated more generally with functional psychotic syndromes (Strauss, 1983). It has been pointed out that "in the absence of direct evidence that an abnormality of dopamine is involved, we must clearly recognize that the biochemical basis of schizophrenia is unknown at this time" (Davis et al., 1982, p. 197).

In short, a more complex picture of the brain is evolving, and its complete functional correlation with chemistry and psychology is becoming more probable.

Functioning

The summation and discharge activities of the interneuronic system are connected with such intricate operations as perception, memory processes, recall, decision making, and the organization of behavior. The discharge of efferent neurons stimulates afferent neuron discharge—via feedback processes. The system is bombarded with afferent impulses produced from the feedback processes, as well as from the sensory impact of the outer world and of internal bodily processes. Consequently, the sensory influx to be dealt with can be tremendous.

An intermediate degree of sensory influx, which is optimal for the healthful functioning of the interneurons, facilitates maturational processes in the young child. On the other hand, consistent exposure to either weak or strong sensory influx taxes the nervous system. Under these conditions, it calls into play the various methods at its disposal for influencing excitations that threaten psychological survival—such methods as approaching or avoiding stimuli, finding or creating the proper kind of stimuli, and developing defenses against stimuli.

Exposure early in life to proper sensory stimulation initiates the favorable development of neuronic circuits. Interneurons activated by afferent neurons discharge their energy completely into effector neurons, thus producing a sense of satisfaction. Improper sensory stimulation—afferent inputs which the interneuronic system cannot organize and cannot discharge completely—creates tensions in the organism. When discharge into the effector neurons is characteristically blocked, pools of undischarged energy accumulate and charge up the interneuronic system. Patterns of dealing with this overload come into play. In short, excessive stimulation, understimulation, or unwholesome stimulation has the effect of delaying efferent outputs. Energy gets discharged into repetitive patterns (as shown in Figure 2).

Many unexplained microevents intervene between stimulus and response. Observations and theories that have been reported about these, however, shed new light on behavior. To mention a few that are pertinent:

1. Sensory input may exceed contemporary output to an astronomical extent. Motor discharge is apparently influenced by the immediate psychological state of the organism and the type of patterns already laid down, as well as many unknown factors. The outward flow through the final motor pathway is reduced by the imprisoning of some impulses in closed loops or assemblies of neurons. Overly prolonged reverberations or synchronous activity produced in this manner figure in explanations of unconscious processes in dreams, unresolved tensions, anxiety, and the like.

2. The behavior of the organism may be adversely affected by input underload and input overload (both exogenous). These are, in psychological terms, sensory deprivation and excessive stimulation. The negative sensations created by quantitative extremes in stimulation generate aggressive impulses. Interneurons may then be activated to delay the discharge of these impulses resulting from endogenous excitation.

3. The healthful maintenance of equilibrium entails only partial activation of the interneuronic system; an abundance of unactivated neurons is then available to cope with stressful situations. Consequently, optimal nervous functioning is associated with an ample "neuron reserve"—the neurophysiological correlative of uncommitted or unbound psychic energy. Insufficiency of neuron reserve is believed to be a factor in psychosis. An *excessive tie-up of neurons in fixed and pathological patterns and overactivity or underactivity of certain neuronic systems* are generally associated with mental illness. Its various forms may be characterized, in this sense, by the type of fixed patterns in

Neurodynamics of Improper Sensory Stimulation in Early Life

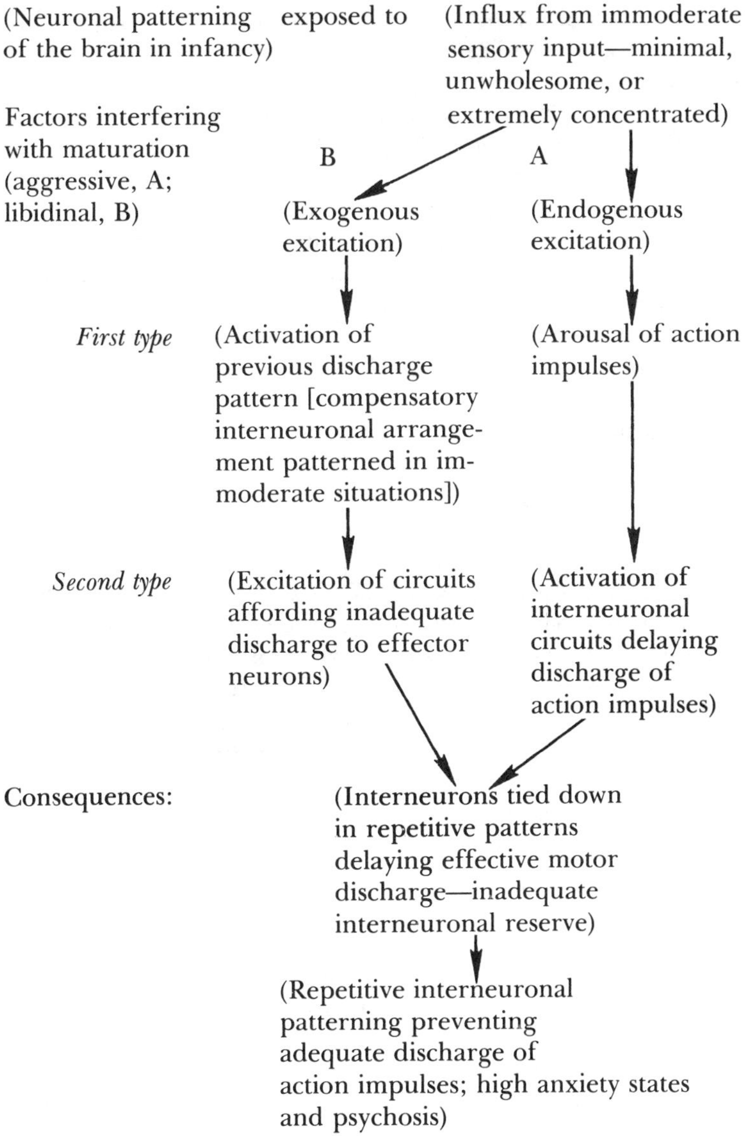

(Neuronal patterning   exposed to   (Influx from immoderate
of the brain in infancy)   sensory input—minimal,
                                                        unwholesome, or
Factors interfering   extremely concentrated)
with maturation   B   A
(aggressive, A;
libidinal, B)   (Exogenous   (Endogenous
                                        excitation)   excitation)

First type   (Activation of   (Arousal of action
                        previous discharge   impulses)
                        pattern [compensatory
                        interneuronal arrange-
                        ment patterned in im-
                        moderate situations])

Second type   (Excitation of circuits   (Activation of
                        affording inadequate   interneuronal
                        discharge to effector   circuits delaying
                        neurons)   discharge of
                                                              action impulses)

Consequences: (Interneurons tied down
                                        in repetitive patterns
                                        delaying effective motor
                                        discharge—inadequate
                                        interneuronal reserve)

                                    (Repetitive interneuronal
                                    patterning preventing
                                    adequate discharge of
                                    action impulses; high anxiety states
                                    and psychosis)

Figure 2

which interneurons are imprisoned and the extent to which the neuron reserve is depleted. One may speculate that the depletion follows a different course in each type of disorder, and that symptoms are an indication of the nature and extent of the depletion.

In all psychogenic illnesses, a disproportionately large quantity of interneurons appears to be committed to the process of preventing discharge. Patterns of motor discharge are so underdeveloped or operate so sporadically in some patients that they convey the impression that inhibiting or delaying the output of overwhelming sensory input is the primary, rather than the secondary, function of the nervous system. The more or less automatic repetition of such behavior demonstrates the operation of regulatory mechanisms developed over the years to cope with noxious or painful stimuli. Failure in the operation of these mechanisms may lead to psychotic states.

Clinical Implications

This interdisciplinary exploration was not undertaken merely to supplement psychoanalytic evidence of the effects of early life experience on the "set" of the personality. Knowledge accumulated through studies of the nervous system also accounts in a material way for much of the clinical experience of the analytic practitioner, notably the time and effort entailed in facilitating long-term changes in behavior. Resistance to change is *more comprehensible* when the analyst is aware of the neural events that are implicated in change. As indicated, these events turn out to be profound physicochemical processes going on in at least seven systems, probably many more.

The obstacles to change that these phenomena present cannot be significantly altered by the patient simply by the exertion of will power—that is, by the systems controlling voluntary action—however crucial such exertion appears to be at times. The change has to be facilitated by the analyst in the psychotherapeutic process. The familiar analytic concept of transference cure might be equated with a particular sensory input that stimulates the interneuronic system to operate in new pathways; however, unless interneurons are freed from the old circuitous pathways (as in analytic cure), the latter are very likely to be reactivated when the patient is no longer under the analyst's influence. What frees the neurons—that is, permits them to be activated in new, more desirable pathways—is a redirection of the *old pathways*. Redirection entails the deactivation of previously used pathways, their reactivation in a new way, and the activation of other pathways.

Freedom to behave with integrity in variegated ways means that an ample supply of interneurons is ever-available to deal with significant fluctuations in sensory input, to make decisions deliberatively, and to behave appropriately in the immediate situation. In neurodynamic terms, the analytic task might be conceptualized as one of shifting from roundabout to more efficient interneuronic pathways, of freeing pathways that drain off interneurons required for personality growth, or of increasing the interneuron reserve.

Clearly, analysts are primarily concerned with improving the functioning of the integrative and controlling neural apparatus; but the structure of the nervous system makes it equally clear that they can apply their influence only indirectly. Interneurons are not accessible to direct environmental influence; they can be approached only via the other two groups of neurons. Behavioral change gets under way when new connections are formed between specific combinations of the receptor and effector neurons. And these receptor and effector neurons have to be freed from the damaging patterns that were the product of pathological experiences in the past.

With the reawakening in the analytic relationship of feelings associated with a significant life experience, "transference behavior" indicates that the specific interneuronal organization set up in response to that experience has been activated. This affords the opportunity to deactivate the pathway originally laid down and to open up other pathways—that is, to connect the emotional state recreated with an interneuronal organization that will express itself in more mature patterns of behavior. With that purpose in mind, the analyst applies himself throughout treatment to facilitating the patient's intake of stimuli that will bring the relevant combination of afferent impulses into operation and secure the output of the desired combination of efferent impulses.

The only instrument applied to arouse the excitatory and inhibitory mechanisms is communication, nonverbal as well as verbal. The parties to the relationship wield the instrument in different ways. The situation is structured to encourage the patient to release impulses through the speech apparatus. *Nondeliberative talking* is most effective because it opens up pathways of discharge for intense feelings. When verbalizing spontaneously, moreover, the patient reveals the specific organization of nerve impulses that is dominant at the moment. To facilitate this revelation and to modify the patient's neuronic organization, the analyst talks with therapeutic intent. And he engages in *no more communication* than is necessary for those purposes (Zipf, 1949).

Besides deactivating circuitous pathways of discharge and activating new ones, the release of psychic energy via the speech apparatus influences the receptor system through feedback. Although other types of feedback operate in psychotherapy, auditory feedback makes the significant contribution. Merely hearing what he says stimulates sensations in the patient, thus exciting afferent impulses, evoking sensations and ideas in the interneuronic system, and activating efferent impulses.

The continous renewal of this sequence of neuronic activity is stimulated by feedback from the patient's own verbalizations and the supplementary stimulus of the analyst's communications. By bridging the three groups of neurons, language makes the patterns of the interneurons accessible to therapeutic influence. Moreover, spoken language is the form of motor activity through which efferent impulses are released, and this release is crucial for modifying organized behavior through the continuing discharge of interneurons. Hence, the analyst operates consistently to organize the discharge of mental energy via the speech apparatus.

Associated with this discharge, it has recently become clear, are certain physiochemical processes that go on in the nervous system. Specific cerebral pathways have been mapped out and studied. The more knowledge we gain about these pathways, the greater the possibility of utilizing biological and psychological measures in combination to resolve mental disorders.

Studies of psychological function have increased our knowledge, in particular, of the different roles performed by the brain's two hemispheres and by the corpus callosum, the densely packed bundle of fibers that knits them together. It has recently become clear that the left hemisphere has more to do with the intellect than the right; the fact that the left is the dominant hemisphere (in most individuals) facilitates intellectual performance. The notion of behavior being controlled by reason would mean that the left hemisphere retains its dominance. The right hemisphere may have more to do with emotional experience and intuitive processes.

Findings of left hemispheric dysfunction in schizophrenic patients have been reported (Wyatt et al., 1982) and may be linked with such symptoms as cognitive problems and disorders in thinking. There are other schizophrenic syndromes, however. Some of these patients manifest primarily affective symptoms; defects in integration are most significant in others. Whereas the foci of deficits in intellectual processes would be looked for in the left hemisphere, those of emotional deficits might be looked for in the right hemisphere; the foci of deficits in integration might be looked for in both hemispheres and also in the corpus callosum (Lishman, 1983).

In this context, psychoanalysis may be viewed as the process of making it possible for the functionally isolated and specialized cerebral hemispheres to express themselves through verbal communication and to work together in an integrated way. That notion would appear to be consistent with the latest findings in neurophysiology and the principles of modern psychoanalysis (Wilson, 1981, pp. 104-112).

Growing understanding of the relationships between the psychological and biological processes underlying schizophrenic psychosis will facilitate the recovery of prepsychotic and postpsychotic, as well as psychotic patients. They will achieve emotional maturity through the appropriate combination of individual and group psychotherapy, and the adjunctive use of chemotherapy when indicated. It is desirable, however, that the chemotherapy be reduced, and eventually discontinued, as soon as possible. Once the basic neurotransmitter mechanisms that went awry have been corrected (Flinn, Leon, & McKinley, 1981), the ultimate goal of treatment is to assist these individuals to function independently with the physical and chemical assets of their own bodies.

APPLICATION OF THE THEORY

The long-range task of resolving the defensive patterns or maladaptations that prevented the patient from completing essential maturational sequences has two aspects. First of all, the maturational blockages must be aroused with sufficient intensity to be identified and understood. The instruction given the patient to talk initiates what is, by and large, an exploratory and testing-out process. It continues until the analyst fully understands the origin and history of the pathological patterns and their significance for the patient's current functioning. The second aspect of the task gets under way when the analyst has acquired sufficient knowledge of the patterns to exert some influence on them; it continues until the termination of treatment. The patterns which have served to foreclose maturation are "dealt with" in such a way as gradually to loosen them up until their compulsive grip has been nullified. Further growth of the personality then becomes possible.

How much energy the analyst expends in talking depends on the immediate stimulus needs of the patient. When the study of the patterns of impulse discharge begins, it is desirable that the patient be protected as much as possible from extraneous forms of stimulation. The analyst, after issuing the instruction to talk, provides *no more verbal feeding (communication) than is needed to help the patient relax and communicate freely—in other words, to maintain the patient in a state of self-propelled discharge.* Auditory feedback is a major source of stimulation during the exploratory period. Later on, the input and output of the specific forms and amounts of energy that will produce fundamental changes in the patient's mode of functioning are stimulated primarily by communications from the analyst. The amount of energy expended in verbal interchanges usually increases as the treatment proceeds.[2]

During the initial phase of treatment, the analyst's silence is, on the whole, gratifying to patients. It communicates attention and interest, which invite them to articulate their impulses to their heart's content. But talking uninterruptedly session after session consumes a great deal of energy, and the talker comes to expect some replenishment—*verbal feedings* from the listener. "Monologizing whets the appetite for dialogue and vice versa," a young man remarked.

Answers to specific requests for information are provided, assuming that the requests are motivated by a desire to facilitate analytic progress rather than to impede or destroy the relationship. When the response of the analyst is satisfying, it tends to alleviate the situation. But whether or not the schizophrenic patient taps this potential source of gratification or continues the monologue, sooner or later he experiences increasing states of tension. These serve to inhibit verbal spontaneity. The patient is then likely to revert to an infantile method of dealing with frustration.

In other words, an interneuronal pattern set up early in life during exposure to sensory deprivation is activated. As has been pointed out, this situation leads to endogenous excitation, which stimulates aggressive impulses. If the release of these impulses is checked, opportunities are created to investigate how the infantile patterns delaying effective motor discharge were set up and why the patient persists in using them.

(Immature patterns) charged with (Transference) ➤(Resistance)

The presence of resistance permits the inference that the interneuronic system is overinvolved in preventing sensory input from being transformed into effective motor output.

[2]It will be noted that the analyst's substantial investment of mental energy in thinking about and developing understanding of the patient does not enter into this formulation. Silent interpretive analysis goes on consistently from the beginning of treatment.

As long as a patient talks spontaneously, he gives expression to impulses resulting from changing sensory input and the activation of diverse interneuronal structures. Moving forward from one idea or experience to another, the patient engages in *progressive* language discharge.

In periods of resistance, on the other hand, the patient either bogs down in silence or his verbal output is characterized by rigidity or repetition. The dominance of a specific organization of neural impulses leads to verbal repetition. The patient sounds like a phonograph record stuck in a groove. This behavior, it has been suggested, is connected with the reverberation of impulses in interneuronic circuits. In neurophysiological terms, resistance might be described as the "locking up" of energy in neural structures which interfere with progressive language discharge.

The analyst's participation in resolving resistance is consistently one of providing communications that will enable the patient to verbalize freely all impulses, feelings, thoughts, and memories. In the course of progressive language discharge, the interneuronic structures whose repetitive activation to limit or delay discharge has served to block maturation are gradually redirected. An intervention that resolves a blockage is therefore referred to as a "maturational communication." The term applies to all *verbal feedings* that are designed to liberate the patient from resistance.

(Resistance) met with (Maturational communication)

(Resolution of resistance)

The variable factor in this generally applicable equation is the *quantum* of communication. It depends on the patient's emotional state at the moment and ability to verbalize it spontaneously without supplementary verbal stimulation. The analyst invests in communication as much energy as is required to help the patient mobilize and discharge energy appropriately, or to shift from repetitive to progressive language discharge.

As transference develops, the patient's responses to the analyst's verbal output of energy are studied to determine how much is optimal for arousing moderate resistance. After it is clearly aroused, the minimal amount of communication needed to move the patient out of repetitive language discharge or silence is determined. This is tantamount to saying that the analyst learns empirically how much limit to place on his own communications (1) to keep the patient in the optimal state of frustration for *arousing a desirable intensity of resistance* and (2) to provide the *minimal* amount of gratification that will reduce the resistance and enable the patient to resume the process of progressive language discharge (Spotnitz, 1966).

Arousal of resistance:

(Impulses
pressing for
discharge)   encounter   (Resistance
                                   force or
                                   counterforce
                                   to communi-
                                   cation) ⟶ (Resistance
                                                 pattern—
                                                 repetitive
                                                 language
                                                 discharge
                                                 or silence)

Resolution of resistance:

(Impulses
pressing for
discharge)   freed by   (Reduction of
                                   resistance—
                                   dissolution of
                                   the counter-
                                   force through
                                   analyst's
                                   communi-
                                   cation) ⟶ (Progressive
                                                 language
                                                 discharge)

A therapeutic range of communication—the dimensions of maturational communication—is gradually established for the case.

In general, the *higher the developmental level* at which the patient enters treatement, the *broader the range of therapeutic communciation* that he can tolerate and the less urgent it is for the analyst to operate strictly within that range. Silence does not mobilize much explosive force in a patient whose problems are oedipal in nature because the capacity for verbalizing emotional energy is well developed. The patient can discharge those high states of central excitation associated with sensory deprivation rather readily in speech. There is relatively little danger that the patient will release efferent impulses into undesirable forms of motor activity. A wider range of communication is therapeutic as well as tolerable. Because of a relatively long course of wholesome development, varying degrees of verbal contact *create situations* which favor the resolution of resistance in the case.

The immediate release of efferent impulses into motor activity—acting out—is characteristic of the most primitive mode of functioning. Patients entering treatment for preoedipal problems have a limited capacity to engage in precise verbal release; they tend to discharge their impulses into indiscriminate forms of motor activity rather than speech. This tendency and the attendant dangers create anxiety, and inhibitory tensions are mobilized. In order not to stimulate the operation of the more primitive action patterns, one therefore refrains from exposing these patients to extreme degrees of sensory input or sensory deprivation in terms of verbal contact. To control the mobilization of aggressive impulses by the patient and secure their release in language, the analyst adheres rather strictly to a narrow range of communication. This militates against the threat of iatrogenic regression.

Schizophrenic patients often appear to tolerate the absence of verbal contact for prolonged periods far better than less disturbed persons. They do not verbalize their aggressive reactions to such deprivation as readily as, for example, the psychoneurotic patient. Some of them go on talking for many sessions without soliciting any communication from the analyst.

However, the misdirecting influence of frustration-aggres-sion is implicit in such behavior. Not being in command of their aggressive reactions, these patients can only conceal them—the schizophrenic reaction. Their tendency to store up aggressive impulses reflects an extreme need to inhibit their discharge.

To prevent a potentially explosive situation from develop-ing, and to deal therapeutically with these defensive reactions, the analyst restricts his gratification of the patient—in terms, that is, of verbal contact. Rather than the moderate dosages at vary-ing intervals to which the psychoneurotic patient responds, the psychologically healthful diet for the schizophrenic patient early in treatment is usually minimal dosages of communication at relatively long intervals. During the first 20 minutes of the ses-sion, in particular, interventions are, in principle, as few and as widely spaced as the situation permits. Toward the end of the session, more communication from the therapist may be needed to facilitate the patient's leaving the office.

What is the actual difference between "moderate" and "minimum" dosages of communication? Since firm measure-ments are impossible, the term "units of communication" is in-troduced to suggest the difference.

One unit of communication, viewed as a verbal feeding, would be the equivalent, say, of a mouthful of milk. It is the briefest of interventions, such as a single question or very short statement. These communications may be ego-syntonic or ego-dystonic. The units stipulated below represent an estimate, on a long-range basis, of the amount of time the analyst spends in talking to the patient.

Quantified roughly, the analyst's communications to a pa-tient being treated for oedipal problems range from 10 to 100 units; the range indicated to deal with the characteristic defen-ses of the schizophrenic patient is from 2 to 5 units. The dif-ference between these two types of verbal feedings is comparable to that between the normal dietary needs of the adult and those of a child who has been conditioned to underfeeding.

In general, in the formative stage of the relationship, ver-bal contact with a schizophrenic patient is rarely in order. It is desirable that the analyst remain under the specified 5 units until the narcissistic transference has been resolved. Between the regular brief feedings at relatively long intervals, 2 additional units are occasionally provided when demanded. Whatever resistance the patient develops to a transference object experienced as being like oneself, or even a part of oneself, yields temporarily to a few appropriate words, preferably spoken when a communication is solicited. The intensity of the resistance can be more easily influenced when the analyst limits and times communications in the manner suggested above.

The development of the case when one tries to deal with resistance through larger dosages of communication at shorter intervals—the customary procedure in other cases—is indicated in the following diagram:

(Resistance) met with   (10 to 100
                         units of
                         communication)———▶(Excessive
                                            sensory input
                                            and inadequate
                                            motor output)
                                                 │
                                                 ▼
                         (Intensification of resistance,
                         and regression too severe to be
                         resolved in the course of the
                         session—overexcitation, which
                         may lead to iatrogenic regres-
                         sion)

The situation delineated above is especially undesirable in the outpatient treatment of schizophrenia; indeed, it was probably a contributing factor in many failures that have been reported in such treatment. The danger of precipitating iatrogenic regression in persons being treated on an ambulatory basis usually mounts when they are exposed to "overfeeding." Too much communication creates more excitation, primarily exogenous, than the patient can discharge appropriately. That situation is averted by respecting the patient's need to develop and work through the narcissistic transference in a state of *mild* frustration-tension controlled by minimal gratification. That, indeed, is my prescription for the psychotherapy of the schizophrenic patient.

Analytic therapists who equate the classical approach with passivity and have been educated to the idea that this is unsuitable for the schizophrenic patient are more apt to exceed the range of 2 to 5 units of communication than to operate below it. Nevertheless, it is possible to veer toward the other extreme; failures that appear to be associated with "verbal starvation," one of the factors contributing to emotional drought, are occasionally encountered:

(Resistance) met with   (0 to 2)
        units of
        communication) ⟶ (Excessive
                      endogenous
                      excitation
                      and inadequate
                      motor output)
                          ↓

        (Intensification of resistance, and regression too severe to be resolved in the course of the session, which may lead to iatrogenic regression)

Too little communication is as deleterious as too much and for the same reason: the relative inadequacy of motor output.

Resistance originating in the narcissistic defense can be resolved without undue difficulty when the analyst consistently limits himself to small dosages of communication at long intervals. After the narcissistic transference evolves and the patient begins to relate more characteristically to the analyst as a separate object, he is more capable of verbalizing feelings. During the transitional stage, the communication dosages are gradually increased and the intervals between them are shortened. The patient develops an increased tolerance for more communication, and finds it pleasurable.

The development of object transference usually signifies that the reorganization and reintegration of the patient's energy system have reached the point where he can respond appropriately to larger verbal feedings. When exposure to from 10 to 100 units of communication reactivates the old resistance patterns, the patient reverts on occasion to the narcissistic defense. In such a situation, it is desirable to restrict one's communications to the initial range of 2 to 5 units. Oscillation between moderate and minimal communication dosages constitutes the main departure from the classical approach after the narcissistic transference has fully evolved.

A.   Stage of Narcissistic Transference

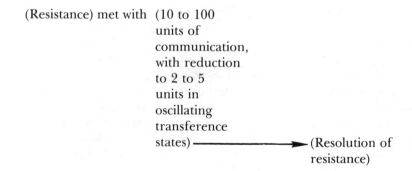

(Resistance) met with (2 to 5 units of communication, with gradual expansion in this range as appropriate) ⟶ (Resolution of resistance)

B.   Stage of Object Transference

(Resistance) met with (10 to 100 units of communication, with reduction to 2 to 5 units in oscillating transference states) ⟶ (Resolution of resistance)

The principles just discussed shed some light on what transpires in the patient's nervous system during the psychotherapeutic process. They suggest that the analyst's communications are designed to help the patient engage in appropriate verbal discharge while helping to free him from old patterns of discharge and to form new ones. That threefold task makes enormous demands on the patient; it entails the reorganization and reintegration of the nervous system, with the multiplicity of physicochemcal changes that, as we now recognize, accompany that transformation. At best, this is a time-consuming task and, the more primitive the level of the pathological patterns, the more time it requires.

In the course of this undertaking, the temporary administration of physicochemical measures may facilitate progress until the "laboratory" of the patient's body can take over the entire process of physical and chemical integration. But whether or not the task is pursued exclusively through psychotherapy or with the adjunctive use of pharmacotherapy, the analyst, by responding to the patient with well-timed and exquisitely specific dosages of appropriate humanizing communications, makes a vital contribution to the success of this mammoth undertaking.

Chapter 5

FROM RUDIMENTARY TO COOPERATIVE RELATIONSHIP

The decision to accept a patient and the precise manner of embarking on the case are influenced by one's preconceptions of the kind of treatment alliance that would lead most expeditiously to the desired results. The more deep-seated the patient's problems, however, the more difficult it is to impose the mode of relatedness that is usually prescribed. The structuring of the relationship with a schizophrenic patient rarely proves to be a unilateral operation. Both parties structure it together, the patient no less by unconscious opposition to relinquishing ingrained patterns of conduct than the analyst by his understanding of that opposition, the techniques he employs, and the contractual arrangements under which he applies himself to secure and stabilize change. The development of a firm treatment alliance can ultimately be facilitated through "sensitive work with" the patient's narcissistic defenses (Rothstein, 1982, p. 185).

When contemplating treatment, however, pathologically narcissistic individuals are rarely interested in change. What they want primarily—and immediately—is relief from emotional suffering. They are likely to feel that they would be investing time, money, and effort just to prove that they are incurable. For them to commit themselves fully to work for real change requires much more time than the interval between their first call for an appointment and the completion of arrangements for opening the case. How they are responded to when making the first moves toward engaging themselves in the analytic situation is of great significance for securing this eventual commitment.

Consequently, the initial phase of coming together, exchanging information, and decision making, rather than being regarded as a mere preliminary to the therapeutic process, is governed by the general plan of treatment. In other words, the treatment relationship, like the mother-child relationship, begins with the first contact between analyst and patient; their initial interchanges influence all subsequent contacts between them.

As soon as the prospective patient mobilizes himself sufficiently to investigate the possibility that he can be helped to "feel better," the principle of providing him with a continuing opportunity to resist direction begins to operate. Usually he labors under the unconscious conviction of having been an "unwanted child," as may well have been the case, and enters the office steeled against the expectation of insistent probing and wounding inspection. For example, the offspring of a fault-finding parent anticipates that the therapist will find fault in the same manner. But instead of being subjected to pressure to disprove unworthiness of time and assistance, the prospective patient finds that the therapist is willing to get together with him to study the situation. Attention is shifted from the patient's ego to the object to convert the exploratory discussions into a therapeutic experience.

The individual who is "screened into" treatment in this manner may have any form of schizophrenia, and may report hallucinations, catatonic episodes, or mixed symptoms. The degree of deterioration is not an important consideration, provided that one is well enough oriented to realities to know one's name and surroundings and how to get to the office at the appointed time and home again. Ambulatory treatment is not absolutely precluded if these criteria cannot be met; in exceptional cases, a relative or hospital attendant has accompanied a patient to the office a few times. However, the closer he is to un-controllable psychotic behavior, the more difficult to treat him in a noninstitutional setting.

Reasonably good physical health and capacity for psycho-logical change at a relatively rapid rate are other important de-siderata. One has to consider whether a person suffering from a serious organic disease, such as a coronary condition, might be exposed to more emotional wear and tear than would be de-sirable. Since flexibility of personality does not invariably equate with chronological age, it is assessed on an individual basis. In-telligence, on the other hand, is a minor issue because the treat-ment is conducted primarily as an emotional process. Moreover, intelligence is rather consistently used—particularly by cogni-tively complex individuals—to oppose rather than facilitate treatment.

Selection is governed to some extent by the preferences of the individual practitioner. One usually achieves the most fa-vorable results with the people one can work with most com-fortably and with those who inspire a determination to cure. Whatever one's predilections, a unique challenge is often found in working with the patient entering treatment in late adoles-cence or the early twenties. At the time of life when the prob-lems of living await solution and the factors that precipitated the disorder are not very remote, the long-range effort entailed in reversing the schizophrenic reaction seems to be especially jus-tified. A powerful incentive for undertaking the case operates when one is confronted with a young person whose intelligence and potentials for creative or social achievement are chained in severe psychopathology.

Earlier views on the analysand's suitability, accessibility, readiness for analytic work, ego strength, and the like—quali-fications that were vague and susceptible to arbitrary interpre-tation—are encompassed as objectively as possible in recent formulations on the therapeutic alliance and Ralph R. Green-son's concept of the working alliance. These new approaches to the situational aspects of the treatment relationship reflect sig-nificant progress in spelling out the demands that standard psychoanalytic therapy makes on each partner. The patient's specific contribution to successful outcome of the case, as

Greenson has conceptualized it, is the ability to work purposefully on his problems, to ally his "reasonable" ego with the analyst's "analyzing" ego (1965, p. 157).

The schizophrenic patient who can cooperate to that extent in the early stage of treatment is rarely encountered. Nevertheless, the patient becomes capable of making that contribution if the *analyst accepts the responsibility* for developing an effectual alliance with him. The eventual formation of a relationship in which the patient engages systematically in memory recall and self-analysis, and the ability to maintain these processes are major indicators of progress in the case.

To continue with Greenson (1965), the vital components of the working alliance are transference reactions stemming from the "reasonable and purposeful part" (p. 157) of the patient's feelings for the analyst. Since such reactions intermix with more regressive and inappropriate reactions, the distinction between transference neurosis and working alliance is not absolute. In theory, however, the two phenomena are parallel and "antithetical properties" (p. 174) meriting equal attention. The patient's "potential for forming" (p. 171) and ability to maintain a "reliable" working alliance are essential for psychoanalytic therapy.

Commenting on a group of cases conducted by himself and other analysts that did not get beyond the preliminary stage or seemed interminable, Greenson (1965) attributes the therapeutic stalemate to the "*failure of the patient* to develop reliable working relations with the analyst" (emphasis added; p. 155). The observation that in the classically analytic patient the working alliance "develops almost imperceptibly, relatively silently, and seemingly independently of any special activity" (p. 160) on the analyst's part strengthens the impression that the onus for the absence of a good working relationship rests exclusively on the patient. Greenson's clinical illustrations of analytic work that proved crucial for the establishment of the alliance were drawn from "irregular" cases, and the "special" activity was apparently limited to the first 6 months of treatment.

On the other hand, the analytic work required to produce a good working alliance with the pathologically narcissistic patient is regarded as regular activity rather than a circumscribed "rescue" operation. Almost invariably, when such a person enters treatment, one observes that the ability to engage in it appropriately is limited, generally or in a particular area of functioning. The practitioner of modern psychoanalysis, as long as he finds it possible to work with that patient on an ambulatory basis, accepts whatever contribution the patient is able to make and works systematically to transform as essentially rudimentary relationship into a cooperative one—a full-fledged working alliance.

The philosophical approach to that task is simplified and integrated with the general theory of the treatment. The initial interview, the contract, the treatment routines established, and the supplementary practices and rules later introduced are all conceptualized in terms of dealing with resistance. In order to describe the formation of the working alliance and its general nature in a case of schizophrenia, I must intrude somewhat into the subject-matter of subsequent chapters.

THE INITIAL INTERVIEW

The prospective patient's efforts to determine the availability of the analyst's services are often heralded by inquiries from a family member or an associate, who may also relay a request for an appointment. It may then be suggested that the candidate for treatment be the one to make the appointment. Direct contact before the first visit is desirable; besides, an appointment made personally is less likely to be broken. Prospective patients are asked when they would like to come in, and are given that time if it is available. If not, and they say that they cannot come at other hours suggested, they are invited to call again. Before a firm appointment is made and honored, they may oscillate for a protracted period between an intense desire to be relieved of their misery and what seems to be an unconscious need to defend themselves against the anticipated stress of the analytic situation.

If for any reason the prospective patient is inadequate to personally making the arrangements for treatment, no objection is raised to the participation of a relative or someone else to make the appointment and escort the person to the thera-pist's office, provided that the subject agrees.[1] The optimal conditions are set up, however, when the latter comes unac-companied and agrees to undergo treatment of his own voli-tion. The feeling of being forced into treatment, combined with a conscious will that is dead set against it, may create formida-ble obstacles. And sometimes these obstacles make the treat-ment impossible, at least for the time being.

An acutely disturbed young man who entered analysis at his father's insistence withdrew after five sessions, communicating the attitude: My father is forcing me to come and I don't want to come. The patient was informed by the analyst that it was preferable that he not be treated contrary to his own wishes. He stopped treatment to convince himself that it was not being forced on him; 10 days later he resumed treatment "on his own." The transformation of the initial attitude that made the creation of the relationship possible was to the following effect: My father is *not* forcing me to come and I *want* to come (Spot-nitz, 1962).

Acceptance of the characteristically irresolute attitude that the candidate for treatment communicates verbally and non-verbally during the first visit helps him to express himself com-fortably. It also helps the interviewer to make a tentative diagnosis, assemble a brief family history, anticipate the various obstacles to change that would arise in the case, and decide whether he wants to deal with them and could do so effectively. In instances where the decision is difficult to make, the analyst may exert slight pressure for disclosure. In principle, however, when a treatment relationship is under consideration, the ana-lyst asks fewer questions than when functioning in a purely consultative capacity, demonstrating a willingness to accept the factual information offered without eagerness to obtain any that is withheld.

Voluntary disclosures about the onset of the illness and the emergence of symptoms strengthen the diagnostic impression but are not essential. The interviewer is concerned primarily

[1]Third-party participation in the drawing up of the contract is dis-cussed later.

with the prospective patient's functioning in their first face-to-face contact, particularly the stresses and deviances that become manifest. When treatment is expected to follow the interview, it is unnecessary to exert pressure on the prospective patient to reveal feelings and thoughts that would definitely establish a diagnosis, as would be done in an interview conducted only for diagnostic purposes. The clinician needs to gather only enough information to help decide whether he could treat that individual effectively and wants to work with him.

There is another reason that it is unnecessary to look for clear-cut symptoms of the illness: In the course of the treatment, when the patient's deviances are dealt with effectively as they interfere with cooperative functioning in the session, the clinical picture undergoes a series of changes.

Those that occurred in a patient I treated many years ago at the New York State Psychiatric Institute were especially dramatic. On admission following an acute psychotic episode, the young woman was diagnosed as an anxiety hysteric. The staff's initial diagnosis was changed twice, first to manic-depressive psychosis and subsequently, at the stage when I was assigned to treat her, to catatonic schizophrenia. As I have reported elsewhere (Spotnitz, 1981a), having developed a strong desire to cure her, I spent several hours a day on the case. In the course of her treatment, the diagnostic sequence was quickly reversed. In other words, she impressed the staff as behaving again like a manic-depressive, and later like an anxiety hysteric. About 6 months after I began to treat her, she appeared to be normal and was discharged from the Psychiatric Institute.

Clinical observation alone generally meets the immediate need of the experienced practitioner, which is to secure enough information on the nature of the emotional problem to begin the treatment. Supplementary diagnostic procedures are rarely required for that purpose. Psychological tests are not employed in a routine manner because they often cause narcissistic injury to the schizophrenic patient (Lucas, 1982). The potentially negative effects of such tests are weighed against their possible value for subsequent evaluations of progress, as research data, and the like. Occasionally, special family or legal considerations dictate the need for psychological tests, or the patient may have to undergo them for reasons not related to the treatment. But the analyst himself refrains from recommending diagnostic procedures that are not agreeable to the patient when they are not essential.

Any suggestion that the emotional problem may be related to organic dysfunction prompts the interviewer to request reports from medical practitioners. In the course of the treatment, this policy is extended to cover all physical complaints. Periodical medical and dental examinations are recommended to the patient, sometimes even to one who appears to be in sound health. It is well to bear in mind that schizophrenic patients may, consciously or unconsciously, try to prove—for example, by neglecting their teeth—that their physical well-being is a matter of indifference to the therapist.

History-taking is not regarded as a routine procedure. When conducted in an object-oriented way, it has the special value of helping excessively self-preoccupied individuals communicate their impressions of other people. It is desirable to obtain information about grandparents, parents, and siblings. Their occupations, marital status, as well as the ages and causes of death may contain clues to familial patterns of illness and also to the childhood experience of the subject. The patient is asked about members of his immediate family; if married, information is obtained about the spouse and any children they have. The more one knows about the family constellation, the better.

The identity of the person who referred the patient to the analyst and the reason for the referral may be of some significance for the case. These subjects are discussed if the candidate is willing.

The patient may request information about the nature of the illness. Such a request requires judicious handling. A forthright explanation of psychopathology during the initial interview is likely to cause severe narcissistic injury (Lucas, 1982); the schizophrenic individual tends to experience it as an attack on his personality by someone who speaks another language and neither likes nor understands him. It is generally more appropriate to characterize the condition in nontechnical terms than to label it diagnostically or, when possible, to counter a question about it with one that will stimulate the prospective patient to give his own impression of his problems.

Why does he want treatment? With what problems does he wish help? Questions to that effect are among the few that I have found it productive to ask during the initial contact. Whatever answers the candidate gives permits one to study his attitude about treatment and to evaluate his willingness and ability to work with the analyst under mutually agreeable terms.

Any attempts by the patient to elicit information about the practitioner are usually investigated. Professional or personal disclosures, even if these are made simply to reassure the prospective patient, are almost invariably interpreted by him as evidence of professional ineptitude. Consequently, his own feelings of insecurity and reluctance to enter treatment, rather than being alleviated, are intensified. Such information also has the effect of diluting the transference and increasing treatment-destructive resistance (Chapter 7).

It is preferable not to volunteer information about the length, emotional impact, difficulties, or anticipated results of the treatment. Promises, explicit or implicit, of a successful outcome, are contraindicated. Assurances of this nature have varying effects, and these are difficult to predict during the first encounter. For instance, a negatively suggestible person may labor under an unconscious determination, whatever the cost to himself, to outmaneuver and defeat the analyst; such resolves may be strengthened by a suggestion of recovery (Perri, 1982). Moreover, a promise of cure may lead to legal difficulties for the therapist; it would justify a claim of breach of contract by the patient should the treatment be unsuccessful (Perri & Perri, 1978). Before responding to a specific question about what the treatment entails or its expected results, it is advisable to explore the question thoroughly with the patient. When its unconscious meaning is fully understood, one knows how much information to disclose in responding to the question.

If the interviewer decides that analytic psychotherapy conducted with the resources at his own command will help that individual resolve his basic emotional problem and that they can work together under mutually satisfactory arrangements, the terms of treatment are discussed. In theory, the initial interview ends when the contract—a verbal agreement—is concluded. One interview I conducted extended over seven visits, but more than two are rarely required. For most of my patients, the formulation and agreement on the terms of the contract are completed during the first visit.

Should the therapist decide for any reason not to undertake the treatment, he communicates this rejection therapeutically by attributing it to his own inability to deal with that patient's problems.

THE TREATMENT CONTRACT

The contract with the schizophrenic patient is not essentially different from the usual psychoanalytic contract (Menninger & Holzman, 1973). It is, however, somewhat differently formulated and implemented.

The contract is provisional in the sense that the relationship is entered into on a tentative basis to test the analyst's ability to work productively with the patient. The trial period usually lasts about 6 weeks. No formal declaration is made when it ends unless the practitioner decides not to continue. In that case, he may explain that he does not believe he can be helpful to the patient.

The patient may leave treatment at any time. He is helped to continue it—without being put under extreme pressure to do so—for 2 years, the minimum duration for significant change to occur. If he wishes to terminate the relationship at that time, he may be given the option to return later if he desires to achieve further progress. The ultimate duration of treatment depends on the mutual willingness of the parties to work together. Although the effective reversal of the schizophrenic reaction requires a minimum period of 5 years, the treatment may continue for a longer period. However, unless they both recognize that consistently worthwhile progress has been made and anticipate that it will continue, termination of the relationship is recommended. But if the patient has a particularly strong desire to preserve the relationship, that recommendation may be held in abeyance until they reach agreement on termination.

The contract defines purposeful participation in terms of what can reasonably be expected of the patient at the emotional level at which he enters treatment. Provided that he agrees verbally to participate to that extent, the analyst assumes all responsibility for the treatment process. He may say so at a time when the patient is functioning cooperatively and castigating himself for failure to improve; but generally the practitioner conveys the idea implicitly through his attitude. This changes, of course; as the patient makes progress, he becomes more and more capable of assuming an increasing degree of responsibility. Eventually he assumes full responsibility for the success or failure of the treatment. The analyst can only help him function in the treatment sessions. The actual work of adjusting to his life situation must be performed by the patient.

The most seriously handicapped patient agrees to meet the baseline requirements for office treatment by the practitioner in private practice: to come to the office at the designated hours, lie on the couch, talk, and pay for the treatment. By spelling out these criteria for cooperative functioning by the patient, the contract keys the rudimentary relationship to mutual recognition and investigation of the difficulties that cluster around these four requirements. Failure to deal with such lapses satisfactorily may jeopardize the success of the treatment.

In the trinity of terms on performance in the sessions, talking is the most vital. By and large, the more severe the illness, the more powerful the opposition to verbal communication. The patient is not asked to say everything that comes to his mind. He is instructed—commanded, actually—to just talk, and the idea communicated is that he can talk about anything.[2] This

---

[2] In recent years, I have from time to time enlisted the aid of a responsible member of the patient's family in training him, either before entering treatment or in its rudimentary stage, to lie down and talk for 50 minutes at home. The relative is instructed to listen attentively while the patient talks, and just interpose a brief question or two about external realities when he is silent. When parents have cooperated effectively in such training, this supplementary procedure has made it possible for some patients with severe disturbances to be treated successfuly on the analytic couch.

is the *first move* in educating someone to free-associate.

Faithful attendance and adherence to the couch position are less important per se than in their respective contributions to verbal communication. Obviously, the time available for talking is reduced if the patient misses or comes late to sessions. Use of the couch (Stern, 1977) enables him to communicate whatever he thinks, feels, and remembers with relative freedom from environmental and bodily stimulation. To a patient discussed by Steiner (1982), for example, the couch apparently "represented a haven where he could feel protected from enormous anxiety" (p. 244). The patient is in the most favorable physical and psychological state to verbalize his immediate intrapsychic experience when lying on the couch in a relaxed position, with legs uncrossed and arms at his side. Moreover, the safety factor cannot be disregarded when one is working on obstacles to the discharge of frustration-aggression. The practitioner has a forewarning of any danger that the patient will behave destructively when his changes of position on the couch can be observed.

In defining cooperative functioning in these terms, the analyst is, in effect, inviting the patient to experience the internally active state associated with the rapid-eye-movement (REM) periods of sleep, when most dreams occur. Summarizing scientific evidence of "tumult within the central nervous system" during REM sleep, William C. Dement (1965) characterizes it as essentially different from other periods of the sleep cycle and from the waking state. During the dream state, laboratory studies indicate that the brain is "by many measures . . . more active . . . than when wide awake" (p. 190). Its periodic upheavals may have remained unrecognized for many centuries, Dement suggests, because "during REM sleep a special mechanism is inhibiting or blocking the effect of the central discharge upon the motor neurons, so that the body does not move. . . . We might conclude that the brain is telling not only the eyes but also the body what to do during a dream. Our probable good fortune is that the muscles cannot obey" (pp. 190–192).

The only "special mechanism" at the analyst's disposal for influencing the schizophrenic patient to desist from motor activity and to discharge psychological energy in verbal activity is the order to appear regularly, place one's body in a state of repose, and talk. This is equivalent to asking someone to behave like an infant babbling on comfortably in his crib. It is difficult for any grown person to engage himself in this way consistently when beginning treatment. The schizophrenic patient especially fights against experiencing and discharging primitive feelings into verbal symbols. To help him relax his pathological defenses, the orders are repeated as necessary. The analyst does not dictate in the absolute sense; he is, in effect, a *strategic* dictator, intervening in whatever way he thinks necessary to facilitate communication—in other words, to help the patient to talk.

Consequently, the patient learns—usually to his surprise—that violations of the terms of the agreement are not regarded as grounds for terminating the treatment. It continues as long as the patient makes every conscious effort to function in the spirit of the agreement and permits the analyst to assist him in giving up the self-defeating behavior, and in reporting his feelings, thoughts, and memories.

Relatively insignificant lapses, such as coming less than 10 minutes late for a session at infrequent intervals, are not responded to as uncooperative behavior in the rudimentary relationship. The inadequacies in performance that are dealt with first are those that substantially exceed the normal range of variations. Pathological, often ritualistic departures from the terms of the contract, such as extreme tardiness session after session, or repeated indulgence in some form of explosive behavior, are investigated with the patient. The more fixed the patterns, the more help he needs in giving them up.

The pace at which a patient is trained to give up the self-defeating behavior is regulated by his immediate capacity to cooperate. The patient may, for example, arrive late or leave early, but he gets to recognize the self-depriving nature of such behavior because standard-length sessions are adhered to and time lost is not made up. When he fails unaccountably to put in an appearance within the first quarter hour of the session, the analyst phones the patient, thus helping him to cooperate.

Rather than comply with the terms of the contract, the patient can defy or rebel. When he does so, he learns that *verbal* defiance or rebellion is desirable and that defiant or rebellious *behavior* is undesirable.

The principle of helping the patient at first to participate comfortably in the specific context of whatever commitments he has already made underlies the whole training process. The contract thus serves as the pivotal factor in the acceptance, investigation, and understanding of the patient's limited capacity to participate and in the reduction of the major obstacles to more adequate participation in the treatment.

As in the treatment of minors, a relative or other responsible adult may officiate in the drawing up of the treatment contract with the therapist. Third-party participation is in order for a prospective patient whose ego is so defective at the time the treatment arrangements are made that he cannot make decisions affecting his own welfare. The services of an alter ego to assist in making these arrangements may be needed, for example, by a person who, though not actively psychotic, demonstrates incompetence by erratic behavior, gross inability to keep appointments, and the like.

In these cases, the third party should maintain contact with the therapist on a mutually agreeable basis until the patient is competent to negotiate on his own behalf. The initial contract is either confirmed at that time or revised. Thus it eventually becomes a contract between the patient and the therapist.

The rules and practices just described apply to the early stage of the relationship, and tend to change as the treatment proceeds. The timing of such changes is flexible, depending on how the relationship with the patient is developing. Two guiding factors in assessing the appropriateness of the specific practices introduced at the beginning of treatment are the patient's ego functioning and the strength of his object attachment to the therapist. The general principle is that these procedures are applied to help the patient continue the treatment when he wants and needs such help.

FREQUENCY OF SESSIONS

Characteristically, the treatment of the schizophrenic individual begins on a nonintensive basis, usually once a week. It may be administered at the same tempo until the tapering-off process gets under way, or vary at different stages. In the latter case, changes in the spacing of the regular sessions almost invariably plot a rising curve of intensity. Requests made for extra sessions may be granted at a period when the practitioner believes that they would serve a long-range therapeutic need. It is desirable, however, that therapeutic interchange be maintained as consistently as possible at the same frequency no matter how difficult the patient's life situation may be at a particular time.

When the contract is formulated, the patient is asked how frequently *he* wants to come to the office and what *he* wants to pay for each session. If the frequency desired by the patient differs from that at which the therapist wishes to work with him, the difference is discussed. The patient's economic situation may also be discussed if the session fee he has mentioned falls under the minimum fee of the practitioner. Primarily, however, scheduling of the sessions is governed by the amount of time and effort the patient wishes to devote to the treatment and the therapist's opinion on the optimal intensity of contact. When the patient's wishes and the therapist's opinion do not coincide, the schedule and other particulars are discussed until mutually agreeable arrangements are worked out on session frequency, fees, and related issues.

Frequently the patient's wishes and the therapist's opinion on the treatment schedule do coincide. On entering treating the patient, seeking little more than the alleviation of suffering and handicapping symptoms, is not particularly interested in coming to the office more than once or twice a week. The therapist, on the other hand, recognizes that serious obstacles to the formation of a cooperative relationship might arise if the treatment were to be conducted at a faster tempo. It could become too onerous an undertaking for the patient or, if he felt worthless or beyond help, he might develop strong guilt feelings about taking up more time than he thought he was entitled to. These and other reactions may stimulate overwhelming desires to abandon treatment. In structuring the working relationship, one needs to bear in mind the danger of creating too much treatment-destructive resistance at any one time.

Unless there is some compelling reason for seeing the patient at shorter intervals, my own practice is to initiate the treatment on a schedule of one session a week and, during the first few months, investigate the optimal tempo for conducting the case. If it becomes evident that one weekly session does not provide sufficient contact, the patient is asked for his opinion. If he wants psychological assistance on a stepped up basis and feels that he would benefit from it, the schedule is revised accordingly. As a rule, however, no more than two sessions are indicated, at least until the need for immediate relief is transcended by a real desire to develop and mature emotionally in the analytic situation.

In other words, to prevent the patient from accumulating more frustration-aggression than he can verbalize in the formative stage of the relationship, the analyst tries to provide a relatively pleasurable and comfortable treatment experience. As long as the patient's primary concern is the alleviation of his presenting problems, it is preferable that his sacrifices in time, effort, and money impress *him* as commensurate with the progress he feels that he is making toward "feeling better right now." It is borne in mind, however, that high-frequency sessions can be inordinately taxing for the analyst if the patient is difficult to work with, as he well may be. The initial interview may not prove to be an accurate reflection of the length of time and amount of effort that will be entailed in training him to function cooperatively in his sessions.

Many years ago, I treated a pathologically narcissistic man in a postpsychotic condition. During the initial visit, he had expressed great eagerness to talk out his emotional problems. He complied faithfully with the other terms of the verbal agreement. However, several series of electroshock therapy undergone years earlier had induced mental disorganization, rendering him virtually incapable of expressing himself coherently during his first year in psychotherapy. He was helped to talk about his routine activities, such as his lunch or trip to the office that day; and his need for prolonged periods of silence was respected. Even in the second year, there were occasions when he was too confused or troubled by his jumbled ideas to complete a sentence. I talked to him about current events, books, and the theater. Two years passed before he began to do most of the talking and to address himself effectively to his fundamental emotional problems.

Difficulties that emerge unexpectedly because of physical handicap are rarely encountered; but psychic obstacles to the formation of a cooperative relationship characteristically entail a great deal of patience, frustration-tolerance, and "baby-sitting" for the goal-oriented practitioner. If, out of eagerness to make progress as rapidly as possible, he begins the therapy on an intensive basis, he usually observes that the schizophrenic patient tends to use time nonconstructively, clinging to one thought or feeling or lapsing into silence because he has "nothing in mind" to communicate. The neurotic is capable of making an attempt to talk even when he does not have the urge to do so. For the potentially psychotic individual, the same attempt may entail more strain than it is desirable for him to be exposed to before he is capable of verbalizing his immediate reactions to the analytic situation.

Unlike the pressure *not* to talk—the counterforce to communication whose reduction is the essence of analytic process—the pressure to talk is influenced by the frequency of the sessions. The time contracted for seems too precious to waste when the patient is in the state of wanting a little more than he is getting; and as he experiences more pressure to talk, the range of topics he covers broadens. From the point of view of the constructive use of time, it is desirable that, from one session to the next, he became slightly impatient to return to the office. Optimal intensity might be equated with that interval between sessions which keeps the patient mildly "hungry" to resume his communications to the analyst.

At any stage of the relationship, the hunger may become more insistent, prompting the patient to ask for extra sessions. Relatively intense cravings at an early stage may be connected with a desire for the relief of anxiety or tension. If the patient is "rewarded" with time only for that purpose, he is likely to have more anxiety attacks. (Acute or prolonged states of anxiety that seriously incapacitate him signal that the treatment is not being conducted properly or that he is too disturbed by special environmental pressures to undergo it on an ambulatory basis without drugs.) Since analytic psychotherapy is not a consistently effective tranquilizer, an extra session may fail to abate his anxiety appreciably. In that case, the patient's objections to working for significant change intensify, and he may decide to abandon treatment. That eventuality may be avoided by telling him that an extra session would probably prove disappointing to him at that time.

If, on the other hand, the patient wants more time to explore a specific problem and seems bent on enhancing his understanding of it, requests for extra time are usually granted. He is helped to verbalize his impressions of the problem and his own ideas about how to solve it. For instance, a person who was striving to lead a more satisfying life was reinforced in his discovery that alienation from human companionship was causing much of his suffering. He then made a greater effort to engage himself socially. Rather consistently, after a patient is firmly ensconced in the relationship, his requests for extra sessions or more intensive treatment reflect a strong desire to verbalize dissatisfaction over an environmental situation or to improve his current functioning.

As the pathologically narcissistic individual acquires information and emotional experiences that help him mobilize himself to meet his own psychological needs, the analytic experience becomes more absorbing and valuable to him. When he acquires the capacity to focus more effortlessly on his fundamental problems, the immediate cessation of suffering seems much less significant than the potential contribution that treatment may make to his well-being and sense of fulfillment in life. In the process of verbalizing impulses, feelings, thoughts, and memories in the sessions, his psychic pain becomes less acute; the patient should also be experiencing the maturational effects of the analytic monologue and dialogue. In that case, he may want to devote more time to them.

The subjectively beneficial effects of treatment should be discussed regularly (Perri, 1982). It is important that the patient come to feel that emotional progress is being made or, if not, to investigate why that feeling is lacking. Failure to experience wholesome effects from the sessions may mean that the patient and therapist are meeting too frequently or that a change of therapists is indicated. These possibilities should be explored until they reach agreement on a course of action.

It should be pointed out that the spacing of the sessions does not appreciably influence the duration of the treatment. Whether it is conducted on a low-frequency or high-frequency basis, maturation of the schizophrenic personality, as I have already mentioned, requires a minimum of 5 years of analytic psychotherapy. In other words, its sustained benefit—*therapeutic* effectiveness—does not depend primarily on the frequency of the sessions. I have observed that, other variables being equal, their spacing at longer intervals leads to results similar to those obtained through four or more weekly sessions. It is my impression that the best results are achieved when treatment is conducted at a frequency that is comfortable for both the patient and the therapist.

Optimal frequency may correlate with more intensive contact with the therapist beginning in the middle or late stage of the relationship. The patient's early anxieties and fears about treatment tend to subside at that time. He derives safety and security from the now familiar analytic situation. He is often impressed with the general improvement in his functioning and, if his financial status has improved accordingly, he may regard the additional investment as reasonable and worthwhile. What the patient derives primarily from more intensive treatment is increasing ease in the management of his life affairs, the feeling of "always being on top of things," as one man expressed it. Maintenance of that feeling is a valuable prognostic asset.

FINANCIAL TRANSACTIONS

Preservation of the patient's capital resources and the progressive expansion of his earning power may have a direct bearing on the outcome of the case. It is desirable that he be better off financially at the end of the treatment than when it started.

One way of preventing immediate financial pressures from contaminating the climate of transference and countertransference is to negotiate a *mutually agreeable* fee—one that does not entail undue hardship for the patient or significant sacrifice for the practitioner. Insurmountable obstacles to treatment may arise if the amount agreed on exhausts the patient's resources or constitutes an intolerable drain on his current income. (The same considerations apply when a relative or another third party finances the treatment.) The ideal fee, from the patient's point of view, is one that he can pay for regularly out of current earnings. For the therapist, the fee should represent a mild incentive, being neither so low that he feels he is giving away his services nor so high that he feels he is "bleeding" the patient.

If the therapist's customary fee is substantially higher than the amount the patient contemplates paying for treatment, he may be referred to a practitioner who would treat him at a fee the patient can afford. Many therapists embarking on practice are extremely interested in working with schizophrenic and other preoedipal patients. Because of their interest, such therapists may achieve better results with these difficult patients than more experienced practitioners who are not so interested in working with them.

Some patients derive considerable gratification from having family members carry the financial burden of their treatment; others resent their dependency. But whether the problem is one of outgrowing dependency cravings, or accepting the need for help, these schizophrenic patients become aware of a growing desire for independence. Generally they experience a great sense of achievement when they can pay for the treatment themselves.

Unilaterally imposed changes in fee are not desirable (Perri & Perri, 1978). Although reality considerations may justify such a change in the course of a long-term treatment, many patients strongly object to a raising of the fee they agreed to on entering treatment and therapists sometimes have problems in dealing with such objections. Practitioners who try to *impose* a higher fee tend to get angry at the patient who doesn't agree to it immediately and to characterize one who has greatly benefited from their services as an ingrate. The patient's negative reaction to a proposed change in fee, instead of being regarded as a rejection, should be accepted as a subject for further discussion. In other words, the objection should be dealt with as a resistance that needs to be analyzed and resolved.

It is a good idea to broach a contemplated change in fee well in advance, and to help the patient verbalize his reactions to it. After it has become clear that overwhelming resistance to continuing in treatment will not be mobilized by the proposed alteration of contract, it is made with the patient's agreement.

When the contract is established, the patient is informed that the handling of payments for the treatment is entirely his responsibility. The analyst explains that he does not present written statements and that oral accountings are given only when these are specifically requested. The patient is expected to keep track of the number of sessions he has each month and to present properly executed checks for the amount due at the end of the last session of the month. The discharge of this responsibility, besides being viewed as one aspect of training the patient to function cooperatively in the relationship, provides a wealth of opportunities to study his modes of resistive functioning. While ego deficiencies are tolerated, in the process of helping the patient outgrow them, they are called to his attention as uncooperative behavior. The patient is helped to transform the patterns of behavior so categorized into cooperative behavior.

Schizophrenic individuals entering treatment often demonstrate difficulties in the management of money. During the first 2 years of treatment, they usually have trouble paying precisely what they owe the therapist or making the payment at the right time. Some want to pay in advance or overpay; others underpay, miscalculate the number of sessions, or present postdated or worthless checks. One allows for the normal range of variations in these matters. However, when a patient deviates consistently, as in making the same type of error or disregarding dates month after month, these manifestations are dealt with as resistance. For example, with an individual who makes a practice of overpaying or underpaying, it is desirable to review the number of sessions conducted that month, because he may be trying, consciously or unconsciously, to find out whether the analyst will take account of the error or overlook it. The patient is helped to verbalize his attitude about the trustworthiness of the analyst.

Occasionally, a patient presents himself as completely help-less in handling money. He may try to cast the analyst in the role of banker. If resentment over being expected to operate in that capacity influences the conduct of treatment, it may become a realistic obstacle to continuance of the case. But the analyst tends to demonstrate a more tolerant attitude toward the pa-tient's inadequacies in financial matters than the patient ex-pects. Rather than putting him under pressure to adhere more strictly to the terms of the treatment contract, the analyst inves-tigates why the patient has not been fulfilling the contract and tries to help him fulfill it.

Treatment is not automatically terminated because the pa-tient cannot pay for it. A flexible approach to this contingency often leads to mutually agreeable arrangements, based primarily on realistic considerations. How each situation is handled de-pends on the patient's attitude. If he wants to withdraw for lack of funds, his resistance to being carried financially until he is able to resume payment may be worked on. If, on the other hand, he feels that he is entitled to such consideration, discon-tinuance of the treatment sessions, at least for the time being, may be in order.

In recent years, instead of adhering to the general practice of paying for treatment at the end of each month, some pa-tients have preferred to pay at the end of each session. They view this procedure as easier; the number of sessions held each month does not have to be kept track of, and disagreements with the therapist about their accountability for sessions missed without advance notification are avoided. Session-by-session payment is a departure from the classical tradition on financial arrangements, but if it is more convenient for the patient I see no objection to it. I am disposed to go along with any reasona-ble modification of the standard contract requested by the pa-tient. The governing principle is that any special arrangements that are proposed by either party should be mutually agreeable and mutually salutary.

Failure to adhere to whatever payment schedule has been agreed on is usually handled expeditiously. In recent years, I have dealt with repeated infractions of that nature more firmly than I had earlier in my practice because, in my experience, permitting a patient to go heavily into arrears for treatment may well be offering him an incentive either to discontinue treatment entirely or to abandon the present relationship and start afresh with another analyst. Some schizophrenic patients have done this repeatedly, leaving a train of debts in their wake. Other schizophrenic patients, permitted to go into arrears for their treatment, will utilize it to make progress. Whether to permit a patient to defer payment for the treatment or to discontinue it if he becomes seriously delinquent is therefore a matter of clinical concern.

However, to permit a patient to run up a debt *without intervening* to point out the potentially negative therapeutic implications of the situation is an error of omission. The purpose of such an intervention is to help the patient fulfill the treatment contract, not to punish or injure him in any way for failure to pay. Any impression the patient may have that he is being penalized for that reason should be corrected.

A woman whose serious problems in managing money had led to many embroilments with relatives and friends responded to her therapist's discussion of her failure to pay him promptly by insisting on paying for treatment session by session. Several weeks later she told the therapist, "Not getting another appointment until I've paid for the last one is very helpful to me. It means I can't fight with you about money, I can't go into debt, and I don't have to worry about leaving treatment because I owe you money." With this patient, it would have been a technical error for the therapist to have given her an appointment for another session until she had paid for the current one.

Sessions that are cancelled because of physical illness are usually not charged for. A person who phones earlier in the day that he has a temperature of 100° or over is instructed to remain in bed. Frequently, after the relationship is well established, the patient will argue the importance of coming, perhaps offering to do it by taxi and then returning to bed. Defiance of the advice of a physician consulted about a serious illness is discouraged. The analyst communicates the idea that he is more interested in the patient's long-range well-being than in his adherence at that juncture to the treatment schedule.

However, sessions cancelled for nonmedical reasons at less

than 24 hours' notice are charged for unless the time can be allocated to someone else. This policy is firmly enforced, especially when the patient phones 23 hours and 59 minutes in advance that he will not come. Acute personal emergencies and acts of God are not excepted, though an extra session may be offered without charge after the patient has fully verbalized his resentment about paying for the one that was missed. In the event that the time was filled, the patient may be so informed during the next session if his attitude is apologetic; if it is vituperative, the pleasant surprise that he will not be charged for the session may be defered until the end of the month to help him go on venting his resentment. Although some analysts don't want the patient to continue saying how angry he is, it is important not to interrupt the verbal release of anger unless the analyst decides that the patient is being abusive just for the fun of it.

As the treatment proceeds, the rules on cancellations may be modified. To discourage any tendency to abuse the privilege, the patient may be told that he must pay for all nonmedical cancellations. However, he discovers later, if his time is taken by another patient, that he is not charged for it. The patient thus learns that the analyst may present himself dogmatically, but he behaves reasonably.

The operational principles discussed above apply to the early stage of treatment. Later on, the handling of each repetitive pattern is governed by what is going on in the relationship.

OTHER PRACTICES

Practices and policies on aspects of the therapeutic relationship that are not mentioned in the treatment contract are not routinely explained to the patient when the treatment begins. Communications on these matters are usually deferred until the patient asks specific questions about them or the investigation of his reaction to one or another of these practices would serve a therapeutic purpose.

For example, to announce at the beginning of treatment

that the patient refrain from making irreversible changes in his life situation would introduce potentially troublesome ideas before he is confronted with the necessity of committing himself to a course of action. But in the course of treatment, before a major decision of that nature is made, the patient is told it would be better to defer making it until the situation has been thoroughly explored with the analyst. After being helped to balance the pros and cons of the action under consideration, the patient makes his own decision on how to proceed (Greenwald, 1973).

What the patient does outside the office is of much less concern to the analyst than its effect on the patient's functioning in the sessions. The idea communicated to him is that he is free to do anything he really wants to do outside the office as long as it does not interfere with analytic progress.

The analyst may prohibit one or another pattern of behavior in the sessions, such as smoking or getting off the couch, as a matter of therapeutic strategy. Similarly, any setting of limits on the patient's behavior outside the office is a communication designed to facilitate personality change.

In general, rules are formulated and applied simply to help the patient behave cooperatively in the relationship. To convey the impression that he is being *punished for failure to obey is an error in technique.* An unyielding attitude may be demonstrated to help him build up a sense of self-control but a ritualistic approach to arrangements and rules is avoided. Although the patient may not be made aware of the fact, each practice is analyzed in terms of its unconscious meaning to him in the immediate situation, to help him function appropriately with a minimum of effort.

Telephone Calls

A severely disturbed individual needs to know that he can get in touch with the therapist between sessions. The first time he inquires whether he may telephone, he may be asked, "Why not?" Knowledge that this is permitted is ego-reinforcing and, moreover, diminishes the urge of a negatively suggestible person to phone. When the idea is conveyed that the therapist will accept their calls, few patients abuse the privilege. Those who do are educated to exercise it more reasonably. For example, a woman who made a practice of phoning every few hours of the day and night was instructed not to call under any circumstances. After expressing her resentment, she said that the ban helped her control her impulses to phone.

Letters

The practice of writing letters to the therapist is one I recommend to patients. A letter may be no more than a sheet or two of paper on which the patient has spontaneously set down some thoughts and feelings that came to mind following a treatment session. Letters from patients may be answered before the next session with a few comments or questions.

The opportunity to pursue a train of associations with a writing tool is one from which some schizophrenic patients derive considerable benefit. "Writing down my ideas opens me up to thoughts and memories that don't occur when I'm on the couch," one woman said. New areas of psychological significance may be unexpectedly uncovered. The "writing cure" may aid the productive continuance of associations to ideas that were verbalized during a recent session (Spunt, 1979).

Writing has been a helpful supplement to talking for some of my patients; the more they write, the better they tend to communicate. "Whenever I get stuck in the analysis, I write you some letters and that seems to free me," one young man on the verge of recovery remarked. The fact that a patient does not phone or write occasionally may be refered to in a session; often this helps the patient to do so.

Vacation Periods and Other Interruptions

The therapist's vacation, especially during the furst 2 years of the treatment relationship, are difficult for a seriously ill person to tolerate. The more extended this interruption, the more adverse its consequences may be for a psychotic or near-psychotic individual. For that reason, I usually limit my own vacation periods to 2 weeks at a time. In general, I recommend that practitioners working with very disturbed patients make an effort to plan their vacations so that they are not away from the office for longer periods of time.

At least a month in advance of the analyst's vacation, it is desirable to ask the patient how he would feel about keeping in touch with the analyst by mail or phone during the interruption in the regular treatment schedule. (The recent development of telephone therapy also opens up the possibility of maintaining contact with a severely disturbed patient, when indicated, during the vacation period in circumstances where 50-minute treatment sessions over long-distance wires are feasible and affordable.) The patient is also asked if he would like to have the name of another practitioner he might talk with during that period. Such referrals are customarily made during lengthy interruptions in practice.

In general, patients are not influenced to take their own vacation at the same time (or charged for sessions missed when it does not coincide with the therapist's). However, those who have a choice of vacation time may be asked early in the relationship why they do not take it during the same period. Later on, a compulsively compliant or defiant individual may be asked why he does not take his vacation at another time.

Analytic Group Therapy

After a minimum of 2 years of effective individual treatment, if recovery from the illness is well under way, the analytic group experience is recommended to some schizophrenic patients as an adjunctive procedure for dealing with specific problems. In combination with the monologue and dialogue of the one-to-one relationship, "groupalogue" creates a powerful force for change. Under its emotional impact, many resistances are resolved (Spotnitz, 1957, 1961a, 1974; Ormont, 1981; Rosenthal, 1985).

One particular value of analytic psychotherapy in the group setting is that the shared treatment experience tests the patient's continuing vulnerability to emotional stress, however much improvement he has already achieved in the individual relationship. The group experience first exposes and then eventually reduces the vulnerability of the schizophrenic patient to verbal attack.

Another value is that patients engage in more symbolic and other nonverbal communication in the group situation. It is much easier to recognize and utilize such communication therapeutically in the group setting than in the individual relationship.

CONTACT WITH THE FAMILY

As much as possible, the patient is helped to resolve extraoffice interferences with analytic progress. A physical change from an environment that is a source of continuing pathological stimulation, such as his home or place of employment, may be advised; but the modification of any pressures connected with family attitudes is attempted first through less drastic measures. In the treatment of adults as well as of children and adolescents, tactful guidance of the family is usually undertaken with a view to facilitating the patient's improvement.

When the treatment begins, the attitude of members of the patient's family is assumed to be cooperative unless they demonstrate otherwise. With his permission, members of the immediate family may confer with the analyst when they wish to do so. But the analyst is particularly concerned with the parent or spouse whose reactions to changes in the patient's behavior are in some way obstructing the progress of the case. (Schizophrenic patients often succeed in inducing such reactions in those close to them.) One or another of the "backlash" reactions may motivate a member of the family to request a conference, or the relative may be invited to come to the office when the patient believes that the analyst's intervention in the situation would be helpful. Information disclosed by the patient in his sessions is not communicated to members of his family without his knowledge and consent. Exceptions to this ethical principle may have to be made, for example, to secure the cooperation of the family of a totally self-destructive patient in dealing with suicidal tendencies or to alert the family of a potentially violent patient to his homicidal threats (Spotnitz, 1981b).

Provided that the therapist can protect the patient, in particular an adolescent (Spotnitz, 1975), from emotional confrontations that would militate against therapeutic progress at that time, the patient's participation in a discussion of family problems is helpful. The patient's presence also helps the practitioner to identify the focal point of the immediate conflict and to promote recognition of the psychological needs of each member of the family unit.

The therapist rarely limits himself to answering questions. He is interested primarily in ascertaining why they are asked, and in exploring family attitudes. But instead of appearing to "pump" the patient's relatives for information, it is important that he permit them to do most of the talking. If he does not reproach them for inappropriate attitudes and refrains from aggravating any guilt feelings they may have about the patient's illness, harmful pressures on the patient can often be nullified.

Meetings that are oriented to deal with the patient's problems, and are held at mutually agreeable intervals, are good policy. But they will not substantially reduce disequilibrium if a family member in intimate contact with the patient suffers from a serious emotional disorder.

The latter may wish to enter treatment with the same practitioner. There are differences of opinion on working simultaneously with two or more members of a family, and some inexperienced psychotherapists find it difficult. In such circumstances, treatment by someone else may be suggested. The practitioner who can undertake the allied case ably and comfortably is, however, well advised to do so because it usually leads to better results for each patient.

Family conferences are continued throughout the case. These are usually held with the consent of the patient. However, situations may arise when such conferences need to be arranged by the therapist without the patient's knowledge and consent (Spotnitz, 1981b).

COOPERATIVE BEHAVIOR: ULTIMATE CONCEPT

When the principles governing the patient's participation in the working alliance are integrated with the general plan of helping him recognize and outgrow the immediate obstacles to change, the concept of appropriate functioning undergoes significant alterations. The approach to contract, routine arrangements, and rules reflects the inverse relation between the strength of resistance and the degree of cooperation demanded of the patient.

When the pathologically narcissistic individual enters treatment, his capacity to work analytically is assumed to be extremely limited. Consciously and unconsciously, he reacts negatively to requirements that force him to feel his own helplessness and inadequacies. Primitive ideas and explosive emotions that are difficult to verbalize dominate his erratic behavior. Therefore, rather than being expected to fulfill his tasks under the treatment contract, the patient is slowly trained to do so. Few supplementary demands are imposed as long as he remains in a maximal state of preoedipal resistance.

The process of tying up feelings and thoughts with words has a dampering effect on the patient's behavior. His ability to examine his verbal disclosures objectively is enhanced by identification with the analyst's attitudes and communications. The more the patient understands the significance of what he has been talking about, the greater his ability to influence his own functioning and achieve his life goals.

As the early obstacles to implementation of the contract are outgrown, tasks that entail more coordinated functioning, discrimination, and judgment are introduced. Finally, the concept of cooperative behavior is redefined to encompass systematic collaboration in the recognition, investigation, and interpretation of the obstacles to personality maturation that appear in the last stages of treatment. One works ultimately with a patient who is fully cooperative, an individual who is dedicated to the task of recognizing and analyzing his own resistance and utilizing the analyst's assistance in functioning as a mature individual.

The patient trained in this way experiences a growing desire to engage himself in the treatment. He recognizes the purpose of the arrangements and rules under which he operates, and appreciates the necessity of regulating his functioning accordingly. Beyond the long-range benefits derived from cooperating with the analyst as fully as possible in each stage of treatment, the patient understands and acquires the capacity to apply the principles governing his engagement in the analytic situation to the broader spheres of human relations. No longer a prisoner to his own impulses, thoughts, and feelings, he senses that they are now elements of his own personality that give him the freedom to behave as he wants to, and to derive pleasure and satisfaction in living.

Chapter 6

RECOGNITION AND
UNDERSTANDING OF RESISTANCE

The effective application of a theory of dealing with resistance naturally rests on the recognition of its presence. But the detection and identification of the significant forms of resistance in a case of schizophrenia, as well as understanding what they communicate about the patient's immediate state of being, are actually more difficult than dealing with the resistance itself. The present chapter is addressed to these tasks.

Formulations on resistance reflect what one is striving to accomplish through the treatment. As long as the recovery of memories was regarded as the goal of psychoanalytic therapy, the forces that interfered with memory work were equated with resistance. In that context, Fenichel defined it comprehensively as "everything that prevents the patient from producing material derived from the unconscious" (1945, p. 27).

Subsequent developments in the theory of psychoanalytic technique substantially broadened the scope of phenomena admitted to the status of resistance (Marshall, 1982). It has come to be recognized as something other than the artifact of the analytic situation that it was originally thought to be; that is, the nuisance that reared up only when an individual was under pressure to free-associate. Of interest in this connection is Freud's brief reference in 1897 to resistance as "nothing but the child's character"—a notion, he continued, that made resistance something "objectively tangible" for him (1954, p. 226). Rather than viewed as a phenomenon isolated from the patient's habitual behavior and attitudes in life, resistance is now associated with the defenses mobilized by the ego in the interests of mastery of the environment and psychic survival. These protective devices, activated in the analytic situation by transference, are recognized as characteristic expressions of the living personality.

It is also recognized that resistance, once equated with the cutting off of communication, actually performs a communication function. To the observer who can decipher its meaning, it conveys otherwise unobtainable information about the patient's life story.

In whatever way resistance manifests itself, it always denotes opposition—conscious or unconscious—to the analytic process. Menninger (1958) defines it as *"the trend of forces within the patient which oppose the process of ameliorative change"* (p. 104).

Forces *without* as well as *within* may thwart such change in a patient whose ego functioning is inadequate to cope with the immediate realities of his life. Although this is not the case with all schizophrenic individuals, rather characteristically in the course of treatment they experience states of ego weakness, generally or in a specific area of functioning, when progress hinges on the mastery of an outside interference. Since personality maturation is regarded as the goal of treatment, *all* of the forces that prevent the patient from functioning with the analyst in an emotionally mature way are recognized as resistance. Such forces encompass a larger field than interferences with communication in the sessions; but eventually they do interfere with communication or threaten the continuance of the relationship. In either case, the external obstacles are perceived as resistance in the technical sense of the term.

EXTERNAL RESISTANCE

Although Freud enunciated the dictum, *"Whatever interrupts the progress of analytic work is a resistance,"* a footnote appended 25 years later to that statement in *The Interpretation of Dreams* (1900, p. 517) points out "something both true and new" behind that exaggeration. Even though the patient cannot be charged with responsibility for a circumstance or event in his life that interferes with the treatment, how great an interruption it becomes "often depends" on him. Resistance shows itself unmistakably in the "readiness with which he accepts an occurrence of this kind or the exaggerated use which he makes of it." Thus the perception of external obstacles as resistance is not a new one.

Freud often used "resistance" and "inner resistance" synonymously, by and large implying the latter in most of his recommendations on technique. In a review of failures in treatment (1917), he attributes most of those that occurred in the early years of psychoanalysis to unfavorable environmental circumstances. Such resistances, he continues

> are of small theoretical interest but of the greatest practical importance . . . . In psychoanalytic treatments the intervention of relatives is a positive danger and a danger one does not know how to meet. One is armed against the patient's internal resistances, . . . but how can one ward off these external resistances? No kind of explanations make any impression on the patient's relatives; . . . . We had in fact undertaken something which in the prevailing circumstances was unrealizable. (p. 456)

It is my impression that Freud avoided or postponed dealing with external resistance as long as possible for two reasons. Apparently, he was unable to cope successfully with the antagonistic attitudes of the patients' relatives, with social prejudice, and other unpropitious environmental influences in the early years of his practice. Moreover, after he had helped patients deal effectively with their internal resistances, he may have found that they did not need his assistance in mastering the external obstacles. Such a finding might account for the "small theoretical interest" he attached to these external resistances. The only weapon at his disposal for dealing with them, on the basis of this statement, was an explanation to the relatives of what was going on, and such explanations were not helpful.

Even though the theory of psychoanalytic technique does not direct attention to interfering realities as reducible resistances to therapeutic progress, many practitioners today view them in that context. However, persons with relatively capable egos may not require the analyst's assistance in dealing with their environmental concerns. Usually they are able to conduct themselves in accordance with what they regard as their own best interests after their inner resistances are resolved. Meanwhile, some protection is afforded by the instruction to defer vital decisions about personal and professional matters until they are fully discussed and the patient feels adequate to make them. The impending decisions are usually subjected to thorough analysis.

But the individual whose foothold on reality is precarious often comes up against mundane difficulties whose solution will not brook avoidance or delay. Obstacles to personality maturation that are not specific for his illness often hamper his progress in treatment or threaten its continuance. In the interests of helping him master his intrapsychic problems, the therapist recognizes an adverse environmental circumstance that *becomes a factor* in the treatment as resistance to analytic progress. In theory, rather than ignoring these external resistances, the therapist assumes responsibility for helping the patient deal with them.

This approach entails separate judgments. First of all, does the currently adverse reality situation reported by the patient interfere with his functioning in his sessions? If not, it is of little significance to the analyst. If it does interfere, it is investigated. In short, whatever interferes with the analytic situation and the patient's capacity to continue the treatment is regarded as external resistance. That is the governing principle.

The fact that a patient has a headache, for instance, may not prevent him from using his treatment time productively. But if he spends a session complaining about it, attention to his physical condition is justified. It may become clear from what he reports that the headache is stimulated by elementary ignorance or neglect of bodily needs. A simple explanation that hunger pangs or lack of sleep create an unhealthy frame of mind may suffice to counter a tendency to skip meals or pursue other harmful habits. If not, a medical examination may be suggested, or the possibility that significant psychological factors are implicated in the physical complaint may be explored.

During his first winter in treatment, the communications of a highly intelligent college student were interrupted by paroxysms of coughing. He apologized repeatedly. His physical health was sound, he asserted. He was confident that his bronchial condition would clear up shortly. But the coughing bouts persisted, and were investigated. Possible sources of bronchial infection were ruled out until the youth disclosed, in response to questioning, that he wore summer-weight underwear throughout the year. The idea that he might not be coughing if he wore warmer clothing in cold weather surprised him. He had always dressed the same way, he said, and the coughing had started just a few months earlier. However, acceptance of the suggestion followed the discussion. The coughing stopped when he took to wearing warmer underwear.

Obstructive attitudes of members of the patient's family are a common source of external resistance. A young woman who had been functioning cooperatively began to indulge in vague expressions of dissatisfaction about her progress. She said she wanted to give up treatment but was unable to explain why. When this was probed, it became clear that it was not the patient herself but her father who wanted to terminate the analysis. After perceiving the connection between his attitude and her current state of resistance, she asked the therapist to intercede on her behalf with her father. This proved unnecessary; she was able to resolve the problem herself. However, failure to recognize and analyze the external threat she had been concealing would have halted a relationship that ultimately produced the sought-for results.

What initially appears to be an external resistance may, on the other hand, prove to be an internal one. The report that a parent or spouse is opposed to the continuance of treatment or is hostile to the therapist personally may represent an unconscious maneuver of the patient to sever the analytic relationship. It was suggested to a student-analyst that he explore that possibility when he expressed genuine concern that the enraged husband of a patient had threatened him with physical violence. Investigation of the situation helped her recognize that she had been forcing her husband into the role of provocateur. His threats expressed her own opposition to treatment, of which she had been totally unaware. Such maneuvers are commonly observed.

The fact that the therapist admits external resistance to his province of responsibility does not mean that he will be able to help the patient deal with it. Obviously, there are here-and-now realities that are not susceptible to psychological influence. Recognition does mean that the practitioner is in a position to investigate the nature and strength of an interfering factor, determine whether it would respond to analytic understanding and communication, and decide whether he wants to make an attempt to deal with it, either directly or with the cooperation of other individuals. This approach enlarges the analyst's area of responsibility, but it substantially reduces the risk of failure.

INNER RESISTANCES

After discovering that opposition to the recovery of memories was not the only kind of resistance used by his patients, Freud studied the other methods by which they interfered with free association. Later he called attention to five forms of resistance, describing the dynamic processes related to each in terms of the mental structure from which it originated (1926). All of these forms are observed in a case of schizophrenia.

The first group—opposition to remembering emotionally significant life experiences—is repression resistance. It is instituted by the ego. The schizophrenic patient resorts to it primarily while verbalizing memories of situations that were highly charged with aggressive impulses. Prefeelings of hatred and ideas of discharging it to objects are repressed.

To be more specific: at the beginning of treatment, the schizophrenic patient is very dedicated to *not* remembering the feelings of hatred he experienced for other people; any memories that are recalled at that stage are therefore communicated without affect. Subsequently, when the patient has advanced to the point where he is able to express hostile feelings comfortably, he develops a new resistance to engaging in the recall of memories with feelings.

Through secondary gain resistance, the ego's manipulations are gauged to maintain whatever special benefits or consideration the individual has been accorded because of his illness. In cases where the illness has afforded a great deal of infantile gratification, primarily of dependency cravings, this is an especially powerful type of resistance in schizophrenia.

Superego resistance is characterized by the sense of guilt and the need for self-punishment. At times the deeply narcissistic individual becomes immersed in feelings of incurability, hopelessness, or worthlessness. Conscience tells him that his impulses to destroy, as well as ideas that he may be a homosexual, a dangerous pervert, or a potential criminal, are too "shameful" to divulge. When the impulses are too ego-dystonic to reveal and when the ideas are denied, they give rise to hallucinations. But in the course of the analysis, as the impulses and ideas become acceptable to the ego and are recognized as part of the human condition, the attacking voices disappear.

An exacerbation of symptoms or suffering late in the treatment—the so-called negative therapeutic reaction (Freud, 1937; Perri, 1982)—may be an expression of superego resistance. Elements of ego and superego resistance—primarily the former—combine in the feelings of depression and suicidal wishes often mobilized when the patient starts to improve and to recognize that his deep cravings for mother's love will never be gratified. Actually, the suicidal impulses are enhanced by an ego resistance—an unwillingness to accept feelings of hopelessness and futility.

Another type of resistance emanates from the id. Id or repetition-compulsion resistance expresses itself in strong cravings for physical contact and an insistence on action. Murderous impulses linked with memories too deeply repressed for the schizophrenic patient to recall when alone are reawakened in the presence of the analyst. These impulses, derived from unforgiving hatred for the early object, alternate with, and are often masked by cravings for affection and sexual contact.

The four types of resistance described above are primarily

of theoretical interest. They demonstrate how the patient characteristically relates to strangers in frustrating situations. However informative in that respect, they are of minor significance for technique until they become fully charged with affects. This occurs after the patient develops an emotional interest in the analyst as an individual, a development that facilitates progressive communication for a while but eventually interferes with it. This fifth type of opposition to change—transference resistance—is of primary import for the clinician, his "daily bread," in Greenson's words (1967, p. 183). Characteristic patterns of transference resistance in the schizophrenic patient are described later.

SPECIAL MANIFESTATIONS

In the interval between the preliminary overtures and the completion of contract for treatment, the pathologically narcissistic individual often engages in a series of breakaway maneuvers. He backs and fills before committing himself more intensively and extensively than the average candidate for treatment and manifests deep reluctance in special ways. Whereas the latter may be uncertain whether he has selected the "right" analyst and may harbor a few misgivings about the ordeal ahead, the schizophrenic individual is often convinced that he has selected the "wrong" one and that his condition is hopeless. He thinks—and eventually says—that he may be "going crazy" if he is not already. There is no point in involving himself in treatment, even though there is nothing better to do.

An insistent and demanding attitude during the initial interview is a characteristic expression of pre-analytic resistance. A seriously disturbed person is apt to talk confusedly about his problems and complain of severe anxiety or horrible feelings experienced at that very moment. On the other hand, when a willingness to help him is communicated, he may find that he cannot come at any hour the practitioner can arrange to see him. Similar patterns of pre-analytic resistance have already been described (Chapter 5).

When the contract has been agreed on, the patient customarily maneuvers to avoid or delay communicating significant information about himself. To talk about anything may be a tormenting experience when he becomes aware of feelings that give rise to acute states of tension. Moreover, he is not disposed to reveal his poor opinion of himself to someone who, whether or not he is the "right" analyst for the patient, is apparently a superior individual. Perhaps the patient cannot think of anything to talk about; or he may say that he really doesn't know what the therapist wants to hear. One schizophrenic youth responded to the initial instruction to talk by saying, "Well, I was born and here I am."

In the early stage of treatment, and even in the pre-analytic phase, very early arrival, tardiness, and absence are common patterns of resistance. Some patients carry one or another pattern to an extreme, such as arriving a minute before the session is scheduled to end. Others present themselves on the wrong day, and appear surprised or offended that they are not expected. As already indicated, difficulties in the payment of fees is another area in which ego deficits are observed.

The couch position creates other problems. However, a refusal to assume it, or to remain on the couch throughout the session, cannot always be attributed exclusively to the patient's uncooperative attitude. Resistance to use of the couch is frequently reinforced by the patient's perception that the therapist is uneasy about his being there. Numerous forms of such resistance are explored by Stern (1978) and Eigen (1977).

Schizophrenia gives rise to highly specific forms of ego resistance that eventually operate as transference resistance. In other words, disturbances in ideation, inappropriate affects, and the other symptoms of the illness eventually are mobilized in the service of resistance.

The patient may state that he has difficulty in thinking or that his thoughts confuse him. One of his ideas may block off another. He may report hearing voices or sensing that strange impressions go through his mind; attempts to understand them seem to intensify the confusion.

A schizophrenic young man claimed that his previous therapist produced the voices that troubled him by making him feel very hostile. As he put it, the therapist "blew his mind"; in other words, the hostility he experienced disrupted his ego boundaries. The patient's repeated insistence that the voices would never go away operated as a self-fulfilling prophecy, a form of resistance that persisted for many months.

Another patient refers to sensations and affects that are equally disagreeable, among them feelings of resentment and danger. He objects to sexual feelings and does not want to report them. Unwelcome too, he says, are eerie feelings of not being himself or of being dead, and the therapist may be accused of generating them. "I feel like a cadaver," a male patient said. "What has happened?"

The schizophrenic patient may complain that nothing he does is enjoyable. He may mourn the loss of his sense of reality. Feelings of emptiness or a total absence of feeling are reported in a querulous manner.

Impulsive actions that short-circuit verbal communication are other manifestations of the same special form of resistance. In this connection, I am reminded of a woman who used to spring up from the couch to bang at the office door. After indulging in such behavior repeatedly, she said, "You ought to be grateful that I bang at the door instead of at you."

Although thought, feeling, and action are the main areas in which malfunctioning is observed, it also invades the patient's fantasies and dreams. He is not disposed to report them because what he experiences in imagination is often as torturous as what he thinks and feels.

The type of resistance just described reflects the fragmentation or disorganization caused by the illness. Cooperative functioning in the analytic situation entails the prompt release of frustration-aggression in feelings and language, but the pathways through which such release occurs are inadequate or blocked. The analyst observes both the erosive effects of the preoedipal pattern of bottling up aggressive impulses and the repetitive activation of that pattern. The unconscious purpose motivating the pathogenic pattern, as has been indicated, is the need to protect the object. The massive clinical evidence of the damage sustained by the personality brings to the fore the nuclear problem of the damming up of frustration-aggression.

There are two reasons that the severe symptoms connected

with the narcissistic defense come into operation. Their appearance may be incidental to the tapping of past sources of information. Some deterioration in psychic functioning may occur simply because the patient is moving backward in memory. The retrograde process may take him down the rungs of the developmental ladder to the areas where ego boundaries scarcely exist. It is often difficult to differentiate the distorted perceptions and disturbances in thought indirectly produced by regression from clinical manifestations related to the sudden fragmentation of the personality by an intolerable amount of frustration-aggression. Patterns of the latter type are similar to those associated with the organic psychoses, cerebral intoxication, and secondary psychosis, such as that induced by LSD. I refer to these patterns as "personality-fragmentation" resistance.

Is the schizophrenic patient experiencing more frustration-tension than he can release appropriately in the immediate situation? It is extremely important to explore that possibility as soon as such patterns are observed. One needs to bear in mind that the release of rage in moderate feelings and language requires a certain degree of maturation of the mental apparatus. As the treatment progresses and the patient experiences more positive feelings, he becomes more capable of expressing negative feelings "safely"—that is, without experiencing emotional flooding or hallucinations from the mobilization of intense feelings of hatred and anger. Thus, in dealing with schizophrenic patients, one refrains, on the one hand, from being so frustrating that the patient becomes overwhelmed with negative feelings and, on the other hand, from creating so positive a climate that the patient tends to bottle up negative feelings.

The other special type of resistance is a concomitant of regression. The schizophrenic patient often has trouble saying precisely what he means to say, and he tends to employ primitive modes of communication. Instead of expressing his thoughts and feelings in the language expected of a person his age, he may convey them in unconventional signs and body language. He communicates much that he is not aware of as he crosses and uncrosses his legs, lies on his side, kicks at the couch, jumps up when distracted, as well as through his facial expression, mannerisms, gestures, and even the clothes he wears. In the therapeutic group setting, emotional communication in the guise of body language is a common form of preoedipal resistance against verbalization.

The nonverbal as well as the anachronistic verbal communications to which the schizophrenic patient unconsciously resorts are perceived as resistance because they interfere with the vital process of connecting impulses, feelings, thoughts, and memories with words. Nevertheless, for the clinician who has acquired a general understanding of symbolic communication and the language of young children, the presence of "language resistance" is not difficult to recognize or decipher. The focus is on helping the patient verbalize the communication.

TRANSFERENCE RESISTANCE

To facilitate the prior development of negative transference, the analyst functions primarily as a frustrating object. This does not mean that he treats the patient in a discourteous or unfriendly manner on arrival or departure; I refer to his general attitude when the patient is functioning on the couch. Moreover, as already mentioned, one needs to balance frustration with sufficient gratification to help the patient verbalize his aggressive reactions. The message implicitly conveyed to the patient is that the analyst's role is to help him verbalize all of his immediate thoughts, feelings, and memories.

The danger of precipitating psychotic regression is avoided by asking the patient a few object-oriented questions during the session—unsolicited communications that are designed to prevent the patient, during periods of silence, from experiencing too high a degree of frustration-tension. In addition, the analyst responds to the patient's *contact functioning*—that is, his occasional verbal attempts to gratify an immediate need for words from the analyst. This might be equated with the "infant's struggling attempt to make contact with the distant, preoccupied mother, a kind of loss known at times to us all" (Oremland, 1980, p. 311). Contact functioning in the patient (Margolis, 1983a) commonly takes the form of a question posed about procedure or a request for information or advice. Factual information is provided by the therapist from time to time when the patient is making a sincere attempt to function cooperatively.

But, in responding to the patient's contact functioning as a cue to intervene to help the patient continue to communicate, the analyst does not provide any information or advice. Rather, he attempts psychologically to reflect the verbal attempt at contact through some brief communication. The effect of such communications—in essence, brief verbal feedings on a self-demand schedule—is to minimize the amount of frustration-tension to which the patient is exposed while lying on the couch and talking. The purpose of the analyst's interventions is to create a relatively tension-free atmosphere in the session in which the patient, feeling comfortable and at ease, goes on talking.

Although exposure of the patient to an inordinate degree of frustration-tension is thus avoided, there is always enough in every relationship so that he has to learn how to deal with it. By and large, responding to contact functioning enables the therapist to provide, symbolically, an agreeable breast; but even the most sensitively attuned mother cannot always offer one to her baby at the precise moment he wants it or pick him up whenever he wants to be picked up. Hence, sooner or later the patient's customary patterns of dealing with a frustrating object are activated; the more emotionally significant the analyst becomes, the more vividly these patterns come into play. The pathological defenses become charged with emotion for the analyst as a transference object.

These patterns are carefully studied before attempts are made to deal with them because they require different procedures. It is first determined whether the transference object is being related to at the moment as a separate and distinct object; in other words, whether the transference is object (oedipal) or narcissistic in nature. When the patient is clearly object-oriented, the immature pattern is identified as object-transference resistance. When he relates to the analyst more or less uncertainly as "*me*" or as nonexistent, or does not feel the analyst's participation or influence (even though the analyst can observe that his presence has a profound effect on the patient at that moment) the pattern is classified as narcissistic-transference resistance.

Object-Transference Resistance

In a state of object transference, a resistant schizophrenic patient repeatedly makes such statements as: "You sit there and do nothing to help me"; "I don't feel like talking to you"; and "I don't enjoy being in your office." A man who pleaded with his therapist time and again to "do something to help me" was reminded that he was supposed to talk. "I'm too far gone to talk to you," he asserted, "so I guess you can't help me." Responding to the same reminder, another person said, "I must warn you that I'm falling apart." Still another patient said, "If you can't help me, I'm incurable." Reflection of the patient's contact functioning also stimulates unpleasant reference to the analyst: he has disagreeable traits; he is cruel; he is somehow missing the mark; he does not justify confidence, and so on. Such manifestations of resistance indicate that the patient is sufficiently in touch with reality to perceive the frustrating object as a force separate from the self.

Intermittently, as his patterns of contact functioning are reflected, the schizophrenic patient reacts to questions and other "verbal feedings" with feelings of affection. But it is repeatedly difficult for him to verbalize them—to say, for example, that he likes the analyst, or that the analyst pleases him in any way. In a state of object transference, the patient dissembles in the customary way. He may report, "I'm too embarrassed to tell you what I think (or feel) about you." In lieu of progressively verbalizing—providing analytic material in a cooperative manner—the patient repeats some such statement over and over again when the object transference is positive.

Narcissistic-Transference Resistance

The equivalent repetitive pattern in a state of narcissistic transference gives the misleading impression that the patient is talking to himself, or to the therapist as a part of his mind. Agreeable affects or reactions to the therapist's syntonic communications are not reported as such. The therapist's responses to the attempts at contact appear to have no immediate effect on the repetitive pattern when the patient is in a state of narcissistic-transference resistance.

These patterns, however, are much less significant than the patient's *repeated* self-attacking maneuvers, in states of keen psychological discomfort, to prevent himself from saying, "You are frustrating me and I hate you for it." Instead of recognizing and reporting that truth, the schizophrenic patient unconsciously blots it out, conceals, masks, or submerges it. In short, instead of saying to the analyst, "You are frustrating me so I hate you," or "You are pleasing me so I like you," the patient, when experiencing hate for the frustrating analyst, will say, "I hate myself" and, when feeling pleased with the analyst, "I'm pleased about the way I feel."

When the transference is both narcissistic and negative, the patient functions cooperatively when he reports, "I loathe myself when I am frustrated." In a state of resistance, he either repeatedly conceals his self-hatred or does not attribute his psychological discomfort to the therapist. Something is the matter with *me* (Freeman, 1982), the patient repeatedly communicates, something that has nothing to do with the realities of the relationship. He may say that he doesn't feel like talking, that he would like to run away or "jump out of his skin." As he buries his aggressive impulses, he may say that he is "falling apart." Unbearable feelings and sensations are mentioned. The patient may report numbness or tenseness in some part of his body, that his eyes hurt, that he is unable to relax. He may assert that talking out his thoughts and feelings would serve no purpose because they are already known to the analyst. What is the use of talking to someone who is reading his mind?

If he accepts the idea that talking is essential even if the therapist "knows everything," the deeply narcissistic individual tends to become frightened or confused by his tendencies to experience anger or rage. He may then talk about suicide or about mutilating himself; when such thoughts are too threatening to voice, he often finds fault with himself for having nothing new or important to report. Or he may talk in an affectionate vein, making reference to sexual fantasies in which the analyst figures, and perhaps hinting at a strong need for sexual satisfaction.

Eventually, the patient may report repeatedly that the person to whom he turned for help is trying to manipulate and control him by stimulating evil cravings. Then he often veers away from that idea, confusing his impressions of the therapist as a malignant figure with his impressions of himself. For example, instead of saying that he is holding back information because he does not trust the practitioner, the patient may repetitiously complain that he cannot trust himself. On the other hand, at moments when a thought of his own disturbs him, he may say again and again, "You think I'm terrible."

OBJECT FIELD AND EGO FIELD

Understanding of the psychodynamic processes implicated in narcissistic-transference resistance is imperative, both for diagnostic purposes and for analytic progress.

The mélange of ego-object impression transcends the notion of momentary confusions due to projections and introjections. The resistant patient's more or less severe disturbances of identity and memory are more readily comprehensible in terms of personality fragmentation and regressive processes, triggered by undischarged frustration-aggression, that lead to a loosening of the boundary between the mind's two fields of awareness—the object field and the ego field. What is then observed is psychic functioning characteristic of the early stages of ego formation. The patient's states of confusion regarding nonself and self reflect the residue of undifferentiated feelings associated with primitive object relations (Freeman, 1982).

As far as we know, the mind of the infant is like a blank screen on which are recorded whatever impressions the brain has been capable of receiving—since birth, and even before birth. (Evidence is accumulating that the fetus too receives impressions; it registers sensitivity to sounds, such as the mother's voice, and other sensations.) Impressions of the infant's own bodily sensations as well as those of his mother's ministrations during his first few months of life are recorded in the *first object field*; the infant has no sense of separateness from the external world. That experience of oneness with the universe and total engulfment was likened by Freud to the feeling of "something limitless, unbounded [and, quoting Romain Rolland]—as it were, 'oceanic' " (1930, p. 64). This seems to be the *emotional* state[1] connected with the first object field.

With the quantitative sorting out of the impressions of the self, a part of the object field becomes the *ego field*. Although their differentiation is a slow process, usually the boundary between them has developed sufficiently for an ego to exist in the two-year-old child. Demarcation of the boundary is completed by the age of thirteen, and it is fully distinct in the mature personality.

When one is awake and receiving a great deal of external stimulation, it is difficult to distinguish between the object field of the mind and the outer world. When one is asleep and dreaming, however, the object field is activated primarily by internal stimuli. Hence, dreaming provides an excellent example of the functioning of the object field when relatively free from external stimulation. The dream conveys the experiences of the past, reproducing them in somewhat the same way as external realities are reproduced by the motion-picture camera, though much less faithfully. In the dream the object field gives a distorted picture of past realities. Generally, too, the ego field is represented to a minor degree; in the dream state, the ego is a relatively nonparticipatory viewer. Other people usually figure more prominently in dreams than the self.

In the psychoanalytic situation, as in the dream state and to some extent in daydreams and fantasies, experiences of previous object-ego fields are revived. The analysand is thus provided with opportunities to report the noxious effects of inner stimuli to which he was exposed in the past. His impressions of these past events are not necessarily accurate even when he is

---

[1]This has to be distinguished from the child's cognitive state. I refer here primarily to feelings. Early in life, objects can be differentiated cognitively before they are *felt* to be different.

reporting conscientiously. But the communications of a schizophrenic patient, when his earliest ego patterns are activated as
a defense against the release of frustration-aggression, are distorted to an exceptional degree. Objects previously established
in the object field are talked of as though they are part of the
ego; object patterns that moved into the ego field early in life
(identifications) are referred to as though they are in the object
field at the moment. The ego field is much less clear, and attempts are made to highlight it in some way. The boundary between the two fields frequently changes location and fluctuates
with varying degrees of distinctiveness. The severe loss of
awareness and obliteration of memory that may be experienced
by a patient in a transient state of psychosis suggests that the
boundary is virtually wiped out.

A patient describing that state said, "I suddenly felt as
though I was being swallowed up. I was losing my mind and
memory." Another patient, reporting a dream, said that she had
"fallen into one of those heavy sleeps, heavy in the sense that
there is something like weight, like the pressure of being inside
a closed sack of liquid, pushing against any attempts to move,
open my eyes, be in the world." Enveloped in this sack, as in the
intrauterine state, she recalled a series of difficulties she experienced while trying to communicate with an external object.
Analysts who report on their work with pathologically narcissistic individuals refer to similar communications of patients—for
example, fantasies of being enclosed in a "glass bubble" (Volkan, 1979) or encased in a "cocoon" (Modell, 1976).

The defective communications adhere to two general patterns. Impressions made on the object field, object representations, are *egotized*; that is, they are misidentified as experiences
of the ego field. The patient may refer to feelings that he originally experienced from a significant early object as his own
feelings. Conversely, feelings that originated in the ego field are
objectified.

What are commonly referred to as introjection and projection are what I have reformulated as "egotization of the object"
and "objectification of the ego." (Federn and Edoardo Weiss also
preferred the term "egotization" [Federn, 1952, p. 7] but con-

ceptualized the process differently.[2]) Inasmuch as introjection and projection are described as active mechanisms of the ego, the reformulation is more accurate in the present context. What one observes in the schizophrenic individual talking on the couch is an involuntary fusion and defusion of his ego and object fields with fluctuations in the distinctness of the ego boundaries.

In addition to the impulses and feelings that the patient experienced *for* his earliest objects, he may transfer simultaneously those that he experienced *from* the objects. Whole chains of hostile impulses flowing in opposite directions may be mislabeled when the patient is in a state of narcissistic transference.

Patterns of this nature are unconscious and involuntary. The patient is not aware that he is being frustrated or that he is defending himself by burying his aggressive impulses. He is aware only that he is supposed to keep on talking. In the process, he may report the disagreeable sensations produced as the defenses check the impulses. But usually he communicates, tirelessly and monotonously, his belief that the analyst, like his original object, does not really want him to relax his defenses.

Since a patient in this state has little ability to verbalize his hostile reactions, his reporting on the residue of feelings associated with the patterning of the schizophrenic reaction is both inaccurate and scanty. Full verbalization of the preoedipal state is usually impossible without the therapist's aid. The feelings that are induced in him by the patient are utilized to facilitate the sorting out of the patient's own feelings from those of the early objects. The patient is unable to participate in the work of reconstruction until the object transference has been stabilized (Zimmerman, 1982, p. 196).

In brief, recognition of the various mental operations by which the patient in a state of narcissistic transference prevents the release of frustration-aggression to the analyst is the key to effective treatment. These operations involve the use of highly

---

[2]In Weiss's interesting concept of "ego passage" (1957), the object becomes part of the ego and is then projected back into the object field— "externalized" after being "internalized."

specific early patterns of egotizing an object experienced as excessively frustrating. When aggression accumulates in the analytic situation, instead of verbalizing it, the patient unconsciously activates these primitive patterns of attacking the internal object in the ego field (experienced as "me") to protect the transference object.

The same type of resistance is sometimes observed briefly in a patient functioning on the oedipal level. Usually it is not dealt with because it is not strong enough to produce psychosis. Nevertheless, its existence interferes with personality maturation. Failure to recognize and deal with it may account for some of the unsatisfactory results reported in the treatment of oedipal problems.

With an increasing number of analysts working with patients who experienced developmental failure in earliest psychic development, the professional literature of the last decade has devoted ever-greater attention to narcissistic-transference resistance and narcissistic-countertransference resistance. The recognition, understanding, and resolution of these phenomena are essential for the effective treatment of preoedipal patients and also of those suffering from psychologically reversible psychobiological conditions.

Chapter 7

MANAGEMENT AND MASTERY
OF RESISTANCE

The sum and substance of the practitioner's active participation in analytic therapy are virtually encompassed in what is referred to in clinical shorthand as dealing with resistance. Tracing the acceptance of this multi-faceted process as the essence of analytic technique, Freud (1923) pointed out that psychoanalysis was "in the first resort . . . an art of *interpretation*" (p. 239), of discovering the hidden meanings of the patient's associations. After the elaboration of the technique of interpretation had gratified "the analyst's curiosity," more attention was paid to the "problem of discovering the most effective way of influencing the patient" and helping him to achieve permanent mental change (p. 249). It was discovered that the analyst could apply himself most constructively by making the patient aware of his resistances and in facilitating the "task assigned to the patient of overcoming" them (p. 251).

There are, indeed, analysands who require little help in liberating themselves from the grip of crippling emotions and self-defeating patterns of behavior. Usually, however, the schizophrenic individual requires much more than the nominal assistance that Freud (1917) referred to as "the help of suggestion operating in an *educative* sense" (p. 451). With many of these patients, the analyst appears at times to be making the major contribution. However, it is reasonable to anticipate that if he does much of the spadework in a difficult case his partner will tilt the balance in the other direction. Ideally, in the course of the treatment the patient gradually masters the technique of resolving his own resistance, and makes the major contribution to that task in the final state of the relationship.

Various aspects of this vital undertaking are discussed in this chapter and those that follow. The general principles in terms of the overall development of the case are presented first. Chapters 8 and 9, although focused on intrapsychic experience—first the patient's and then the analyst's—elaborate on some of these principles. Their verbal implementation is discussed more specifically, and illustrated, in Chapter 10.

GENERAL STRATEGY

When the case opens, the therapist demonstrates the attitude that the patient has the right to resist. The survival function of the narcissistic defense is respected. Though primitively organized, it has served to stabilize his mental apparatus in his interpersonal relations and insulate him against unwanted feeling states. Until more healthful defenses have been patterned in the analytic relationship, the narcissistic defense is not attacked. Freedom from pressure to overcome it leads to a relative reduction in the need to activate it (Spotnitz, 1961b).

The development of more appropriate defenses does not prevent the patient from reverting to his old patterns of bottling up aggressive impulses, but it does liberate him from doing so as a compulsive or involuntary maneuver. He is then in a position to defy, comply, or cooperate as a matter of choice. Resolving resistance means helping him become fully capable of mastering it, analyzing it, and giving it up voluntarily. Eventually the patient is able to recognize his own resistance and resolve it, unaided by the analyst or anyone else, through self-analysis.

In resolving resistance, the analyst utilizes the most effective tools at his disposal to nullify the immediate effects of the forces that hampered the patient's emotional growth, and to catalyze maturation.

Distillation of Standard Procedures

The standard procedures for dealing with resistance, as formulated by Greenson (1967) are confrontation, clarification, interpretation, and working through. A distillation of these procedures is necessary to enable the schizophrenic individual to keep on working productively and safely on his fundamental problems. An additional dimension of the treatment plan, less necessary to contemplate in the analysis of a psychoneurotic patient, is the *quantitative* management of resistance.

The instruction to talk arouses contrary tendencies. Growth impulses are mobilized and help the patient comply; but the instruction also mobilizes disruptive impulses, which unite to create in the patient a counterforce to communication. Overly regressive tendencies and psychotic manifestations may be observed in a severely disturbed individual if the counterforce is permitted to become unduly powerful (either because of too much pressure on the patient to talk or because the sparsity of the therapist's communications is excessively frustrating to the patient). The counterforce expresses itself through innumerable forms of resistance; in intervening to manage resistance, the practitioner is actually working on the counterforce. Thus, throughout the treatment, he carefully controls the pressure for progress.

Among the various measures employed for that purpose, the therapist reflects the patient's direct attempts to establish contact (Loewenstein, 1956). If the patient does not solicit contact during the session, the therapist intervenes to provide him with opportunities to verbalize pent-up emotions. The patient is helped to verbalize any form of hostility that becomes manifest, especially when *treatment-destructive* patterns of resistance emerge. The patterns signal that some communication from the therapist is in order to lower the frustration level.

To head off increasing resistance of that nature, the therapist promptly investigates any new symptoms or exacerbations of old ones, such as narcissistic delusions, that the patient complains of during the session. The purpose of the investigation is not to provide or obtain information, but to take pressure off the ego. No attempt is made to influence the production of psychotic material. The patient is not discouraged in any way from revealing it but its significance is not called to his attention or explained to him. No effort is made to help him understand it.

Experience indicates that resistance is kept at a minimum when a seriously disturbed person is instructed simply to talk and is permitted to choose any subject and tempo he pleases. *Minimal* pressure is then exerted for progressive communication rather than for "telling everything." The analyst's attitude communicates the idea that the patient may feel, may think, may remember, and may talk, but may not act while on the analytic couch.

Focus on Verbalization

Primary reliance on interpretive procedures is a distinguishing characteristic of the classical method. "The ideal analytic technique consists in the analyst's doing nothing other than interpreting," Fenichel observed (1941, p. 87). Menninger (1958) regards other types of interventions as inappropriate unless they serve as "precursors of interpretation proper" (p. 130). Interpretation, according to Greenson (1967), is the "ultimate and decisive instrument" (p. 39), and the goal of the analyst is to provide insight.

The therapeutic value of insight for the psychoneurotic patient is accounted for in various ways. To cite one explanation: When he falters in the task of connecting his impulses, feelings, thoughts, and memories with words, ideas voiced by the analyst help the patient establish the connections. After *specific memory constellations* that have interfered with his functioning in one way or another are thus brought into awareness and verbalized, the patient is able to express his immediate impulses, feelings, and thoughts freely and comfortably.

But insight via words alone fails to kindle the memory-images that interfere with the functioning of the schizophrenic patient because the interchanges between the primitive self and the earliest objects in which the narcissistic defense was patterned consisted primarily of impulses and prefeelings. He has to be helped to re-experience these interchanges symbolically. A study of the development of the narcissistic transference and countertransference helps the therapist to reconstruct the object relations of the preverbal period.

The patient's self-dissecting tendencies are often intensified when he is given insight into his defective functioning. He has, moreover, many time-consuming ways of defending himself against the wounding impact of unnecessary interpretations. Early in treatment, intensive or extensive explanations of unconscious mechanisms equip him with new weapons for self-attack and are often experienced as intolerable pressure for progress. Thus, interpretation to the patient is undesirable unless the analyst is convinced that the patient really wishes it and will not experience it as hurtful (Hayden, 1983) or "poisoning" him (Zimmerman, 1982, p. 194; Lichtenberg, 1963).

The ego-damaging effects of interpretation in a case of multiple personality are graphically portrayed in Stephen Marmer's (1980) account of the analysis of a woman whose unverbalized negative emotions were pushing her close to psychosis. In reporting a dream, she told the analyst, "You were sticking needles into me . . . hitting the raw spots" (p. 444). His eventual shift from interpretation to functioning as an ego-syntonic object and helping her verbalize her painful emotions was the crucial factor in her recovery.

Nevertheless, *silent* interpretation—the analyst interpreting to himself what is going on in the relationship—is an essential ingredient of a successful analysis. It should go on throughout the treatment.

Resistance is analyzed—silently and unobtrusively—but instead of trying to promote recognition, perception, or conviction, the therapist intervenes to facilitate verbalization as a connective, integrative process. The patient is helped to discover for himself the genetic antecedents of his resistant behavior, explore it in terms of the analytic relationship, and articulate his own understanding.

When the patient is made comfortable and becomes "truly

cooperative" (Wilson, 1981, p. 126) in expressing the ingredients of internal speech in spoken words, insight emerges as a by-product of the connections established between his impulses, feelings, thoughts, and memories and his words. The principle of working to produce verbal communication is an initial step toward making the unconscious conscious. In a sense, the standard approach is delayed until the patient reaches the oedipal stage and wants interpretation.

Negative Transference

The policy of providing insight into resistant behavior and help in controlling it as soon as the treatment gets under way encourages the development first of positive feelings for the transference object. Freud, after instructing a patient to free-associate, apparently called attention to any type of resistance that emerged, liberally demonstrating and interpreting it. Such an abundance of attention, communication, and understanding, given in a relatively painless way, has the effect of producing a positive transference; for the time being, negative feelings are "pushed aside." Of interest in that connection is Freud's (1917) observation that "hostile feelings make their appearance as a rule later than the affectionate ones and behind them" (p. 443). That is usually the case when patient and analyst work together to understand and dissolve other types of resistance and more or less ignore the signs of negative transference.

Inasmuch as the development of transference on a strongly positive basis prolongs and compounds the task of analyzing and dealing with the nuclear problem in schizophrenia, virtually the opposite approach is pursued with a schizophrenic patient. A state of negative narcissistic transference is essential for arousing the schizophrenic reaction with sufficient intensity to understand and reverse it. Rather than thwarting or postponing the negative transference, the strategy therefore is one of securing its expeditious development without exposing the patient to undue pressure to act on aggressive impulses and feelings he is unable to verbalize.

Early in treatment explanations of the ordinary functional resistances, such as repeated tardiness or refusal to lie down on the couch, are withheld because they put the patient under pressure to change, thus promoting a sense of unreality. He strives to understand himself, and this is undesirable when his mental energy should be wholly dedicated to saying whatever he thinks and feels and remembers at the moment. Rare indeed is the patient who achieves change in behavior and feelings through understanding alone; for the schizophrenic individual, change comes from an increase in the capacity to verbalize—that is, as a by-product of the ability to communicate freely whatever is experienced. The more the patient strives to understand, on the other hand, the more confused and emotionally withdrawn he becomes. Absorption in the quest for understanding creates a barrier to communication, inhibiting progressive verbalization and facilitating repetition. The striving to understand thus becomes, in a sense, a form of resistance to verbal communication.

Moreover, understanding of the functional resistances is not really necessary. Most of them disappear after the negative transference has been effectively dealt with (through the resolution of resistance to the verbalization of the negative transference reactions).

Interventions in the opening phase of the treatment are therefore strictly limited, being governed primarily by the need to manage the frustration level (Chapter 4). If the infrequency of the therapist's communications becomes excessively frustrating to the patient, giving rise to treatment-destructive patterns of resistance, the therapist intervenes to the extent necessary to nullify their immediate influence. Chronic and relatively stable defenses may be briefly investigated at times, but other obstacles to communication elicit little comment. They are silently analyzed, in order to determine precisely how excessive frustration interferes with the functioning of ego, superego, and id. Meanwhile, in order to secure the verbalization of negative feelings, the therapist limits his interventions to dealing with the transference resistances mobilized by the stresses of the relationship.

Control of Regression

In view of the tendency of the schizophrenic patient to take flight, mentally or physically, from a frustrating object, his capacity to engage voluntarily, for therapeutic purposes, in a psychologically retrograde process is assumed to be extremely limited. Even when he commits himself to that undertaking with a firm sense of self-control, the move backward in memory may give rise to severe defensive regression and tempt him into the ultimate refuge of psychosis (Rothstein, 1982). To counteract any inclination to utilize the retrograde process to eliminate awareness and shut out feelings, defensive regression is carefully checked (as illustrated in Chapter 10).

So-called schizophrenic associations are discouraged by the initial instruction to talk on any subject and by the practice of responding to the patient's contact functioning. The therapist communicates briefly to reflect the pattern of each of the patient's verbal attempts to secure a response; in other words, he is given minimal verbal nourishment on a self-demand basis. Discussions of his immediate complaints, involving the posing of questions that have to have to be answered on a realistic basis, also militate against regressive tendencies too severe to be dealt with in the course of the session. The interventions are noninformative, designed simply to facilitate the verbal release of the patient's mounting frustration-tension.

Until he understands its origin and can both verbalize hostility comfortably and check its expression in nondamaging ways, retrograde pressure that threatens the whole personality is undesirable. A brief and selective verbalization of memories helps the patient contemplate the past without losing his foothold in the present. Mild pressure is therefore exerted to facilitate the recall of events in relation to one problem at a time. Such pressure may be necessary to help the patient remember the past; his own preference is simply to repeat it in behavior. The better he remembers it, the less danger there is that a traumatic situation will recur.

Concept of Priorities

Departing from the customary practice of dealing with whatever resistances crop up, the therapist recognizes the importance of addressing himself urgently to the forces that block the patient from verbalizing frustration-tension. No attempt is made to be *therapeutic*, to help the patient solve any problems, indeed to help him do anything but verbalize freely whatever he is thinking or feeling at the time. The therapist remains on the lookout for one or another repetitive pattern that expresses the patient's tendency invariably to defend himself against the release of frustration-tension. Thus accorded first priority are the personality-fragmentation patterns (Chapter 6) and other treatment-destructive resistances (that is, any mode of behavior that, carried far enough, would break off the treatment), as well as external resistances of an equally threatening nature.

In other words, the therapist's primary goal in the opening phase of treatment is to preserve the analytic relationship and to deal with any factor that threatens its therapeutic unfolding. In addition, the therapist is especially concerned at that time with nullifying the potentially damaging consequences of the nonverbalization of frustration-tension.

Meanwhile, other interferences, as I have pointed out, are bypassed until they become transference resistances. These patterns are then dealt with in a sequence that will facilitate forward movement in the analytic relationship. In the order in which they are responded to, these are status-quo resistance, resistance to analytic progress, resistance to cooperation, and resistance to termination.

Various principles for dealing with these five categories of resistance are suggested later in the chapter.

Approach to Dreams

The schizophrenic individual tends to flood the analyst with dreams when eager to please, and not to report any when eager to defy. These tendencies are discouraged if the analyst does not indicate a particular interest in dreams and does not work actively to secure associations to them.

Early in the relationship, any dreams that are reported are studied primarily as a source of information on problems that the patient is not consciously reporting. Dreams are regarded as part of the total communication of the session, rather than as material for independent study.

From time to time, a few questions are asked about a dream that has been reported; these are asked primarily for the purpose of clarifying details of content. But usually whatever is reported is included in the therapist's summary of unconscious problems revealed in the session. This approach, which is in line with one of Freud's later papers on dreams (1923) minimizes the danger that the patient will be influenced by the therapist's attitude to provide one or another kind of material.

It is important that the analyst consistently interpret *to himself* dreams that are reported by the schizophrenic patient; for dreams are a major source of material on significant preoedipal experiences that the patient cannot communicate verbally. Understanding of the dream as a form of communication aids the analyst in the process of reconstructing these events. In due time, his impressions of them will either be confirmed or corrected by further dreams. Silent analysis of the dreams may also help one decide what is causing the patient's misbehavior or how to help him give up the pathological patterns.

But in the early stages of the analytic relationship, the interpretation of dreams directly to the schizophrenic patient is, in general, not helpful, and will often prove to be a source of resistance. For example, the patient may solicit an interpretation to a dream so that he can challenge the analyst's understanding of it, inciting arguments about whose interpretation is correct. Eventually the patient and the analyst need to work together at achieving understanding of the preoedipal experiences that traumatized the patient.

The formal interpretation of dreams begins late in the treatment, when ego and object are differentiated clearly and the patient expresses a desire to understand. Although understanding for the mere purpose of satisfying his curiosity is discouraged, it is appropriate to provide understanding for the purpose of opening up avenues to more memories and more communications—a therapeutic way of facilitating change.

POSITIVE AND NEGATIVE WISHES

A clinical formulation I have found useful in regulating the intensity of resistance reflects the recognition that resistance is the product of an unconscious attempt by the patient to secure more gratification than he is deriving at the moment from verbal self-expression.

As he follows the instruction to talk, he falls under the influence of certain inner needs. Some evoke memory-images of situations in which his early objects engaged in activity in response to his needs. If the patient experienced that response as gratifying, the memory secures verbal expression with less effort than if the response was experienced as painful. He thus drifts spontaneously into words that reawaken memories of experiences in which the need he is aware of at the moment was responded to in a pleasurable way. He also strives unconsciously to induce the therapist to respond in the same way. On the other hand, the patient unconsciously defends himself against talking when under the influence of needs that evoke memories of painful experiences. Mental mechanisms operate to fend off the recurrence of these experiences and to prevent the transference object from responding to the needs in the same painful way.

In the *Project for a Scientific Psychology* (1954) Freud refers to these mechanisms, the residues of experiences of satisfaction and experiences of pain, as "primary wishful attraction" and "primary defense." He points out: "A wishful state produces what amounts to a positive *attraction* to the object of the wish, or rather to its memory-image; an experience of pain results in a repulsion, a disinclination to keep the hostile memory-image cathected" (p. 383). To highlight the contrast between these motivating forces, I use the term "positive wish" in place of "wishful attraction" and designate the painful memory-image against which the defense operates as "negative wish."

The patient does not resist the realization of a positive wish unless he feels unable to control his behavior at the rate at which the wish is being intensified. His security is threatened when the wish is being realized more slowly or more rapidly than the tempo to which he has been conditioned. Then the patient tends to repeat himself. In such circumstances, a pleasurable wish may become painful because of the danger that it may lead to action.

Another type of resistance develops with the anticipated accentuation of a negative wish. Again, it is not the accentuation per se that may constitute a problem but the possibility that it may lead to action. The patient is not supposed to act on either his positive or negative wishes while on the analytic couch. Thus he fights against the arousal of wishes—that is, impulses that frequently appear to the individual as wishes—that might lead to action.

In a sense, the amount and type of resistance mobilized depends on whether the approaching wish is a positive or negative one. Relatively little resistance is aroused when the patient is afforded some opportunity for the fulfillment of a positive wish. The therapist encourages that expectation when he recognizes the patient's momentary needs to bring the object close or to keep it at a distance (in terms of understanding the patient's positive and negative wishes and verbalizing that understanding). The optimal distance, in that sense, varies at different stages of the relationship. And when it is achieved, the patient often describes the immediate need and tells how it was responded to in the past. In other words, when the analyst succeeds in verbalizing the defense the patient is using against an immediate need, the patient frequently describes the need and tells how it was responded to by significant people in his past.

The negative wishes of the schizophrenic patient in the opening phase of treatment are connected primarily with his strong opposition to re-experiencing situations in which he learned not to act on hostile impulses. The fear of loss of control in the process of releasing hateful impulses is a powerful deterrent to verbalizing them. The patient may betray that situation, for example, by remaining silent with hands rigidly clasped.

The notion of positive and negative wishes provides a useful conceptual tool in dealing with the special forms of resistance observed in the schizophrenic patient at times when maximal arousal of these patterns would imperil the treatment. Although the treatment-destructive resistances cannot be effectively influenced until the transference situation reaches a climax, their intensity can be modulated if the therapist is able to recognize the nature of the wishes being mobilized during the sessions. Through his communications he can increase the intensity of a positive wish or decrease the intensity of a negative one—whichever would serve the purpose of assisting the patient to verbalize it. Conversely, negative wishes can be accentuated or positive wishes diminished through appropriate and timely interventions.

In essence, we have been discussing the fact that the patient comes under pressure to act on positive or negative wishes. (Positive wishes are to get close to the analyst and negative wishes to move away from him.) This pressure can be controlled by the analyst's interventions.

A reserved attitude in the opening phase of the treatment facilitates the management of resistance that may be mobilized through the influence of negative wishes. On the one hand, the patient is frustrated sufficiently to highlight his resistance to verbalizing hostility. On the other hand, in order not to mobilize too much hostility at any one moment, the therapist symbolically gratifies a few positive wishes by asking some object-oriented questions. This approach has the effect of making the patient aware of the therapist's presence, and likewise aware that the therapist is interested in him and would welcome communications from him.

TREATMENT-DESTRUCTIVE PATTERNS

The types of resistance that claim prior attention early in treatment include disturbances in affects, delusionary ideas, and other reflections of fragmentation. These patterns evoke *no* comment unless they interfere with progressive communication during the sessions. Whereas the relatively stable patterns are just studied silently, the analyst does speak to lower the frustration-level and help the patient verbalize frustration-tension when a sudden intensification of such patterns is observed. Inasmuch as silence can have a soothing effect or exert increasing pressure on the patient, the analyst needs to regulate the amount of verbal communication he engages in, depending on whether he wants to intensify or to diminish pressure on the patient to verbalize.

Various statements conveying a disagreeable reaction to the analytic setting or to the attributes of the therapist are clues to the potential emergence of modes of functioning that may imperil the treatment. The patient may complain, for example, that the couch is sticky, that he dislikes the color of the office walls, or that the therapist's voice grates on him—and then stop talking. The brief venting of such impressions often suggests that the patient will soon be talking about stopping treatment. When the patient remains silent, the analyst may ask for an impression of his own presence, thus drawing attention to himself as a factor in the situation. The mobilization of treatment-destructive resistance can often be recognized by what the patient talks about and influenced by the type of intervention the analyst utilizes.

After talking for a considerable time in a detached manner, a patient may report a delusive idea; his mind is "in a daze" or he feels now that he is "falling apart." Instead of expressing interest in the content of the delusion, the sensation, or feelings conveyed, the analyst calls attention to *himself* as a factor in creating the situation. Did he have anything to do with producing the daze? Was he too silent or did he talk too much? Questions about the analyst at such a juncture help the patient function more cooperatively. The analyst, as he mirrors the patient, gets to sound like an inordinately self-centered human being; he may also get to feel that he is talking too much about himself.

If the patient reports that he is thinking of quitting treatment, and no interest is shown in the statement, he may, without mentioning the intention again, fail to appear a few sessions later. If, on the other hand, the analyst asks a brief question about his own performance, this often helps the patient verbalize his dissatisfaction. The analyst may ask what *he* has done or has failed to do that has led to this dissatisfaction. These interventions have a temporizing effect; they may influence the patient to put off acting on the withdrawal pattern. The threat of disengagement remains, however. It is impossible to resolve the withdrawal pattern until it becomes a maximal transference resistance. Then the relation between the withdrawal pattern and the analyst's performance needs to be studied.

A resistance that has recently come into prominence in treatment of the schizophrenic patient, and which is difficult to deal with, I refer to as the "negative judgment" pattern. Engaging repeatedly in negative evaluations of the analyst's conduct of the treatment, the patient reiterates, for example, that the analysis is getting nowhere, that what the analyst is saying to him doesn't make sense, that the analyst hasn't helped him at all, or hasn't helped him "fundamentally."

The negative judgment resistance needs to be distinguished from the negative therapeutic reaction, which is associated with a patient whose condition worsens (Freud, 1937; Perri, 1982). On the other hand, the patient employing negative judgment resistance is actually making progress. (Usually this pattern of resistance represents a wish to "get even" with a parent who was highly critical of the patient in early childhood.) But it needs to be dealt with promptly as a resistance destructive to the relationship because, should the patient eventually become convinced that his negative evaluations are correct, he may abandon treatment.

In dealing with this resistance pattern, the practitioner calls attention to the fact that the patient is using negative judgment resistance and that this interferes with his doing what he is supposed to—communicating all of his feelings, thoughts, and memories. The patient is educated to the idea that, instead of repeating vague criticisms, he should cooperate with the analyst by soliciting help in solving specific problems. The analyst suggests that the patient give up his negative judgments—at least for a while—and work instead on recalling his memories. The recall of the feelings that were originally linked with the memories makes it possible for the patient's feelings about the analytic relationship to change. In the course of the ensuing verbal battle, the patient is asked questions to help him communicate the particular problems he wants the analyst to assist him in resolving.

Whether silence is dealt with as a resistance depends on the anxiety level at the moment. When the patient is comfortable and relaxed in a period of silence, especially at the formative stage of the relationship, there is no reason to interrupt it. He may be encouraged to remain silent if he wishes. But protracted silence is undesirable for a seriously disturbed person who is tense, suffering, or in a state of conflict. It is important to find out why he is not talking and, if he wants to talk, to help him do so. What he says is of no immediate consequence; com-munication on any subject is preferable to remaining mute (Liegner, 1974).

Talking may be facilitated by instructing him to put his thoughts into words, by asking questions, giving explanations, joining the patient's silence, or interpreting it to him; on the other hand, the analyst may talk for a while, preferably about impersonal matters. This often stimulates the patient to follow suit; moreover, his resistance to talking diminishes temporarily when he observes that the analyst does not insist that he do so. The counterforce to verbal communication is thus worked on by controlling the display of eagerness. It is important slowly to diminish the power of the counterforce by appropriate inter-ventions (preferably in the sequence described in Chapter 10).

Serious violations of the treatment contract are called to the patient's attention without delay. Since he is educated to the idea of telephoning the therapist if he does not plan to attend a ses-sion or will predictably be more than 15 minutes late, such no-tification evidences an effort to cooperate; if it is not received, the lapse is queried. If the patient makes a habit of arriving late, the questions put to him are preferably free of any insinuation that he is reluctant to come or that his functioning is below par. Did the therapist fail to make the session time clear? Was the patient delayed by traffic? The appropriate query safeguards his ego from pressure by focusing on the object (Margolis, 1983b).

Although the mastery of intractible resistance by resorting to telephone sessions was reported decades ago (Reiss, 1958) analytic psychotherapy by telephone, as a regular practice, is relatively new. Its use may greatly diminish a patient's resis-tance to continuing treatment. The counterforce to coming to the analyst's office may remain strong, but is circumvented. How-ever, the use of phone sessions to master resistance requires keen judgment.

The individual who fails to arrive on time may be dilatory in leaving the office at the end of the session. Such resistance when strong and persistent, may be responded to by permitting the patient to get up from the couch about as many minutes ahead of schedule as he habitually overstays his time. The strat-egy of helping such a patient to talk while standing during that brief interval also may be effectual in drawing him out of a regressed state and restoring him to reality.

In the course of departure, a patient may seek to gratify a desire for physical contact. He may, for instance, want the therapist to help him on with his coat or accompany him to the door. Since such experiences arouse the expectation of more intimate gratification, the patient will then tend to become more emotionally explosive, or his difficulties in verbalizing hostility may be intensified. As long as he is dominated by dependency cravings, any kind of physical contact is to be avoided.

The approaches just described are, in a sense, emergency measures to protect the patient and preserve the relationship. He is permitted to retain the resistance pattern but discouraged from intensifying and acting on it. The analyst calls attention to the behavior without explaining why. It is simply described, and its implications for treatment noted in such a way as to facilitate verbal communication. After observing the patient sufficiently to understand what brings the pattern into operation, the practitioner is in a position to supplement these preliminary measures.

OTHER CATEGORIES

Status-Quo Patterns

As the schizophrenic patient becomes adjusted to the analytic situation, he at times manifests the attitude that he is completely satisfied with the progress he has made since entering treatment and is primarily interested in maintaining his present state. Shakow (1971), in reporting on psychological aspects of schizophrenia, describes neophobia—that is, an exaggerated clinging to the old and an intense fear of the new or unfamiliar.

When trainees have difficulty understanding this pattern, I liken it to the attitude of the young child who clings to a pair of old shoes that no longer fit or wants to keep on wearing a piece of clothing that has become threadbare. The message communicated, "I want to keep the old," is also conveyed by status-quo (inertia) resistance.

Status-quo resistance commands attention when the treatment-destructive patterns are not in operation, and may become a significant factor after the first 6 months of treatment. The patient conceals his "bad" feelings and ideas, represents his need for ameliorative change as slight, and builds up the idea of being the "good" patient. When such attitudes become transference reactions, for instance, he may communicate the notion that he is stalling because the analyst would welcome a standstill. The patient may then be invited, through questioning, to account for the analyst's desire to drift along aimlessly. The immediate emotional state of the patient determines the choice of other procedures.

Resistance to Analytic Progress

From a clinging to the old situation, the focus gradually shifts to the potentially undesirable effects of venturing into new experience. The patient now communicates the message, "I don't want anything new."

Reluctance to learning how to move forward is expressed in various ways. The patient may try to avoid talking out his thoughts and feelings by asking for rules and directions. For an inordinately long time, midway in treatment, schizophrenic individuals appear unwilling to move ahead, to say what they really think and feel without weighing the consequences. Moving ahead verbally into unknown territory impresses them as being a perilous venture.

The temptation is strong to deal with these so-called resistances to analytic progress when the case opens, particularly for the beginning analyst. To achieve manifest results as quickly as possible, he tends to address himself immediately to the factors that impede forward movement and to defer working on the negative feelings.

As I have suggested, this orientation is undesirable with a schizophrenic patient. The more impressed he is with the benefits of the relationship, the greater his reluctance to verbalize hostility to the benefactor. Efforts to be helpful by providing interpretations of such resistances early in the case encourage the development of positive transference, thus intensifying the patient's tendencies to bottle up his frustration-tension. Moreover, treatment-destructive resistance is activated if he feels that he is being "pushed" ahead.

Hence, the resistances to analytic progress are accorded third priority. They are dealt with when they entail a significant degree of emotional involvement with the transference object. For example, if a patient communicates the notion that the analyst does not want him to bring up any more problems or is opposed to investigating new activities or ideas, the analyst asks him to explain why the analyst opposes progress.

Resistance to Cooperation

By the time the patterns that interfere with cooperative functioning dominate the relationship, the first three categories of resistance have been somewhat resolved. The patient has moved into the normal range of variability in fulfilling the terms of the treatment contract. He has been educated to speak freely, and he engages in negative catharsis without undue effort. Having outgrown his tendencies to run away from present realities into the uncontrollable past, he can be trusted to move backward in memory without loss of orientation. He can also voluntarily check the expression of hostility without damaging himself. By and large, he demonstrates that he is capable of purposeful participation in the solution of his problems.

At times, however, he demonstrates the old narcissistic attitudes. He may seem unaware of the importance of verbalizing *all* of his feelings, refuse to give information, or appear unwilling to listen to the analyst. Instead of discussing what he is experiencing in their interchanges, the patient may concentrate exclusively on himself. He may communicate the attitude that talking is all that is required of him. The analyst would enjoy his cooperation, but why give him such satisfaction? Why help him do his job? Such attitudes may be responded to with questions or interpretations.

When the patient is really cooperative, he solicits communications that will help him verbalize spontaneously and uncover the immediate obstacles to this. Then it is desirable for the analyst to interpret and answer questions with a view to facilitating the patient's understanding of the analytic process. The spontaneous statements of the reasonably cooperative patient usually encompass five topics in a session: current activities; past events; sex life; dreams and fantasies; and what is going on in the treatment relationship. He has some awareness of the practitioner as a real person and of what he is trying to communicate.

Resistance to Termination

An important factor in resolving the patient's resistance to termination is to educate him to the idea that becoming a well-adjusted person does not mean that the analytic relationship has to be terminated. Even though he has given up the patterns of the illness—is cured—he usually possesses a potential for, and a desire to achieve, further personality maturation. Assuming that the patient and the therapist agree to work toward that goal, the analysis can continue until they both decide to terminate it.

When the time for dissolving the relationship does draw near, the schizophrenic patient usually manifests intense opposition to that prospect. (This category of resistance is also observed earlier in the relationship before temporary interruptions in the treatment. The patient is therefore notified well in advance of the therapist's vacation schedule and other planned absences from the office, and given repeated opportunities to verbalize his reactions to such interruptions.) Termination is suggested as soon as there is a basis for doing so because the working through of the resistance to it is a prolonged process.

Frequently, during the terminal period, old problems that seemed to have been completely resolved much earlier in the case show up again. In addition to the reappearance of the initial difficulties, the patient points to various new ones not previously reported. Despite long years of working with the analyst, the patient may complain, he has not been helped at all—even though he has repeatedly said otherwise.

Emotional communication is engaged in to test out the permanence of behavioral change and the patient's tolerance to more severe stress. When the feelings induced in the therapist by the patient's behavior are "returned" to him, the emotional impact of the confrontation serves either to reawaken the old patterns or demonstrates that the patient is now immune to situations that once had toxic effects on him (Spotnitz, 1963; Hayden, 1983).

STEPS IN RESOLVING RESISTANCE

Recognition.   This refers to identification of the type of resistance that has put in an appearance. Labeling of the pattern is an aspect of the therapist's silent study of why and how the resistant behavior came into play in the immediate situation. He begins to investigate its significance in terms of the patient's life history. The practitioner, on the basis of his analysis, decides whether the pattern should be tolerated, should be psychologically reflected (joined) because it serves a useful purpose at the time, or should be discouraged and eventually resolved. When more than one type of resistance is detected, he also decides on the order in which they should be dealt with.

Control of intensity.   Control (of the counterforce to communication) applies specifically to managing of resistance that has been classified as treatment-destructive, including the personality-fragmentation patterns. The intensity of the counterforce mobilizing these resistances, which is controlled by communications from the analyst, is consistently dealt with on an emergency basis to nullify their immediate threat to the relationship. The patterns are not interpreted, however, until the patient is capable of modifying them.

Verbal descriptions.   A resistance is called to the patient's attention in due time, when it has been sufficiently aroused to be demonstrable. Arousal, though primarily a function of the intensity of transference, is to some degree a matter of technique; the therapist has to decide whether increased verbal starvation or a specific intervention would better illuminate the pattern. A brief description may be given to help the patient discharge his impulses in a manner appropriate to the occasion, thereby reducing any pressing need to utilize the resistance. The therapist does not attempt to get the patient to acknowledge that he is being uncooperative. If he denies it, his view of the matter is accepted. He may be asked if he has noticed that he tends to repeat himself in the session in some way.

The verbal description of a transference resistance is usually brief and timed to the patient's contact functioning. A question or comment that he makes is reflected or joined in some way to help him speak of his resistant behavior. The therapist does not explain why he is calling attention to the resistance until the patient has made sufficient progress to verbalize hostility comfortably.

Temporary resolution.   The patient is helped to understand the origin, history, and present meaning of the repetitive pattern and to give it up without detriment to his psychic economy. The therapist's verbal conceptualizations of its antecedents help the patient "feel into" its defensive aspects and talk out his feelings about it. It is not necessary for the patient to understand what is being done.

Joining techniques and emotional communications are utilized to resolve preoedipal forms of resistance. Interpretive techniques are utilized to the extent to which they prove effective at that stage in facilitating progressive verbalization by the patient.

After the first year of treatment, explanations of unconscious mechanisms are provided—when the patient requests them—to control the frustration level, not for understanding. Formal interpretations of oedipal problems are given late in the relationship when the patient is in a state of object transference. Any preoedipal patterns to which he reverts at that time are resolved through the procedures that removed them earlier in the treatment.

Permanent resolution (working through).   In the process of removing resistance patterns temporarily, the therapist develops various hypotheses about their origin, history, and immediate significance, and investigates their validity. These hypotheses are communicated over and over, intellectually and emotionally, in many different contexts, and when they repeatedly influence the patient to give up the resistant behavior, they are regarded as correct interpretations. In other words, instead of working through an interpretation—putting the cart before the horse—the therapist works through *to* an interpretation. Subsequently, the validity of the therapist's assumptions is discussed with the patient.

Communications designed to loosen up the pathological defenses and facilitate emotional growth are made early in the relationship. However, working through on a methodical basis gets under way when the patient is communicating consistently in adult language, demonstrating genuine interest in analyzing his resistances, and relating to the analyst as a separate person.

All components of transference resistance are investigated and dealt with at all levels. No specific period is assigned to the task; it goes on throughout the analysis. Eventually, the patient is helped to free himself from the unconscious domination of the impulse patterns that interfered with meaningful communication. He is also helped to form new patterns of adjustment in the analytic situation if and when he indicates that he wants such assistance.

The development of verbal and other action patterns (out of the office) for the appropriate release of frustration-aggression leads to the disappearance of treatment-destructive resistance, including the personality-fragmentation patterns. Emotional communications and reflective procedures drain other patterns of gratification and facilitate healthy new identifications.

The old narcissistic patterns remain at the patient's disposal, and he will tend to revert to them until he has firmly achieved a healthful adjustment to his current life situation. These patterns have, however, been liberated from their original compulsive force, and respond rather quickly to the procedures that resolved them over and over again early in the treatment. When he perceives that the new modes of behavior patterned in the relationship lead to more enjoyable and desirable experience and afford consistent security for the personality, the patient finds these adult patterns of human relatedness easier to use than the early inadequate patterns. Thus he becomes anchored to life in the real world.

Chapter 8

NARCISSISTIC TRANSFERENCE

References have been made in the preceding chapters to the complicated transference situation in a case of schizophrenia. It has been pointed out that, unlike the patient functioning at the oedipal level of development, the pathologically narcissistic individual does not invariably relate to the analyst as a separate and distinct person. In their relationship, the schizophrenic patient transfers feelings that he developed for himself as well as for others during the first two years of life. He may also confuse the analyst's feelings with his own. In short, a two-way emotional transaction is revived and communicated as originating in one locale—the mind of the patient. That transaction, suggestive of a re-experiencing of the ego in the process of formation, is identified as narcissistic transference.

The present chapter explores this conceptual tool first in the general framework of transference. The analyst's task in dealing with resistance is reformulated in terms of the therapeutic management of narcissistic transference—its induction, dissolution, and transformation into object transference. Affects and sensations experienced by the schizophrenic patient at various stages of the analytic relationship are described.

IN HISTORICAL PERSPECTIVE

Freud's Views on Transference

The discovery of transference and deepening understanding of it are lucidly described by Freud. Reporting it first as an unexpected occurrence in the treatment of hysterical patients by the cathartic method, he eventually described it as an unconscious phenomenon operating in all human relations.

In the *Studies on Hysteria* (Breuer-Freud, 1893-1895), transference is referred to as the "false connection" of the patient's material with the person of the practitioner— a *"mésalliance"* that occurred regularly in some cases and "greatly annoyed" him because its resolution entailed time and effort. However, he "came to see that the whole process followed a law; and I then noticed too, that transference of this kind brought about no great addition to what I had to do. . . . The patient, too, gradually learnt . . . it was a question of a compulsion and an illusion which melted away with the conclusion of the analysis" (pp. 302–304).

The metaphorical allusion to transference as "new editions or facsimiles" that was to reappear in Freud's later discussions of transference is found in his postscript (1905) to the brief case of Dora, which foundered because the transference was not mastered:

> . . . a whole series of psychological experiences are revived, not as belonging to the past, but as applying to the person of the physician at the present moment. Some of these transferences have a content which differs from that of their model in no respect whatever except for the substitution. These then . . . are merely new impressions or reprints. Others . . . will no longer be new impressions, but revised editions. (p. 116)

In this, his first systematic discussion of transference, Freud also expresses and explains his opposition to the full development and verbalization of negative transference toward the therapist: "If cruel impulses and revengeful motives . . .

become transferred on to the physician during treatment, before he has had time to detach them from himself by tracing
them back to their sources, then it is not to be wondered at if
the patient's condition is unaffected by his therapeutic efforts"
(p. 120). Freud appears not to have explicitly recognized Dora's
basic hostility to men (Krohn & Krohn, 1982).

Explanations of transference in terms of the compulsion to
repeat were advanced later. *Beyond the Pleasure Principle* (1920)
contains Freud's first reference to the repetition-compulsion as
a manifestation of the death instinct. The same hypothesis figures in his discussion of protracted negative transference in
Analysis Terminable and Interminable (1937).

The definitive exposition of his views on the phenomenon,
in *An Autobiographical Study* (1925), contains the clearest statement of Freud's misgivings about negative transference. These
observations also have relevance for his views on countertransference, and are therefore quoted extensively below:

> Transference is merely uncovered and isolated by analysis.
> It is a universal phenomenon of the human mind, it de-
> cides the success of all medical influence, and in fact dom-
> inates the whole of each person's relation to his human
> environment. . . . When there is no inclination to a trans-
> ference of emotion such as this, or when it has become en-
> tirely negative, as happens in dementia praecox or
> paranoia, then there is also no possibility of influencing the
> patient by psychological means. (p. 42)

Here once again Freud reveals his belief (cf. 1912a) that
negative transference nullifies the possibility of therapeutic effect. Accounts of the great difficulty he experienced in managing his own potentially destructive aggression (e.g., Kavka,
1980; Roazen, 1969, 1975; Wilson, 1981) may help to explain
Freud's efforts to discourage the development and expression
of negative transference. In his analytic work he apparently
strove to detach the negative transference from himself. To operate in that manner, however, makes effective treatment of the
schizophrenic patient impossible. It precludes the full develop-

ment of negative transference, which is indispensable for resolving obstacles to the verbal release of aggressive impulses and feelings (negative transference resistance).

To quote further:

> It is perfectly true that psycho-analysis, like other psychotherapeutic methods, employs the instrument of suggestion (or transference). But . . . in analysis it is not allowed to play the decisive part in determining the therapeutic results. It is used instead to induce the patient to perform a piece of psychical work—the overcoming of his transference-resistances—which involves a permanent alteration in his mental economy. The transference is made conscious to the patient by the analyst, and it is resolved by convincing him that in his transference-attitude he is *re-experiencing* emotional relations which had their origin in his earliest object-attachments. (1925, pp. 42-43)

To operate on this assumption leads to failure. The key to reversing the schizophrenic reaction is not "convincing" the patient of the genetic antecedents of the negative feelings that are transferred to the therapist but resolving the resistance to their expression.

The handling of transference, Freud continues, "remains the most difficult as well as the most important part of the technique of analysis" (p. 43). This is as true today as it was in 1925. However, the crucial element of this task in a case of schizophrenia, as already indicated (Chapter 7), is the therapeutic management of negative narcissistic transference.

Another passage re-echoes, but with significant modifications, Freud's explanation of unsatisfactory results in the analysis of psychotic patients. The crux of the problem, as restated in 1925, is that they are "as a rule without the capacity for forming a *positive* transference" (emphasis added; p. 60). The element of positive transference whose absence he regarded as most troublesome was that of rapport or the "reasonable" and purposeful cooperation implicit in the notion of therapeutic alliance. Nevertheless, Freud continued, there are a number of methods of approach to be found. Transference is often not so completely absent but that it can be used to a certain extent; and analysis has achieved undoubted successes with cyclical depressions, light paranoiac modifications, and partial schizophrenias. It has at least been a benefit to science that in many cases the diagnosis can oscillate for quite a long time between assuming the presence of a psychoneurosis or a dementia praecox; for therapeutic attempts initiated in such cases have resulted in valuable discoveries before they have had to be broken off. (1925, p. 60)

This is, in a sense, an admission that treatability depends less on diagnosis than on the analyst's ability to deal effectively with the individual patient. Zimmerman points out that a person may be deemed unanalyzable because his psychopathology coincides with "non-resolved infantile conflicts of the psychoanalyst" (1982, p. 198).

Also of interest in the present context is Freud's statement that sufferers from the narcissistic neuroses reject the therapist "not with hostility but with indifference" (1917, p. 447). He did not connect the indifference with the obliteration of positive by negative feelings.

Federn, who identified himself as "one of the first to oppose the dogma of 'no transference' in psychosis" (1952, p. 142) commented on the development of Freud's views on transference. On the basis of conversations with him in the last years of his life, Federn wrote:

Transference is needed to shift object attachments from the unconscious to the psychoanalyst. . . . . Lack of transference in neurotics was unknown to Freud, so that he suspected an underlying psychosis when such a lack was noted. . . . Freud himself detected later that the narcissistic type of libido distribution affords a foundation for aggression and independence, and this type may refuse any transference through extraordinary pride and spite. Some analysts are apt, much more than Freud, to provoke this kind of resistance. W. Reich has called it "narcissistic armor" which has to be broken down before positive transference can be established. (1952, pp. 136-137)

Specific recommendations on the management of transference that are relevant to the treatment of the schizophrenic patient are found in Freud's essays on technique. He suggested (1913) that *"so long as the patient's communications and ideas run on without any obstruction, the theme of transference should be left untouched"* (p. 139). He also suggested that the analyst withhold his first explanations until a "strong" (p. 144) transference has been established. An "intimate" attitude on the part of the analyst, Freud observed (1912b, p. 118), makes the resolution of the transference difficult.

Other Views

Delving beyond the customary explanations of transference in terms of suggestion, repetition-compulsion, displacement and the like, many theorists have sought to explain the phenomenon on a rational basis. The notion that it meets a need or performs a restitutive function has been elaborated in various ways.

Michael Balint (1952) has conceptualized transference as a "new beginning." Some patients, he writes,

> regress to primitive stages in their development, in order to begin the process of adaptation anew. . . . Primitive, undifferentiated states are elastic, capable of new adaptation in various directions. . . . if a radically new adaptation becomes necessary, the highly differentiated organization must be reduced to its primitive undifferentiated form from which a new beginning may then issue. (p. 216)

Daniel Lagache (1953) based his formulation on the finding of B. Zeigarnik, an experimental psychologist, that the tension motivating a task persists after its failure. Transference, according to Lagache, represents the "activation . . . of an unsolved conflict; injury to the narcissistic drives . . . is not just a reason for defense, it evokes an unconscious demand for reparation . . . a main function of transference" (p. 9).

Elaborating on the need-fulfilling function of various transference states, Joost A. M. Meerloo and Marie Coleman Nelson (1965) refer to negative transference as the "patient's quest for a means of handling hostile feelings" (p. 59). A need to repeat the relationship of infancy is implicated in narcissistic transference. One of several patterns these authors associate with it is fear of loss of control. They suggest that regression to an infantile psychological state "may be understood as a self-imposed control against the discharge of a lifelong accumulation of rage" (p. 34).

Reports that patients in a state of negative transference responded to analytic influence challenged the assumption that the formation and safeguarding of the positive transference relationship were indispensable to effective treatment. In one of the earliest explanations of both aspects of transference in schizophrenic patients, Melanie Klein (1952) expressed the view that transference originates in object relations of the first year of life, and reflects the presence of hatred as well as love—"the mechanisms, anxieties, and defenses operative in earliest infancy" (p. 436).

Dexter M. Bullard (1960) advises against attempting to establish positive transference when beginning the treatment of a patient who has rarely experienced interpersonal relationships that were warm and uncomplicated. According to Bullard, an approach "which assumes that he has had these experiences is doomed to failure" (p. 139).

Among others who have expressed similar views, L. Bryce Boyer (1967) writes that the schizophrenic patient "is terrified of the potential destructiveness of his impulses and when the emergence of hatred of former love objects is discouraged, he interprets the therapist to fear the patient's or his own hostility (p. 166).

CONCEPTUALIZATION OF NARCISSISTIC TRANSFERENCE

The evolutionary development of the transference relationship with the schizophrenic patient is illustrated in the reports by Nunberg (1948) and Hendrick (1931) discussed in Chapter 2. Manifestations of both narcissistic transference (though not referred to as such) and object or oedipal-type transference are described in both reports.

Federn commented in 1936 on the appearance of mixed transference states:

> Often there are several infantile ego states existing facultatively at the same time; these must be recognized in order that one may establish contact with them, as one does with a child. . . . Both object libidinal and narcissistic cathexes are transferred in varying proportions; the latter in most cases through the renewal of early identifications. (1952, p. 327n)

Early Use of the Term

Robert Waelder (1925) introduced the use of "narcissistic transference" as a technical term. He proposed a method of treatment oriented to the sublimation of narcissism, and described a case in which a transference of that nature had proved sufficient to sustain the relationship.

Referring to Waelder's theory, L. Pierce Clark (1926) described a "fantasy method" of analyzing the narcissistic neuroses. In the absence of the customary transference leverage, one may conduct treatment with a "conscious will and a narcissistic transference" (p. 226). Clark characterized such transference as of the "mother type," contrasting it with the "lover" type that evolves in the transference neuroses (p. 227). Woven into "emotional feelings of the infantile life," which the patient may first regard as actual memories, are actually "automorphic retroprojections having all the affective value of infantile memories" (pp. 227–228).

"The Narcissistic Transference of the Juvenile Impostor," by August Aichhorn, published in 1936, was abstracted by Anna Freud (1951) in her obituary tribute to the author of *Wayward Youth*. He could therapeutically influence the young delinquent who could not form a meaningful object relationship other than through an "overflow of narcissistic libido," Aichhorn reported, when he presented himself as a "glorified replica" of the patient's "delinquent ego and ego-ideal" (p. 55). Undergoing experiences that undo anomalies and make up for deficiencies in early libidinal development in such a transference relationship, Aichhorn claimed, enables the delinquent to "complete the structure of his personality, which was arrested at a primitive level" (A. Freud, 1951, p. 54).

Blum (1982) refers to Aichhorn's claim as the "entire theory of the use of the transference to undo a developmental deficiency and defect and to complete structure formation . . . a very optimistic formulation" (p. 964). Kohut (1971), on the other hand, stresses the importance of Aichhorn's "pioneering theoretical and technical steps" (p. 161). Marshall (1982) points out that Aichhorn pioneered in the use of mirroring techniques "deliberately and with rationale" (p. 74).

Aichhorn appears to have presented the first description of the ego-syntonic transference object. Robert Bak (1952) was another early advocate of such functioning. He recommended that the therapist "represent a narcissistic object, appearing as part of the patient" (p. 203).

Gustav Bychowski (1952) refers to a schizophrenic patient who greeted his therapist with the declaration, "You are me. We are the same person. You are a woman, a daughter, a man, a horse, a bear, and I too am all this. Everything is one" (p. 41).

Herbert Rosenfeld (1952b) reported that a particular type of object relationship developed in all of his cases of schizophrenia: "As soon as the schizophrenic approaches *any* object in love or hate, he seems to become confused with this object" (p. 458). He also stated (1952a) that "in the same way as a transference neurosis develops in the neurotic, so, in the analysis of psychotics, there develops what may be called a 'transference psychosis' " (p. 112). In a later report (1964), Rosenfeld described a "marked narcissistic transference" in a patient who showed no sign of psychosis (p. 333).

Generalizing from personal experience and the observations reported by other investigators, Leo Stone elaborated on the theme of narcissism and transference at a meeting of the New York Psychoanalytic Association in 1954:

It would seem that the conception of narcissistic incapacity for transference rests to some extent on a terminological-historical basis. For it is true that the original transference love of the hysteric or the transference fear and aggression of the incest complex are different from the primitive phenomena of the narcissistic transferences, although all gradations between them may occur. . . . In those many instances where the transference does break through, insatiable demands may appear; or the need to control or tyrannize over the therapist; or failing that, the polar alternative—to be completely submissive, passive, obedient, to be told what to do, or indeed whether things can be done, whether a symptom will appear or disappear; or the transference may be literally "narcissistic," i.e., the therapist is confused with the self, or is like the self in all respects; . . . or the therapist and patient—alternatively—are, in effect, parts of one another. . . . In the fantasy of the analyst's omnipotence . . . it has been my impression that the guilt about primitive destructive aggressions plays an important part. . . . One may speak with justification of a transference psychosis, in the sense of a still viable variant of transference neurosis, in the extreme forms. (pp. 583–585)

Thomas Freeman (1963) in a discussion of pathological narcissism in schizophrenic states, presented some interesting data from a case in which an "intense positive" narcissistic transference led to an intractable "resistance of idealization" (p. 296). The patient, a young woman, freely discussed her hatred of her mother but in the "new version" (p. 297) of an infantile separation trauma, she "securely internalized both the therapist and the sadistic phantasies which were directed against him" (p. 296). In her auditory hallucinations, the analyst spoke reassuringly to her. She believed she had irritated him and that he had, in turn, arranged for her landlady to harass her. The ventilation of her persecutory ideas proved therapeutic but eventually the patient developed a "full-blown delusional complex" (p. 297). She felt that the therapist had sexual feelings when she herself experienced them, and that he was upset and wept with her when she was upset. These are not uncommon narcissistic-transference phenomena.

In a lecture entitled *The Narcissistic Defense in Schizophrenia* (originally published as a monograph (1961b), I discussed the nature of the narcissistic transference in the schizophrenic patient and the role of the analyst in promoting its development.

> The patient is permitted to mold the transference object in his own image. He builds up a picture of his therapist as someone like himself—the kind of person whom he will eventually feel free to love and hate.
>
> My immediate objective at the start of treatment is to help the patient develop a narcissistic transference. On the surface it looks positive. He builds up this attitude: "You are like me so I like you. You spend time with me and try to understand me, and I love you for it." Underneath the sweet crust, however, one gets transient glimpses of the opposite attitude: "I hate you as I hate myself. But when I feel like hating you, I try to hate myself instead." (Spotnitz, 1961b, p. 33)

Related Terms

Various descriptive terms that are roughly synonymous with "narcissistic transference" are found in the literature. There are references, for example, to infantile or infantile-level transference, and especially to primitive transferences. Kernberg (1976) uses the term "primitive transference" specifically to indicate the reactivation of "part-object relations—units of early self- and object-images and the primitive affects linking them" (p. 163).

Stone (1967, 1981a) has described three levels of transference. The lowest level is designated as primordial transference, the middle level as transitional object transference, and the highest level as the mature transference. Stone discerns an "irredentist urge toward bodily reunion" (1981, p. 97) in the primordial transference state; the patient is propelled by "parasymbiotic" needs and seems to be attempting to recreate the symbiotic relationship with the mother.

Morton Berg (1977) points out that patients with border-line-type disturbances, instead of displacing affects from one object to another, develop an "externalizing" transference in which "internal structures" are allocated to the therapist. In this essential narcissistic process, the transference "becomes rather more an occasion for the revival of narcissistic preoedipal, pre-genital and prestructural elements and rather less an object-libidinal, oedipal, genital and structural matter" (p. 235).

Harold Searles (1963) reports that transference in the therapy of patients suffering from chronic schizophrenia "is expressive of a very primitive ego organization, comparable to that which holds sway in the infant who is living in a world of part-objects" (p. 252). The patient's transference to the therapist is basically a relatedness to a mother figure from whom the patient has never become "deeply differentiated" (p. 253).

Searles generally refers to this phenomenon as "transference psychosis," which he defines (1963) as "any type of transference which distorts or prevents a relatedness between patient and therapist as two separate, alive, human and sane beings" (p. 257). On the basis of clinical data derived from work with many hospitalized schizophrenic patients, Searles identifies transference psychosis with (1) "transference situations in which the therapist feels unrelated to the patient" (p. 257); (2) situations marked by a clear-cut relatedness but which the therapist feels to be "deeply ambivalent" (p. 260); (3) transference situations marked by the patient's effort to complement the therapist's personality or help him become established as a "separate and whole person" (p. 263); and (4) situations in which the patient ambivalently tries to "perpetuate a symbiotic relationship" and, through a sadistic or castrative nullification of the therapist's efforts, expresses "a determination to be a separately-thinking, and otherwise separately-functioning individual" (p. 266).

Margaret Little has introduced an analogous concept, that of delusional transference. She discusses a transference state in which the analyst "*is*, in an absolute way, . . . both the idealized parents and their opposites, or rather, the parents deified and diabolized, and also himself (the patient) deified and diabolized" (1958, p. 135).

Later Contributions

Thomas McGlashan (1983), drawing on experience with borderline patients, observes that they organize their sense of self around a primitive and symbiotic selfobject, which he refers to as the "we-self." In this primitive unit of internal relatedness, a fusion of self and object becomes transferentially enacted and actualized within the context of close relationships, such as that of individual psychotherapy.

Heinz Kohut (1968), in one of the earliest of his numerous references to narcissistic transference, described two types—idealizing and mirror transferences. In a later outline of the concepts and theories of the psychoanalytic psychology of the self, Kohut and Wolf (1978) state that the discovery that patients suffering from these disorders "reactivated certain specific narcissistic needs in the psychoanalytic situation, i.e., that they established 'narcissistic transferences', *made effective psychoanalytic treatment possible*" (emphasis added; p. 413).

In *The Analysis of the Self* (1971), Kohut identifies three types of mirror transference. In the most archaic, "the analyst is experienced as an extension of the grandiose self" (p. 114). In a less archaic form, the analyst is experienced as "being like the grandiose self or being very similar to it" (p. 115). This type of mirror transference is referred to as the alter-ego transference or the twinship. In the third and most mature type, identified as mirror transference in the narrow sense, the analyst is "most clearly experienced as a separate person" (pp. 115–116).

The "decisive factor on the road to therapeutic success," Kohut (1971) states, is the analyst's ability to "remain noninterfering as the narcissistic transference unfolds" (p. 208).

In shifting from the term "narcissistic transference" to "selfobject transference," Kohut (1977) characterized the change as a conceptual refinement (p. xiv).

Kernberg (1975), reporting on his theoretical and clinical approaches to borderline and narcissistic personalities, details the nature of their transference manifestations and occasionally refers directly to "narcissistic transference." He states, for example, that these patients treat the analyst as "extensions of themselves or vice versa" (p. 247). Those transference states that Kohut identifies as mirror and idealizing transferences are viewed by Kernberg as the "alternative activation of components belonging essentially to a condensed, pathological self" (p. 279). He presents brief clinical vignettes that reflect features of the narcissistic transference. The premature activation of "very early conflict-laden object relations"—regarded by Kernberg (1982a) as one of the most striking clinical characteristics of borderline patients—reflects "a multitude of internal object relations of dissociated or split-off aspects of the self with dissociated or split-off object representations of a highly fantastic and distorted nature" (p. 472).

Kernberg (1976) attributes the failure of borderline patients to integrate libidinally and aggressively determined images (self and object) to the "pathological predominance" of the aggressively determined images and to a "related failure to establish a sufficiently strong ego core around the (originally nondifferentiated) good self- and object-images" (p. 163). Kernberg recommends that the predominantly negative transference of these patients be systematically elaborated only in the "here and now" (p. 161).

Vamik Volkan (1976) refers to narcissistic transference as dominating the treatment of a young man with an inflated self-concept. The patient "glorified himself and saw me as an extension of this glory—or, he devalued and discarded me as someone far beneath him" (p. 256). In highlighting the appearance of similar narcissistic transference manifestations in another narcissistic personality, Volkan writes, "I was either a jewel in his crown or, at the other extreme, a sewer in which his resentments could be flushed away" (p. 281). Considerably more complicated is the transference situation with a psychotic patient, Volkan points out, because the patient's "self-images are not differentiated from his object images, and he merges with what he externalizes onto the object" (p. 320).

Although the narcissistic transference and the transference neurosis may appear simultaneously, "one alternately overlying the other" (p. 270), as Volkan states, it would be useless to analyze the latter until the narcissistic transference has been adequately analyzed. It will "return again and again until it is fully worked through" (p. 270). In a later publication (1979), he calls attention to the necessity of tolerating the narcissistic transference without interfering with its development.

Following Modell's conceptualization (1975) of the first phase of the psychoanalytic process for patients with narcissistic character disorder as the "cocoon" phase (p. 295), Volkan (1979) refers to the dissolution of the "cocoon transference," from which the patient emerges "feeling considerably more alive" (p. 407).

Benjamin Margolis states (1981) that the narcissistic transference "is not a given, with which the narcissistic patient automatically begins treatment. With rare exceptions, he does not bring it with him—he arrives with a potential for it and gradually develops it. . . . In order to say correctly that a person is in a state of narcissistic transference, we must observe that he . . . gives *evidence* of it by his behavior" (p. 173). A patient who, though seeming to be emotionally oblivious to the analyst's separate presence, accords major importance to the stimuli issuing from the analyst, gives significant evidence of the existence of narcissistic transference.

MAJOR IMPLICATIONS FOR TECHNIQUE

The Transference Conflict

It is desirable to approach narcissistic transference, not as an illusion or an anachronism, but rather as the patient's unconscious attempt to reveal the basic maturational needs for objects that were not met in the course of his development. These needs arouse impulses, feelings, thoughts, and memories. It is their attachment to the present transference object that makes it possible to liberate the patient from their pathological influence. The more traumatic the early situation in which the schizophrenic reaction was patterned, the higher the intensity of transference needed to repeat and master that situation. For example, a person who was exposed to a great deal of emotional deprivation early in life experiences intense cravings to be taken care of; the analyst often becomes the focus of those cravings.

Through the vehicle of narcissistic transference, the schizophrenic patient attempts to rid himself of damaging object impressions that were egotized during the first 2 years of life. The patient overvalues these narcissistic object imagos out of need but experiences them as intensely frustrating, and thus the source of intense psychic pain (Day & Semrad, 1978). According to Ogden, the patient "unconsciously attacks his thoughts, feelings, and perceptions, which are felt to be an endless source of unmanageable pain and irresolvable conflict" (1982, p. 166). Impulses to hold on to the damaging object imagos battle with impulses to wipe them out of the mind. That is my understanding of the transference conflict.

The Continuum

The transference phenomena observed are broadly viewed as a continuum of essentially similar reactions ranging from transference psychosis to object transference and reflecting the amount of undischarged frustration-aggression being mobilized in a schizophrenic patient. The earlier the period of object relationship involved, the greater the danger that the ego will be shattered by the mobilized frustration-aggression that is blocked from discharge.

In the clinical picture referred to as transference psychosis, the narcissistic object imagos—the nuclei of the ego—appear to have succumbed to that danger. In the fully developed narcissistic transference of a less severely disturbed patient whose ego has not suffered total fragmentation, the transference object is experienced as nonexistent or as part of the mind. In a milder preoedipal condition, the analyst is experienced as outside the self but like it. In disturbances connected with oedipal development, the analyst is experienced as a separate and distinct object. Awareness of this continuum of transference states is a clinical aid in determining whether a case is moving in a therapeutic direction.

Transference psychosis as Searles has defined it (1963) may be observed in ambulatory schizophrenic patients; Searles' clues are equally applicable to transference situations that develop in their treatment. But psychotic manifestations that *freshly* attach themselves to the transference of a patient in office treatment are an indicator of regressive movement. When the ambulatory patient is helped to re-experience the maturational failure gradually, at the developmental level at which it occurred, he swings backward as well as forward; nevertheless, when he is making consistent progress, he observably becomes more and more oriented to reality. Narcissistic transference slowly gives way to object transference.

General Characteristics

The theory of classical technique places its emphasis on defective superego or ego imagos that were originally perceived more or less clearly in the object field of the mind. It is relatively easy to deal with these patterns; they emerge as elements of the object transference. Defective object impressions that were experienced in the ego field during the first 2 years of life—the crucial imagos in schizophrenia—cannot be mastered in the same way. Initially they operate as resistance when the patient is in a state of narcissistic transference. The resolution of narcissistic transference involves, in a sense, the reversal of the process by which they were egotized (Bychowski, 1956). With their "return" to the object field of the mind, they become elements of the object transference.

Apparently the recognition of narcissistic transference as a conceptional tool, as well as the understanding of its behavioral aspects, have been obscured by its major characteristics. Often, a schizophrenic patient in this state, after appearing to be devoid of emotion, will suddenly experience great anxiety. In addition to its deceptive quality, narcissistic transference may be anxiety-provoking. (The feelings it induces in the therapist are discussed in Chapter 9.)

The patient's capacity to transfer feelings to the therapist as a separate person varies from case to case, reflecting inversely the severity of his disorder. Transference is never "purely" narcissistic. But the slow development of maximal narcissistic transference is focused on when the treatment begins, in order to resolve the nuclear problem. The ambulatory patient is helped to re-experience the emotional charge of his earliest object relations without significant impairment of his immediate functioning. The narcissistic transference usually takes from 6 months to 2 years to reach a climax.

During that period, situations may arise when object-transference patterns have to be dealt with, particularly resistance to the verbalization of hostility. In principle, however, narcissistic-transference resistance is dealt with more urgently. Whatever object transference exists is retained as long as it is needed, because it is the source of the analyst's decisive influence.

When the patient is successfully trained to inhibit action and the treatment-destructive resistances (Chapter 7) are temporarily nullified, the main obstacles to analytic progress during the formative stage of the relationship are silences that are obviously not part of self-mastery processes, such narcissistic activities as smoking and napping, and ruminative monologues. To the extent to which the patient denies the reality of the interpersonal relationship, it is difficult at times to detect any note of progress in his early communications. In that sense, the state of narcissistic transference invariably serves the function of resistance. Nevertheless, primitive communications per se are not regarded as resistance. Unless the patient is totally blocked or is merely repeating the same thoughts and feelings over and over again, there is no reason to intervene.

It is an interesting fact that, when one focuses on the narcissistic patterns and works consistently to help the patient verbalize frustration-tension, object transference phenomena become increasingly prominent. These are, however, more fluid than in a case of psychoneurosis. The schizophrenic patient frequently reverts to his extremely narcissistic patterns of resistance. The therapist is then called on to return to the techniques that proved effective earlier in the case. Eventually, the patient's transferences are aroused by his emotional perceptions of the therapist as a parental transference figure.

In general, the transference relationship is characterized by periods during which the schizophrenic patient's self-preoccupations or growing preoccupation with the analyst are communicated more or less progressively. Occasionally there are interludes of aggression-catharsis (when the immediate resistance to the verbalization of hostility is temporarily resolved).

The sections that follow illustrate the patient's transference reactions and detail principles underlying the management of transference at successive stages of the relationship.

NARCISSISTIC TRANSFERENCE
(EARLY STAGE)

The Patient's Self-Preoccupations

When the schizophrenic patient begins to talk, he may be somewhat anxious. Usually, however, he is aware of little if any feeling. He soon becomes preoccupied with the functioning of his own body, and may report disagreeable sensations connected with breathing, seeing, hearing, and the like. When talking freely about his presenting problems, the patient tends to become restless and agitated. He may say one day that he remains in treatment only because he would be even more miserable without it.

Any anxiety the patient may have had at the start soon becomes absorbed in feelings of confusion, strangeness, emptiness, deadness, and hopelessness about getting better. He may also express doubts that he "really" exists. Birth fantasies or sexual preoccupations may be reported without any show of emotion.

The more regressed the patient is, the more difficult it is to identify the earliest transference reactions. Because of the patient's well-known flatness of affect, the analyst's influence appears to be nil. A seriously disturbed individual may actually verbalize the feeling that the analyst does not exist. Some patients who have discussed that impression retrospectively have recalled that they experienced cravings for a few words from the analyst even when they did not feel that he was in the room. Patients suffering from severe depression have reported the same impression.

The attitude that the therapist does not exist is one of several types of pre-ego feelings (Margolis, 1981) that may be reawakened in a pathologically narcissistic person. It is reminiscent of functioning in the objectless phase of life. The transference object may also be related to as a part of the self, as outside the self but a psychological twin image, as part of the self but different from it. These primitive emotional attitudes have been mentioned in the order of their significance for the evolution of narcissistic transference. A seriously disturbed individual may pass through all of these stages before relating to the analyst as a separate and distinct person.

In a detailed clinical illustration, Thomas Ogden (1982) conceptualizes the successive steps in the resolution of schizophrenic conflict as 1) the stage of nonexperience; 2) the stage of projective identification; 3) the stage of psychotic experience; and 4) the stage of symbolic thought.

The narcissistic transference may initially have intrauterine qualities. However, oral and anal elements are dominant. The appearance of phallic qualities signals the emergence of object transference.

The Ego-Syntonic Object

As the narcissistic transference develops, the schizophrenic patient begins to reveal the basic object hunger of his personality. The type of audience that helps him talk out his painful feelings with the least strain on his vulnerable ego has been described by Michael Balint (1959): "The analyst should not be an entity in his own right . . . in fact not a separate sharply contoured object at all; but should merge as completely as possible into the 'friendly expanses' surrounding the patient" (p. 97). The patient wants and needs to relate to an *ego-syntonic object*.

The analyst serves as such an object when he applies the principles I have stressed in the preceding chapter for dealing with resistance. To recapitulate briefly: To facilitate the development of narcissistic transference, the analyst intervenes to deal with resistance only to the extent necessary to preserve the relationship. The patient's contact functioning is reflected in some way and a few object-oriented questions are asked in the session to discourage defensive regression. The patient is helped—indirectly—to verbalize frustration-tension promptly and educated to *inhibit action*.

Repetitive reflection of the contact functioning serves to convey to him the message: Stop attacking yourself with your hostile feelings; attach them to me verbally.

Objectification of the Ego

In the early stage of narcissistic transference, a sorting out, by analytic process, of disturbing feelings that were originally experienced from the patient's earliest objects—introjected feelings that were not distinguishable from the infant's own feelings—gets under way. Bychowski (1956), who referred to the release of internal images as a reversal of their original incorporation in the ego, observed that the ego "feels the need to reexperience the object as lying outside the ego boundaries" (p. 335). Marie Coleman Nelson discussed the "externalization of the toxic introject" (1956). My concept of the psychological process of transferring the early object impressions from the patient's ego to the transference object is referred to as the "objectification of the ego."

This is somewhat similar to the well-known mechanism of projective identification, first discussed by Melanie Klein (1946; Ogden, 1982). But whereas the schizophrenic patient engages in projective identification naturally, that is, projects his own feelings onto the analyst, the process of objectifying the ego is one that the analyst facilitates as a matter of *therapeutic strategy*. Objectification of the ego eventually makes it possible to reconstruct the relationship of the patient with his primary objects.

The residue of disturbing feelings that were experienced from objects early in life is transferred as expeditiously as possible, and in a nondamaging manner, when the therapist intervenes with the following purposes in mind:

1. To permit any attitude expressed by the patient to stand uncorrected.

2. To utilize the patient's attitude as a basis for investigating the object. The patient is encouraged to verbalize his impressions of the therapist but his curiosity is not satisfied.

3. To encourage the patient to verbalize his perceptions of external reality instead of concentrating on what he thinks and feels about himself and his ego.

4. To investigate the patient's characteristic preoccupations, especially his worries about himself, when he wants to discuss them. Instead of being given the requested information, he is asked why he wants the therapist to give it to him.

5. To take pressure off the ego as much as possible and shift it to the object. The impression is conveyed that there is nothing seriously wrong with the patient aside from the fact that he was not trained properly. Undoubtedly, he can be retrained; the question at issue is whether his present object is adequate to the task. The patient's views on the analyst's competence are explored.

In short, the process of *objectification of the ego* helps the patient to relate verbally to the analyst as an object like the ego, someone the patient can hate and love as he hates and loves himself. Thus structured, the relationship illuminates and makes it possible to deal with the enormous rage that is recognized as the schizophrenic's "most severe problem" (Day & Semrad, 1978, p. 220). The defective ego is externalized (Berg, 1977) and analyzed as it appears to exist in the transference object.

NARCISSISTIC TRANSFERENCE (FULL DEVELOPMENT)

The Patient

The patient is often preoccupied with autoerotic feelings. He may allude to painful sensations in various parts of his body. Somatic delusions may intensify and become more diffuse. The patient may feel that his body is changing radically, is paralyzed, falling apart, or separating from his mind.

He may experience himself as living in a dream.

He may feel that people stare at him wherever he goes, read his thoughts, talk about him, and call him names.

The patient's psychic discomfort may frighten him. He may run out of the office in the middle of a session, perhaps banging the door behind him. Sometimes he returns a few minutes later.

His attitude is one of extreme suspicion, of remaining on guard in a potentially threatening environment.

The patient may feel that it is "always me, me, me" that has to be talked about because he has no source of love or satisfaction outside himself.

He may feel that he is weltering in words that don't make sense.

At times he feels that he is a superior and powerful human being; at other times he feels "at the bottom of the heap."

He often feels that what he is saying is "wrong" or not what he is supposed to say.

The emotional conviction that his own "rotten self" is wholly responsible for his mental torture may be repeatedly voiced. He feels helpless and has no hope that anything can be done for him.

Talking about his destructive urges, the patient feels, will force him to act on them.

Something is wrong with him, he is certain, when he experiences anxiety, tension, or rage. He worries that he may "blow his top."

The patient fights to conceal thoughts of committing homicide or suicide because they confuse and horrify him.

De-Egotization of the Object

In the fully developed narcissistic transference, the residue of disturbing feelings experienced by the patient in the process of ego formation is reawakened in the analytic relationship. He transfers to the therapist feelings that he experienced during the first two years of life. Some of those that the patient transfers are presumably toxic feelings connected with the undue inhibition of his impulses; there are also feelings of grandeur associated with infantile fantasies of the all-satisfying state. Object impressions that moved into the ego field through such early identificatory processes as fascination (Fenichel, 1945, p. 37), introjection, and imitation are also transferred.

A sorting out of the undifferentiated feelings that were objectified helps the patient to de-egotize the early object representations. As they are moved back into the object field, he relates increasingly to the transference object as a person outside and different from the self. In other words, the objectified feelings become elements of the object transference.

At the time the defective object imagos moved into the ego field, the infant was experiencing great discomfort. These feelings are relatively easy to deal with if they are eventually projected onto the object; in that case they are readily attributed to the therapist. That process is facilitated by the use of joining techniques (Chapter 10).

OSCILLATING TRANSFERENCE STATES

Oscillating between the narcissistic and object transference states, the patient is characteristically in the grip of intense and conflicting emotions. Some of the attitudes and affects experienced during this phase are described below.

The Patient

The patient may worry that he is boring or upsetting the analyst.

Thoughts that the analyst does not like or respect him stimulate feelings of total rejection in the patient.

When he talks about "guilty" secrets and perverse fantasies, he may feel that he is betraying himself and implicating others.

The patient feels tortured and gloomy, more and more convinced that the analyst can do nothing for him and that the treatment should be discontinued.

The patient, after feeling helpless and incurable, begins to feel that he can be helped to get better.

Although he wants to like the analyst, the patient may dislike him very much and get to feel that the analyst is indifferent to these feelings—just a "brain" or "logical piece of machinery" in human guise.

Emerging suddenly from a nonfeeling state, the patient may react explosively to a question or word mentioned by the analyst.

When he feels hatred for the analyst, the patient tries to hate himself instead.

At times the patient recognizes that the analytic process is a factor in his experiencing of thoughts, feelings, and memories that he would rather not be aware of and would rather not put into words.

He does not want to implicate the analyst personally in this intolerable situation and tries to conceal desires to attack him.

The patient fears that, if he reveals his hostility, the relationship will be terminated.

The patient feels that he hates everyone.

At times he feels like leaving treatment to prove that he was right and the analyst was wrong.

When he flares out in rage to get the analyst to talk to him, the discovery that verbal expressions of his hostility make him feel more comfortable often surprises him.

The patient may fear that he is abnormal when he experiences homosexual feelings.

When he becomes immersed in heterosexual or perverse fantasies, he may say something such as that talking about them makes him feel that he is behaving like an alley cat.

He suspects at times that the therapist is trying to manipulate or control him. Although the patient may conceal these malignant impressions, he frequently feels like smashing up things in the office or hurling them at the therapist.

Reconstruction

The patient has no actual recollection of the events of his earliest years. Impressions of some of the events that are beyond recall may appear in retrospective fantasies and dreams, or be acted out in perverse behavior. But the object relations restaged in the narcissistic transference were not originally perceived as such, and are very difficult to discern. Some memory traces may be reinforced when the transference resistance is psychologically reflected. Dreams, verbal imagery, fantasies, and acting-in and acting-out behavior are other sources of information. Nevertheless, the patient's picture of the psychic events of his infancy is, in most cases, indistinct. The high concentration of rage impulses that were attached to the earliest objects, including part-objects and selfobjects, and to the self, are repressed beyond conscious recall. Consequently, reconstruction of the emotional situation in which the schizophrenic reaction was patterned is a major aspect of the dissolution of the narcissistic transference.

Reconstruction of a whole complex of preoedipal experience is a more formidable task than interpreting one or another element of the material; the advisability (even the possibility) of attempting it is still questioned by many therapists. Preoedipal constructs can be developed, however, if one takes the considerable time necessary to accomplish it.

These constructs are not developed in the interests of "thorough analysis," nor are they communicated to the patient in the mistaken hope of eliciting memory traces of the actual events. From the point of view of therapy, recall of the events per se is not important. Reconstruction is engaged in to help the patient articulate those impressions made on the sensory-motor sphere in infancy that interfered with personality maturation.[1] The verbalization of these impressions as freshly perceived by the adult mind and voiced anew in adult language, is crucial for personality integration—that is, the linking of preverbal impressions with verbal impressions of the past. Language serves to link them together in the mind (Glauber, 1982). When the impressions are all linked together, both the fantasies and the perverse behavior disappear, which suggests that the impressions of preverbal life that were unavailable to the conscious mind have been successfully integrated into the ego.

Reconstruction is usually pursued within the theoretical framework of transference, and the constructs developed by the analyst are communicated as questions, hypotheses, or interpretations. But in the reconstruction of the inner realities of the undifferentiated period, the feelings induced in the therapist by the patient's transference feelings and behavior contribute additional—at times indispensable—clues to the early emotional history.

---

[1]The germ of that idea will be found in the first chapter of the *Studies on Hysteria*: "The psychical process which originally took place must be repeated as vividly as possible; it must be brought back to its *status nascendi* and then given verbal utterance" (Breuer & Freud, 1893-1895, p. 6). I believe that a mature level of perception and language was implied by Breuer and Freud.

It is now widely accepted that the feelings induced (objective narcissistic countertransference) represent an important tool in the reconstruction process. Moreover, in the analysis of the schizophrenic patient, the posing of questions plays a larger role than interpretations in the development and communication of constructs. They are a by-product of the joint analytic activity rather than originating exclusively in the analyst's suggestions. The analyst asks questions and the patient asks questions; in this two-way interrogatory process, constructs are indirectly volunteered by one or the other. Often they are explored cooperatively.

The constructs developed in this manner help the patient verbalize impressions of the original emotional situation with a sense of conviction. Changes in feeling and new action patterns subsequently testify to the value of the constructs. For example, an involuntary pattern of complaining may be transformed into a voluntary pattern of asking for what the patient wants; when the new pattern is consistently used, the therapist knows that the original emotional constellation that led the patient to complain like a baby has been outgrown.

In my opinion, attempts to validate the actual events of infancy take one off on a tangent. Nevertheless, there are instances when the practitioner succeeds in reassembling the true picture. If he does so, however, he does not communicate it immediately; blunt presentations of reality can be damaging to the schizophrenic patient. Instead, the patient's own impressions of early experiences, distorted as these impressions may be, are thoroughly probed. Questions are asked about the patient's gross distortions. Queries that help him verbalize his impressions of the factors that led to the distortions are of the utmost value.

If, for instance, the patient says, "In my head my mother was attacking and criticizing me," the therapist does *not* tell the patient that this was a memory trace of something his mother told him when he was a baby. Instead, the patient is asked such questions as: Why was your mother attacking you? Do you hear her voice now? What was she saying? The patient verbalizes his impressions as the investigation continues. Eventually, when the patient is ready to accept it, the reconstruction is communicated to him.

The more freely the patient is able to articulate the feelings connected with the childhood impressions, the more consistently he is able to describe the therapist as a wholly separate person. (This is the point of transition from a narcissistic transference to object transference.) Reconstruction of the preoedipal emotional situation has the effect of "returning" the feelings of objects that were egotized to the object field of the mind, and early ego feelings that were objectified to the ego field. It then becomes possible to deal with these impressions as elements of the object transference.

OBJECT TRANSFERENCE

The Patient

A shift from increasingly evident but primarily intellectual interest to intense emotional concern with the analyst as a distinct and different personality is observed as the object transference becomes more or less stable. Elements of the ego that developed out of contact with the mother tend to become attached to the practitioner. The tendency may be stimulated to some degree by psychological reflection of the patient's contact functioning; but it is not an uncommon observation, even among analysts who do not employ resistance-reflecting or joining approaches, that the transference object, in a sense, *becomes* the parent.

The transference reactions of the schizophrenic patient functioning on the oedipal level are similar to those of psychoneurotic patients. He feels that there is total "safety" in the relationship, that he can trust the therapist with any information. Genital strivings are communicated with growing ease. The patient may express the idea that his love is so great that nothing the analyst might say could diminish it. The latter is incorruptible, his understanding boundless, the patient feels. To spend the rest of his life "going everywhere and doing everything with you" would be paradise.

Despite its increasingly positive trend, the most striking characteristic of the transference relationship is its aggressive charge. This is much more powerful than negative-transference reactions in other cases. The most primitive abuse, threats, and curses are barely adequate to convey the feelings of a schizophrenic patient changing from the rage-withdrawal to the rage-combat pattern.

The patient may complain that the analyst is "making" him feel things that should not be experienced with another human being.

The following is quoted from an earlier publication:

> In one session a man who had been blocked from emotional communication for more than a year began cursing and making the worst threats he could think of. He would start off by tearing my office to shreds. Then he would kill my wife and children. When my turn came, quick death would be too good for me, but he'd figure out something bad enough. I would die through some form of torture. He would stretch it out "inch by inch" and enjoy my anguish as long as possible. Then he dashed out of the office.
>
> He expected to be thrown out the next day, rejected as his mother had rejected him when he lost control. But a few weeks later, he had trouble recalling the outburst. A sort of amnesia settles over such episodes. (Spotnitz, 1961b, p. 37)

STABILIZATION OF MATURE ATTITUDES

Permanent resolution of the stubborn infantile defenses is carried on with a patient who manifests a high degree of co-operation and a strong need to understand the conflict between various aspects of his ego. With the help of the ego-syntonic object, he has mastered the initial obstacles to verbal discharge. Having passed the emotional age of two, the patient is ready to communicate with a different object and, in fact, becomes aware of cravings for a more lively one!

Since the patient is now able to discriminate emotionally between male and female objects, the nuclear conflict expresses itself more prominently through oedipal strivings. Most resistance stemming from the superego operates in relation to the analyst. The patient is usually terrified of, as well as thrilled by, his sexual urges. Sooner or later, the idea that such impulses are permanently frustrated in the relationship may have to be stated; if so, this is communicated in a manner that will not inhibit the patient from continuing to verbalize them freely. The statement may be like that of a parent telling a child that father and daughter (or mother and son) don't get married and that the child will in due time find a more suitable partner.

The patient's feelings for the transference object are regarded as *real* feelings. Reminders that they developed in relation to his parents are out of order as long as the patient communicates them in adult language without acting on them. The object transference is not tampered with until the patient has stabilized the attitude that he would rather verbalize hatred for the transference object than attack or destroy his own ego.

Special Transference Problems

Some patients have no awareness of their feelings of hatred for the therapist as a transference object. One way of dealing with this problem is to ask a series of questions about why the patient does not feel hatred. It is important to recognize the distinction between *provoking*[2] hostility, which is undesirable, and either making the patient aware of its presence or investigating why he does not feel it. In some cases that foundered on this lack of awareness, it was eventually recognized that the thera-

---

[2]Getting the patient to express his anger in language or behavior is viewed by some therapists as a major problem to work on in treating the schizophrenic patient. *This view is incorrect*; the cathartic approach is *not* curative. The problem is, rather, to study and resolve the *forces that prevent* the patient from expressing the anger in language.

pist had been repressing his own negative feelings and that the patient had been identifying with this attitude; thus, a mutuality of nonfeeling states was encouraged.

When such a problem is explored thoroughly, however, it may become clear that, in his earliest object relations, the patient was not aware of rage impulses that were actually aroused. A patient who is repeatedly questioned about the nature of the infantile experience, in terms of investigating the historical prototype of the transference resistance, may eventually become aware of the hatred and its origin.

The opposite problem is encountered among individuals who experienced great hatred from their early objects. Such a patient may verbalize strong suicidal urges in the narcissistic-transference state and later, in relating to the analyst as an external object, demonstrate an attitude of unforgiving hatred. The patient may act out this attitude by denying the analyst the satisfaction of securing the successful outcome of the case. The need to retaliate unconsciously motivates the patient to psychologically "kill off" the transference object. Defeating the analyst may become more important than his own recovery. The *talion principle* of punishment identical to the offense—an eye for an eye—seems to operate in such cases; the patient is usually close to fulfilling his conscious aims in treatment when he leaves his first analyst and seeks another partner in therapy. The defeat of several may be entailed in resolving an attitude of unforgivingness.

DISSOLUTION OF TRANSFERENCE

Before the treatment draws to a close, the illusory aspects of the transference figure have been resolved. Invariably, the patient has some awareness of the practitioner as a real person. But transference phenomena are dealt with only to the extent to which they operate as resistance. It is therefore unrealistic to assume that the patient's attitude will be entirely neutral.

He may be aware of feelings of hostility for one who was responsible for the frustrations he experienced in the treatment. In the final stage of the relationship, the patient is helped to verbalize negative affects appropriately so that, when these are mobilized in interpersonal situations thereafter, they will not interefere with his functioning.

Usually, too, the patient entertains strong feelings of appreciation for the skill and dedication of the treatment partner who helped him achieve a monumental victory over emotional illness. Some degree of identification with the analyst is generally a powerful factor in the establishment of a new object field reflective of emotional maturity.

Chapter 9

COUNTERTRANSFERENCE: RESISTANCE AND THERAPEUTIC LEVERAGE

A person undergoing psychoanalytic treatment enters a quiet, dimly lighted room, lies on the couch, and talks. As he goes on talking in his sessions, he transfers feelings he developed for significant persons in his life to the listener whom he cannot see or touch and is relatively unaware of as a real person. In one way or another, the analyst becomes aware of these feelings and they arouse feelings in him too—fortunately or unfortunately, depending on how they influence his professional functioning.

The unfortunate consequences were the first to be discovered. They are scrutinized in the privacy of training institutes in the spirit of Freud's observation (1910):

> We have become aware of the 'counter-transference' which arises in [the analyst] as a result of the patient's influence on his unconscious feelings, and we are almost inclined to insist that he shall recognize this counter-transference in himself and overcome it. . . . we have noticed that no psycho-analyst goes further than his own complexes and internal resistances permit. (pp. 144–145)

In an essay on technique (1915) Freud again cautioned against any tendency to countertransference. In the interval between these warnings, he discussed the phenomenon briefly in a 1913 letter, categorizing countertransference as "one of the most difficult problems technically" in psychoanalysis but "more easily solvable on the theoretical level" (Binswanger, 1957, p. 50).

Freud's pronouncements on the subject were generally responded to as a warning against experiencing, manifesting, or acting on emotions toward the analysand. The prevailing notion was that of the "mirror analyst" scrupulously safeguarding the transference situation against intrusions of the practitioner's own emotions. Anxiety and guilt about overstepping the consistent and mildly benevolent attitude prescribed by many training analysts often reinforced the strivings to repress all feelings. Apparently, patients expected to be confronted with emotional coldness; some of his own, Fenichel (1941) reported, were astonished at his naturalness and freedom. "Different analysts act differently," he pointed out, "and these differences influence the behavior of patients" (p. 72).

In the early years of analytic practice, however, there were less forbidding attitudes about the analyst's emotional reactions to the "patient's influence," including the recognition that they might be of therapeutic value. Claire Ernsberger (1979) traces the development of that idea.

To cite a few of the early exponents, Helene Deutsch (1926) characterized "the utilization and goal-directed mastery" (p. 137) of countertransference as among the analyst's most important duties. Deutsch also discussed the analyst's tendency, as the patient's ungratified infantile wishes are directed toward him, to identify emotionally with the original objects of those wishes. She called this unconscious process the complementary attitude, a term that inspired Racker's concept of "complementary identification" (1957, p. 323).

Fanny Hann-Kende (1933) stated that the countertransference, when "brought into a suitable equilibrium with the transference . . . not only does not inhibit, but, on the contrary, actually facilitates analytic work" (p. 167). Among others who contributed to the literature on countertransference during the

1930s, Jung (1935) referred to the analytic process as the "reciprocal reaction of two psychic systems" (p. 4), and the Balints (1939) called attention to the inevitability of "interplay" (p. 228). Schilder (1938) commented, "It is a general principle of social psychology that an emotion of a person with whom we are in contact must necessarily provoke an emotion in the other person fitting the situation" (p. 169).

In a highly influential paper presented to the British Psycho-Analytical Society in 1947, Donald Winnicott stressed the importance of countertransference phenomena, especially the objective reactions to the patient, which the therapist needs to be sufficiently aware of to "sort out and study" (1949, p. 70). Maintaining objectivity is one of the therapist's main tasks and, Winnicott added, "a special case of this is to hate the patient objectively" (p. 70).

In another much-quoted mid-century contribution, Paula Heimann (1950) stressed that not only is countertransference "part and parcel of the analytic relationship, but it is the patient's *creation*, it is part of the patient's personality" (p. 83). Heimann referred to the therapist's emotional response within the analytic situation as one of his most important tools and "an instrument of research into the patient's unconscious" (p. 81).

These views gained general currency, even among those who disputed them, as the literature on the subject burgeoned during the 1950s and the 1960s (Ernsberger, 1979). With the gradual tempering of the original wholly negative attitude, the antitherapeutic aspects of countertransference continued to be agreed upon while analysts of various schools explored the possibility of extracting both analytic data and therapeutic leverage from the phenomenon (Epstein & Feiner, 1979).

In a paper presented to the American Psychiatric Association in 1949, I discussed the role of emotional induction in analytic therapy. I stated that the therapist "must be capable of feeling emotions induced by his patient and utilize these feelings to help the patient with his resistances." In a revised version of the paper (Spotnitz, 1976a, chapter 1), the reciprocal nature of emotional induction was pointed out. "As the patient develops a transference, the therapist usually develops a countertransference, which is based on unconscious reactions to the patient's transference attitudes and behavior. The effectiveness of the therapy depends in large measure on the therapist's ability to 'feel' the patient's tendencies toward instinctual discharge. The capacity to sense his latent emotions and help him feel them determines whether their relationship is grounded in genuine emotional understanding or is primarily an intellectual exercise" (p. 29).

With growing recognition of the implications of reciprocal interchanges, Maxwell Gitelson (1952) characterized countertransference reactions as "facts in any analysis" and the therapist who is "open to their analysis and integration" as "in a real sense a vital participant in the analysis with the patient" (p. 10). This attitude is now widely accepted (McLaughlin, 1982).

Parelleling the general literature on countertransference, reports of its special characteristics in the treatment of schizophrenic patients stressed its problematic nature before calling attention to it as a potentially useful phenomenom. Nevertheless, since the early 1950s, countertransference has been identified by many experienced clinicians as the crucial factor. Shortly after practitioners, meeting under the aegis of the Group for the Advancement of Psychiatry, recommended that therapists working with schizophrenic patients make a practice of investigating their countertransference reactions, Frieda Fromm-Reichmann (1952) stated that "if and when" it seemed impossible to establish a workable doctor-patient relationship with a schizophrenic patient, "it is due to the doctor's personality difficulties, not to the patient's psychopathology" (p. 91).

Other practitioners advance the idea that the analysis of countertransference phenomena is at least as important as the analysis of transference. Among them, Arieti (1961) states that "at times the whole treatment depends on" understanding of the "self-perpetuating reciprocal situation" (p. 71). Countertransference is, in the words of Herbert Rosenfeld (1952a), a "sensitive receiving set" (p. 116) and often the "only guide" to interpretation (1954, p. 140). Harold Searles (1967), who has contributed many clinical observations on the subject, refers to countertransference as his "most reliable source of data as to what is transpiring between the patient and myself, and within the patient" (p. 527). And also, I would add, within the therapist.

In the treatment of the schizophrenic patient, the need for an exquisite balancing of evenly hovering attention with emotional sensibility gives rise to special problems. The present chapter focuses on the understanding of countertransference reactions induced by narcissistic transference, the nullification of their resistance potential, and their therapeutic value. By way of introduction to my views on the nature and scope of the therapist's emotional commitment, I shall begin with some early findings—and speculations—on the phenomenon of negative countertransference.

NEGATIVE COUNTERTRANSFERENCE

Breuer and Anna O.

The discovery that negative countertransference, unrecognized and uncontrolled, may force the practitioner out of his therapeutic role antedates the formal history of psychoanalysis. A clinical mishap of this nature, as well as theoretical disagreement, apparently figured in the departure of Josef Breuer from the field he helped Freud to open.

Breuer's treatment of Anna O. in 1880–1882 precipitated reactions in both parties that are not mentioned in the report of that pioneer case (Breuer & Freud, 1893–1895). Freud subsequently referred to the intense rapport created through the use of the cathartic method in that case as "a complete prototype" of transference (1914b, p. 12). On the basis of information provided by Breuer as well as Freud, Breuer's conduct in the final phase of the relationship could now be identified as the prototype of countertransference—unrecognized countertransference reactions that operated as resistance.

Anna O.'s disturbance, diagnosed as hysteria, manifested itself as a "psychosis of a peculiar kind" (Breuer & Freud, 1893–1895, p. 22). Several authors have expressed the opinion that the condition would now be diagnosed as schizophrenia;

others have diagnosed it as a profound mourning reaction to the death of her father (Rosenbaum & Muroff, 1984). Hypnosis was employed to help her talk out her feelings and, as she did so, her symptoms subsided.

Freud emphasized the pathognomic influence of the young woman's sexual feelings for her father. A study of the case material suggests that she also had strong feelings of hatred for her father that she did not want to recognize. Her transference of affects of both kinds to Breuer apparently induced positive and negative counter-reactions that became fused with his own emotions.

When he realized that his wife was jealous of the attractive young woman to whom he was devoting much time and thought, Breuer suddenly abandoned Anna O. in a state of anger (Spotnitz, 1984). Summoned back to her home later in the day, he found her "in the throes of an hysterical childbirth (pseudocyesis), the logical termination of a phantom pregnancy that had been invisibly developing in response to Breuer's ministrations." After calming her down with hypnosis, "he fled from the house in a cold sweat" and went off with his wife on a second honeymoon. Anna O. suffered a series of relapses in the next few years. Breuer told Freud that she was so sick that he wished she might die and thus be relieved of her suffering.[1] The passages just quoted are from volume 1 of the biography of Freud by Ernest Jones (1953, pp. 224–225). Jones stated that the information he disclosed about Anna O. was gleaned from conversations with Freud; but on the basis of subsequent research the Jones report is now regarded as inaccurate, and it is probably based, in some measure, on speculation (Rosenbaum & Muroff, 1984, chapters 1, 2).

Jones also reported that, in order to overcome Breuer's strong objections to reporting the case, Freud told him about one of his own experiences with a female patient in a state of transference love (1953, p. 250). Breuer, eventually persuaded that he had represented a symbolic as well as a "real" person for Anna O., agreed to collaborate in the *Studies on Hysteria*. How-

---

[1]Over the years, analytic interest in euthanasia has probably covered up many wishes to commit patienticide.

ever, the theory of transference did not revive his interest in conducting psychotherapy. He had learned from the first experience, Breuer stated in a letter written in 1907, that "it was impossible for a 'general practitioner' to treat a case of that kind without bringing his activities and mode of life completely to an end. I vowed at the time that I would not go through such an ordeal again" (Cranefield, 1958, p. 319).

Freud's Views

Freud believed that to experience or express negative feelings for a patient was out of keeping with the professional role of healer. Responding to a patient in other than a mildly benevolent way seemed to Freud unwarranted and antitherapeutic.

When he recognized that patients needed to experience positive feelings, Freud did not object. He described some mildly troublesome feelings such as annoyance, irritation, and surprise, but he seemingly had little difficulty managing his feeling-responses to patients in a state of positive transference unless it got too intense. Referring to the "incomparable fascination" (p. 170) of a woman confessing her passion, he recommended that, were a patient to insist on erotic gratification, the analyst should "withdraw, unsuccessful"[2] (1915b, p. 167). The quotation is from his essay on transference love. Freud did not write one on transference hatred or make any reference to negative countertransference. To the best of my knowledge, he did not talk about hatred for patients or did not recognize such feelings as countertransference reactions. He appears to have had a great need to keep negative feelings out of awareness in clinical work, and he tended to act on them in relations with his colleagues (Wilson, 1981).

Fragments of biographical data, personal correspondence, and the like invite the speculation that the posture of the indomitable surgeon that Freud recommended was not an easy

---

[2]Such withdrawal would now be categorized by many practitioners as countertransference resistance, with the recommendation that it be analyzed, not acted on.

one for him to maintain. He was capable of strong emotions, and there is evidence that he somatized his aggression at great personal cost.[3]

There is an interesting simultaneity in Freud's essays on narcissism and the history of the psychoanalytic movement, both written during the early months of 1914. These works, like the shorter essay on Michelangelo's statue of Moses, penned during the previous autumn, were produced during the period when Freud was deeply immersed in and distressed by the ideological struggles with Jung and Adler. In one letter at that time, he wrote that he was "fuming with rage"; in another, he mentioned "strong feelings of vexation" about the paper on narcissism (Jones, 1955, p. 304).

Yet the desertion of his former "disciples" is discussed with cool restraint and scientific objectivity in the historical essay, despite its polemical nature. The essay on narcissism concentrates on the withdrawal of love, making no mention of the role of aggression in the narcissistic disorders—a puzzling omission. But the outstanding clue to Freud's manner of mastering negative emotions is his personal interpretation of the Michelan-

---

[3]Robert Langs' paper (1984) on the Irma dream of 1895, the first of Freud's dreams that he reported analyzing in detail (1900, Chapter II) reflects on some of his painful struggles during the 1890s, the decade when he was trying to evolve a way of dealing with preoedipal impulses. Exceptionally illuminating is the new information that has recently become available on this crucial period with the issuance of the complete texts of Freud's many letters to Wilhelm Fliess between 1887 and 1904—letters published in their entirety for the first time (Freud, 1985).

These letters suggest that one of the reasons Freud was so negative about dealing with psychotic patients was that, in order to tolerate the aggression they mobilized in him, he had to fortify himself with cocaine, nicotine, and/or alcohol. What he called the science of "dreckology" was difficult for him to master. For example, in a letter to Fliess in 1900, Freud writes callously about a woman suffering from paranoia who hanged herself in her hotel room several days after he dismissed her. Apparently, he used drugs and alcohol as a defense against the feelings such patients mobilized.

gelo work. He saw in the Moses statue a "concrete expression of the highest mental achievement that is possible in a man, that of struggling successfully against an inward passion for the sake of a cause to which he has devoted himself" (1914c, p. 233). At that time, and probably even earlier, in the opinion of Jones, Freud "identified himself with Moses and was striving to emulate the victory over passions that Michelangelo had depicted" (Jones, 1955, p. 366).

Freud discussed hostility and aggression, and pointed out that "hate, as a relation to objects, is older than love" (1915a, p. 139). But he was opposed to expressing hatred to patients. This attitude interfered with his investigating the function of hatred and its role in personality maturation.

With his patients, Freud apparently mastered any urge to communicate hostility that they might provoke. His behavior in the analytic situation reflected his compassionate attitude toward all emotionally disturbed people. But his theoretical objections to the analyst expressing hostile feelings to the patient were also linked with his concern about the development of negative transference. That connection is clearly stated in his discussion (1937) of the possible use of the transference situation to arouse the patient's latent instinctual conflicts:

> We must not overlook the fact that all measures of this sort would oblige the analyst to behave in an unfriendly way to the patient, and this would have a damaging effect upon the affectionate attitude—upon the positive transference— which is the strongest motive for the patient's taking a share in the joint work of analysis. Thus we should on no account expect very much from this procedure. (p. 233)

Although he did not believe that expressions of hostile feelings to a patient were in order, it appears that Freud was not opposed, in principle, to the analyst's use of emotional communication. There is no mention of emotional influence in his formulations of techniques; these argue for the control of feelings by suppressing them. However, two of his posthumously published letters indicate that he gave some thought to the controlled expression of feelings by the analyst.

One of these letters, written in 1899, contains the statement: "From time to time I visualize a second part of the method of treatment—provoking patients' feelings as well as their ideas, as if that were quite indispensable" (1954, p. 280). In the other letter, written to Binswanger in 1913, Freud discussed the controlled use of positive feelings, as follows:

> What is given to the patient should indeed never be a spontaneous affect, but always consciously allotted, and then more or less of it as the need may arise. Occasionally a great deal, but never from one's own unconscious. This I should regard as the formula. In other words, one must always recognize one's countertransference and rise above it, only then is one free oneself. To give someone too little because one loves him too much is being unjust to the patient and a technical error. (Binswanger, 1957, p. 50)

To allot too little hate to a patient who needs to learn to experience and sustain it comfortably is also unjust. To give him too little of any kind of feeling because the analyst has too much is a technical error. The patient is entitled to whatever feelings—positive or negative—are needed to resolve his resistance to mature functioning; but rather than giving rise to countertransference resistance, these feelings should be a source, and tool, of communication.

SCOPE OF THE CONCEPT

The formulations on countertransference that follow apply to *the reactions to the patient's transference attitudes and behavior* (Spotnitz, 1979a).

Other types of unconscious reactions figure in the *totality* of the practitioner's response in the analytic situation. He may develop transferences to the patient, and these are often equated with countertransference. Personal needs, bodily as well as psychological, arouse feelings. So too does indecision about how to proceed at a critical juncture, attributable to inexperience or lack of theoretical knowledge. Reactions to personal needs and professional insecurity that may lead to errors of commission or omission receive more attention in training and supervision than in the literature; but some theorists encompass them in their formulations on countertransference.

These three types of feeling-responses are unobjectionable per se; they do not interfere with analytic functioning if the practitioner can sustain them comfortably. It is desirable that he behave undefensively with a schizophrenic individual and accept all kinds of personal feelings. They do not give rise to counter-resistance unless the therapist is unable to account for them, understand them, and consciously control their expression. When the term "countertransference" is broadly applied to these three types of feeling-responses, however, it is difficult to chart clearly the special right-of-way that feeling-responses to the patient's transference merit in the theory of the technique. It is therefore desirable that the therapist's transference attitudes, unrelated as they are to the feelings of the patient, be clearly distinguished from the therapist's countertransference, which, as defined above, is influenced by the feelings the patient transfers toward the therapist.

The initial focus on countertransference as an undesirable phenomenon has created a generally negative attitude toward the conceptual tool itself. But a value judgment—whether true or false in the immediate circumstances—is removed from the basic concept when countertransference reactions to the patient's transferences that impede treatment are clearly identified as such. For that reason, the terms "countertransference" and "countertransference resistance" are employed as reciprocals of "transference' and "tranference resistance."

These distinctions enable one to obtain an uncluttered view of the relationship as it moves backward or forward or grinds to a halt on the double track of transference-countertransference. This, while an oversimplification, is true in the sense that the analysis and controlled use of countertransference feelings are as vital as the analysis of transference to produce significant change in the schizophrenic patient.

Countertransference feelings do not interfere with progress unless they are regarded as the sole reason for interventions. After the transference has unfolded and the patient is able to verbalize frustration-aggression appropriately, there are times when the therapist communicates the feelings that the patient induces. Decisions to do so, however, are based on an understanding of what it is necessary to do to resolve a current transference resistance.

The practitioner who can tolerate the impact of the feelings transferred by the patient, and clearly identify his own feeling-responses, has at his disposal what Donald Winnicott (1949) calls the "truly objective countertransference . . . the analyst's love and hate in reaction to the actual personality and behaviour of the patient, based on objective observation" (p. 70). These realistically induced emotions are to be distinguished from reactions attributable to insufficiently analyzed adjustment patterns in the therapist. It seems appropriate to classify the latter as *subjective countertransference*.

An analogy from the field of optics may clarify the difference between these two types of reactions. Anyone with normal color vision who closes his eyes after looking at a red light gets a green afterimage. But for a person with abnormal vision, the image may be gray or some other color, depending on the nature and extent of the impairment.

Like the green and gray afterimages, both the objective and the subjective countertransference are aroused by the patient's transference feelings and attitudes. The objective is the predictable response of the emotionally mature observer—one that, in Ogden's words (1982), reflects "mature reactions to the realistically perceived current interaction" (p. 71). The subjective response is atypical, altered in some way by unique tendencies in the therapist.

Subjective countertransference phenomena are usually rooted in distortions created by memory processes. Feelings that the therapist developed for persons who were emotionally significant to him early in life are revived by the patient's symbolic recapitulation of his own childhood experience in the analytic situation. Any tendency to communicate the therapist's subjective reactions impulsively to the patient, whether verbally or in behavior, needs to be recognized and mastered, whether through the therapist's own analysis or through continuing self-analysis throughout the treatment. As Margaret Little (1966) points out, "It is all-important to have one's subjective and objective feelings clearly distinguished" (p. 482).

It is relatively easy in self-analysis to nullify the intrusion of the subjective feelings in the treatment of a relatively well-integrated patient. After their influence is detected and understood, the analyst is able to utilize appropriately the feelings induced in him purely through resonance with the patient's affects.

The "analyzing out" of the subjective countertransference reactions is more difficult in the treatment of the schizophrenic patient, who induces feelings that often appear to be entirely unrelated to him. In a state of narcissistic transference, as I have indicated (Chapter 8), the patient often appears to be out of contact. In response to the patient's latent emotions, the therapist experiences feelings that seem to be extraneous to the relationship and tends to attribute such reactions to unresolved problems in himself (Spotnitz, 1981b). These seemingly extraneous feelings turn out rather consistently, however, to be responses to the transference re-enactments of the patient.

As I learned through personal experience, it is highly desirable, when one begins to work with pathologically narcissistic persons, to be in analysis oneself. In the process of detecting and analyzing emotional phenomena grounded in one's own life experience, it usually becomes clear that some of the feelings experienced with such a patient could have no other source than the patient. Because these feelings are induced by the behavior, communications, and emotions of a patient functioning in a state of narcissistic transference, they are identified in modern psychoanalysis as *narcissistic countertransference* (Spotnitz, 1979a).

Prior to the introduction of the term "narcissistic countertransference" in the literature of modern psychoanalysis in the early 1970s, it was rarely referred to. I have come across only two earlier references to the term. The first is of historical interest but unrelated to the phenomenon to which the term is now applied. Ferenczi and Rank (1925), discussing the analyst's narcissism, refer to it as a "particularly fruitful source of mistakes: the development of a kind of narcissistic counter transference which provokes the person being analyzed into making flattering remarks about the analyst and suppressing unpleasant remarks about him" (p. 41). This statement might refer to the analyst's transference to the patient as a neutral object or to the analyst's subjective reactions to the patient's transference attitudes (narcissistic countertransference of the subjective type).

In the other, much later reference encountered, the term is used in the sense in which it is used here. Clarence Schulz and Rose Kilgalen (1969) identify narcissistic countertransference as a particular problem in psychotherapy of the schizophrenic patient. To illustrate the primitive nature of the therapist's feelings and "symbiotic relatedness" to the patient, they report that, during a supervisory session, a therapist reviewing his notes on the inpatient treatment of a mute catatonic patient "came to one quotation where he was absolutely unable to ascertain whether he or the patient had spoken the particular sentence" (p. 221).

Some analysts who conceptualize the clinical process differently employ terms that are more or less equivalent to "narcissistic countertransference" and "realistically induced feelings." Money-Kyrle, for example, wrote about "normal countertransference" (1956). Gerhard Adler (1967) observes that "constructive countertransference has, of course, to be most decisively distinguished from such undesirable countertransference manifestations as unconscious identifications and projections due to the analyst's unanalyzed neurotic complexes and leading to harmful unconscious involvements" (p. 346). Another Jungian, Michael Fordham (1979), applied the label "syntonic countertransference" to reactions that provide the therapist with constructive information about patients.

Ernest Wolf (1979), writing in the framework of Kohut's psychology of the self, predictably refers to "self-object countertransferences" (p. 455). These provide, in Wolf's words, "the major channel for . . . balanced, controlled empathy which is in the service of treatment and not archaic, controlled empathy" (p. 455). Michael Moeller (1977) views countertransference as the necessary complement of transference and defines it as a "specific non-neurotic reaction" of the analyst to the patient's transference (p. 365). Ogden (1982), focusing on the therapist's response to a patient-initiated projective identification as an aspect of countertransference, points out: "Countertransference analysis is the means by which the therapist attempts to understand and make therapeutic use of his response to the patient." (p. 72).

The creeping-in of the subjective element was long regarded as the source of most countertransference resistance. Understanding of what is going on in the relationship is undoubtedly beclouded when idiosyncratic feelings that developed in the therapist's own interpersonal relations are aroused by the patient's transference reactions and accepted as feelings induced through empathy with him. The present view, however, is that objective countransference reactions—the realistically induced feelings—account more significantly for failures in the treatment of schizophrenic patients than the subjective reactions.

But many therapists working with these patients still do not recognize that the feelings that are actually induced in them by the patient have to be experienced, accounted for, and resolved to produce desirable change. On the one hand, a therapist who fears being so swept up by the countertransference feelings that he will be unable to function well analytically may "barricade" himself, consciously or unconsciously, utilizing *emotional neutrality* as a defense against experiencing the feelings. The emotionally responsive practitioner, on the other hand, may interfere with the full development of transference by failing to sustain the induced feelings silently until their communication would be therapeutic. In short, the resistance potential of countertransference resides more in its objective component than in the subjective. *Utilized appropriately, however, objective countertransference—both the narcissistic and the oedipal types—is a diagnostic aid, an impressive source of information, and a major supplier of therapeutic leverage.* The value of the analytic data it provides has been more and more widely acknowledged.

CLINICAL IMPLICATIONS OF OBJECTIVE COUNTERTRANSFERENCE

The feelings realistically induced in the therapist as a transference object, communicated selectively and in a goal-oriented manner, make a major contribution to the resolution of resistance by meeting the patient's maturational needs. In principle, as I have already mentioned, the gratification of maturational needs is not the function of the analyst. He is primarily concerned with identifying them and helping the patient devise socially approved methods of meeting them. Nevertheless, when preoedipal resistance patterns are upheld by maturational needs whose gratification is not being secured through life experience, the therapist may have to meet them—verbally—in order to resolve the resistance. Specific need-satisfying experiences that will help the patient give up the resistance are provided through emotional communication. Interventions charged with the induced feelings tend to create such experiences.

The objective countertransference also makes a vital contribution to reconstruction of emotionally significant preverbal events that the patient cannot remember. The induced feelings are studied and investigated with the patient, to help him recapture and articulate his own impressions of his early life experience and to correct false impressions. Constructs are based on the combined analysis of the patient's transference reactions and the feelings they induce in the analyst. In some cases the objective countertransference makes the major contribution to the sorting out of the egotized object impressions from the patient's own pre-ego feelings.

In working with a patient who has great difficulty in accepting and verbalizing his own feelings, and who is also hypersensitive to the feelings of others, understanding of one's own feelings and their influence on the patient is of the utmost importance. The analyst who is willing and able to experience the induced feelings deeply and undefensively will find it necessary to remain alert to the source and nature of all of his emotional reactions in the immediate situation. He needs to face and analyze any schizophrenic tendencies in his own personality in much the same way as the analyst working with perverse patients has to "recognize and face both his own perverse core and that of his patients" (Chasseguet-Smirgel, 1981, p. 511). Much introspective study of one's own psychological processes and behavioral tendencies is required to function appropriately as an assembler and effective communicator of understanding to the patient (Epstein, 1982).

The usual prescription is to analyze countertransference when it operates as resistance. This policy is, in my opinion, inadequate, however extensive one's clinical experience. In my supervisory practice, I recommend that all countertransference reactions be analyzed throughout the case. Otherwise, reactions related to unresolved personal conflicts and immediate reality needs easily contaminate the reservoir of emotional reactions that serve a therapeutic intent. In other words, countertransference resistances interfere with one's having adequate emotional reactions to help the patient.

There is widespread agreement that the remedy for acting in terms of transference feelings for the patient is further analysis. Subjective countertransference reactions that stimulate technical errors are often brought to light in self-analysis; if not, they are easily uncovered in supervisory sessions or often, indeed, in informal discussions of the case with a colleague. But the pitfalls in the objective reactions to the transference situation in schizophrenia are relatively unexplored areas.

The "Right" to Sustain Countertransference Feelings

An elementary stumbling-block in the utilization of the objective countertransference is the attitude, often encountered in the inexperienced analyst, that he does not have the "right" to have feelings for a patient. When feelings are regarded as taboo, whether because the therapist has been trained to repress them or does so as a matter of preference, the capacity to communicate is impeded. Inappropriate interventions are often associated with attempts to blot out from consciousness the intense and conflicting affects aroused by the schizophrenic patient. The practitioner's reluctance to experience these feelings serves to accentuate the patient's already *strong opposition to accepting and verbalizing all of his own affects*.

But it is important to recognize that freedom is absolute only as regards the *experiencing* of the induced feelings. Selectivity and timing in communicating them are essential. Many technical errors are avoided when one adheres to the general principle that, although the induced feelings are always raw data for analysis, interventions are never dictated solely or primarily by the experienced emotions. These are communicated only at a time when they will serve the specific therapeutic intent of resolving an immediate resistance of the patient. There is no justification for verbalizing the induced feelings impulsively.

If the analyst's understanding of the resistance he is working on is in harmony with his own countertransference reactions, these may be communicated in accordance with the plan he has formulated for dealing with that resistance. But if there is some *discrepancy* between his reasoning and the induced feelings, he does not intervene. He does not function in any way contrary to his own feelings. He may recognize that one or another feeling-response would help the patient give up the resistance pattern but that feeling must be available at that moment. The impact of the induced feelings on the patient, which is directly proportionate to their *genuineness*, provides therapeutic leverage.

Feelings of confusion about something the patient has been communicating over and over again may point to some unresolved problem in the therapist. If, however, such a connection cannot be established through self-analysis, it may be that the patient is inducing the confusion. When one of his attempts at contact is reflected with a question about the therapist, the patient may indicate that he does not feel understood. Eventually, it may become clear that he had a parent whom he could not understand and who did not understand him. An emotional state that initially appears to be related to a blind spot in the practitioner may prove of great value in reconstructing the patient's relation to a significant object in his childhood.

NARCISSISTIC COUNTERTRANSFERENCE

Countertransference reactions stimulated by a patient's identification of the therapist with objects experienced as separate from the self have been widely discussed. Less attention has been given to reactions to the schizophrenic patient's transference of feelings and attitudes experienced in the process of ego formation—the selfobject feelings (Kohut, 1971), a term equivalent to Glover's "ego nuclei" (1949).

Heinrich Racker called attention to two major components of the countertransference feelings induced in the therapist. His

unconscious identifications may be with either the self component or the object component of the emotional experience with
early objects that is being symbolically re-experienced in the
transference. In other words, instead of unconsciously identifying with the patient's object representations—the *complementary identifications* associated with countertransference reactions
to a patient functioning at the oedipal level—the therapist may
identify with the self aspect of the same emotional experience.
Racker (1957) refers to the latter as *concordant identifications*—
"psychological contents that arise in the analyst by reason of the
empathy achieved with the patient" (p. 312). The notion of
complementary and concordant identifications is helpful in ac-
counting for the conflicting and often confusing emotions
aroused by a patient in a state of narcissistic transference. The
patient's self feelings and attitudes, and at other times, those of
early objects, are induced in the therapist; both types may be
induced simultaneously.

The narcissistic transference also arouses emotions that are
not comprehensible in terms of the same antecedents. The patient communicates the need for feelings that he unconsciously
wanted and did not sufficiently experience in his earliest years.
The therapist may then become aware of strong desires to
"nurture" the emotionally deprived patient. Because these feelings are induced by the patient's anaclitic (psychological dependency) state, I refer to them as the *anaclitic* (or nurturing)
countertransference (Spotnitz, 1983). It encompasses feelings
that the patient needed to become an emotionally mature adult.

Margolis (1978) refers to the analyst's "mothering urge toward the patient" and adds that it is often experienced "on the
most elemental mother-infant level, in which the patient's nee-
diness *per se* is sufficient to stimulate in the analyst the urge to
nurture" (p. 136).

The objective type of narcissistic countertransference may
thus be viewed as a multiple induction experience.

Dominant Reactions in the Course of Treatment

As the narcissistic transference begins to unfold, the therapist has to deal with three types of induced feelings: the self

feelings (concordant identifications), the object feelings (complementary identifications), and the desires to nurture that are induced by the patient's anaclitic state. These feelings are expressed by the therapist in different ways.

On the whole, the therapist wants to be helpful and to respond to the patient with kindness—usually an unconscious defense against feeling the patient's hostility and one's own hostility to the patient. Negative feelings are thus blotted out by positive feelings. (Some of these positive feelings may be anaclitic countertransference reactions.)

Some characteristic reactions of the therapist are listed below in the relative order in which they usually emerge in the course of the treatment relationship.

When the patient feels anxious or talks without affect, the therapist may experience mild anxiety or he may feel strangely unmoved.

When the patient experiences murderous feelings for the therapist and denies them by saying that he wants to kill himself, the therapist may feel like killing the patient (Margolis, 1978)—and then become preoccupied with a personal problem.

A patient who experienced a great deal of emotional deprivation early in life often induces feelings of indifference or unrelatedness early in treatment. The therapist may become drowsy and doze off.

A patient experiencing strong sexual feelings may arouse sexual feelings in the therapist (Spotnitz, 1979b).

When the patient feels hopeless, the therapist may feel sympathetic and compassionate, or he may feel hopeless, withdrawn, and disinterested (Spotnitz, 1979a).

When the patient complains or cries, the therapist may feel impatience or contempt. On the other hand, the therapist may become aware of embarrassment or discomfort.

As the therapist's anxiety is mastered, impulses to be kind and considerate are submerged at times in annoyance. The patient's psychic suffering may induce a sense of satisfaction, even elation.

The repetitious verbalization of the patient's self-attacking attitudes may induce feelings of aversion or boredom in the therapist (Altshul, 1977; Kernberg, 1975; 1982a, Chapter 34).

When the patient explodes with rage, the therapist may experience horror, extreme revulsion, and perhaps, too, a need to protect himself (Altshul, 1980). He may become concerned about his physical and mental well-being.

The therapist may get to feel that the patient is a "terrible nuisance." Often the therapist feels restless; in the middle of a session, he may become aware of an urge to end it forthwith, to find a reason to dismiss the patient early.

When the patient gives free expression to suicidal wishes, the therapist may develop a desire to talk a great deal. Interventions that may be rationalized as needed assurance for the patient may appease the therapist's need to reassure himself that he is helping the patient.

When the narcissistic transference is at its height, the therapist tends to oscillate between states of self-preoccupation and anxiety. He may respond to the patient's autoerotic feelings and delusions with considerable alarm, and become aware at times of desires to "tranquilize" or appease in a friendly manner. He tends to feel more and more removed from the patient, and becomes despondent at times about the patient's immediate state.

When the patient feels helpless and hopeless and the therapist is assailed by similar feelings, instead of acting on these feelings, "the therapist attempts to live with the feeling that he is involved in a hopeless therapy with a hopeless patient and is, himself, a hopeless therapist" (Ogden, 1982, p. 30).

Observing the clenching of fists and bodily contortions that often accompany suicidal wishes that the patient verbalizes or the narcissistic rage he vents, the therapist may experience a more or less realistic sense of danger (Altshul, 1980). Will the patient limit himself to verbalizing hate feelings for relatives or associates, or should they be warned that they are threatened (Spotnitz, 1981a)? And when similar feelings are directed toward the therapist, he may feel that his own safety and that of his family are imperiled.

Eventually such anxieties are dissipated. When the patient lies on the couch in a relaxed position and is able to maintain that posture no matter what he feels, the therapist experiences a strong sense of security and control. He also feels more and more at ease with the patient, more and more interested in sharing his understanding of what has gone on in the relationship. The patient's growing desire for information about his functioning dovetails with the therapist's lively interest in providing it (Kirman, 1980).

The therapist becomes aware of admiration and genuine affection for the patient and also, at times, of strong desires to "mother" or "father" the patient, perhaps both. In a case presentation, for instance, Ogden (1982) reports that he experienced "rather intense feelings of pleasurable closeness and maternal protectiveness" (p. 200). Late in treatment, the anaclitic countertransference (Spotnitz, 1983) becomes a powerful propellant.

COUNTERTRANSFERENCE RESISTANCE

It is important to distinguish between countertransference feelings and countertransference resistance. The former, however intensely they are experienced, do not per se constitute countertransference resistance or provide evidence of its existence. As Margolis points out, "Only the *avoidance* of countertransference feelings or their *misuse* in dealing with the patient's resistance constitute countertransference resistance" (1978, p. 140).

In a state of countertransference resistance, the analyst deviates in some way from the analytic task of helping the patient engage in progressive communication—that is, helping *indirectly*, by removing the patient's resistance to doing so. The schizophrenic individual, when in a state of narcissistic transference, induces strong countertransference feelings. If these give rise to resistance in the therapist, it will not be possible to provide the highly specific responses that the patient needs to make progress.

In addition to the intensity of the emotions generated by the patient, the personality structure of the practitioner may be a source of countertransference resistance. A strong and well-integrated ego is essential to function well analytically with psychotic patients and to control one's behavior under the impact of the feelings they induce. Working effectively with them entails the ability to resolve one's own countertransference resistance or to secure the help of a colleague in resolving it.

Clues

Countertransference resistance betrays its presence in numerous ways. Since many general clues have been reported (e.g., Menninger, 1958; Greenson, 1967), I limit myself here to alerts that sound with increasing frequency in the treatment of the ambulatory schizophrenic patient.

Not all of the evidence is in black and white. There is also gray evidence that requires considerable study before one can determine its reliability.

The list that follows has been culled from my own repertory and from discussions with colleagues and student-analysts.

Listed first are examples of resistant behavior that may be connected with either a positive or a negative state of countertransference. Alerts to the presence of negative countertransference resistance constitute a far longer list.

Positive or Negative Countertransference Resistance

Stopping a session early or late. (Usually negative countertransference resistance in the first instance; usually positive in the second.)

Having difficulty keeping quiet. (A sign of positive countertransference resistance—"overfeeding" to convey how much you care for the patient—or negative, reflecting lack of regard for the patient.)

Finding oneself unexpectedly thinking about a patient between sessions, and in a way that interferes with one's functioning with other patients. (Positive countertransference resistance as regards the patient thought about but negative in relation to the patient one is working with at the moment.)

Forcing one's mind to go in a particular direction. (Whether positive or negative countertransference resistance, this usually signifies a battle for self-control).

Expressing feelings when one has no intention of doing so.

(Usually this is not helpful, but therapeutic effects have been reported [e.g., Tower, 1956].) Such expression signifies a lack of self-control.

Unwillingness to communicate emotion. (Usually motivated by fear of losing self-respect; whether such unwillingness will hinder the patient's progress can be determined only by subsequent analysis.

Usually Negative Countertransference Resistance

"Forgetting" an appointment with one patient and scheduling another for the same time.

Not remembering the name of a patient.

Making an appointment in such a way that the patient is not certain when he is expected—for example, at a quarter to nine or a quarter past. (The best remedy, in my experience, is to ask the patient one or another question dictating that he repeat the time specified.)

Impatience at feeling out of touch with the patient, and objecting to that feeling. (Signifies unwillingness to experience disagreeable emotions induced by the patient, including psychotic feelings.)

Behaving in a way to prevent the patient from saying something one doesn't want to hear.

Responding in a hostile tone of voice to the patient's hostility.

Striving to appear more knowledgeable than the patient (an attempt to demonstrate superiority).

Impatience over the patient's unclear communications or failure to provide analytic material.

Clinging rigidly to one technique. (Hostility or fear usually figures in such a pattern.)

States of anxiety before or after, as well as during the session, which do not appear to be connected in any way with the patient. (In such a state, for example, one may open the door to admit him and observe immediately that he is full of rage.)

Accepting the validity of the patient's feelings that he is incurable (instead of analyzing and investigating the feelings with the patient).

Joining the patient in undisciplined discharge reactions.

Various feelings of anxiety or disturbance that interfere with analytic activity.

Cloudy understanding or misunderstanding of some information that the patient is communicating over and over again.

Major Sources

The need not to feel hate.   In my experience, the main source of countertransference resistance in the relationship with a schizophrenic patient is the therapist's need to defend himself against the rage and anxiety induced by the patient's hostile impulses. Suppression or denial of the induced feelings forecloses their use as therapeutic leverage and also makes it virtually impossible to understand the patient's emotional history.

Complete freedom to verbalize hatred and rage is foreclosed when the practitioner has difficulty asking questions about real or fantasied acts of violence or helping the patient discuss them. Many student-analysts experience strong aversion in the course of such investigations, particularly when they have a great need to deny their own murderous feelings.

The need to be liked.   Bullard (1960) has stated, "To my mind, one serious drawback to effective therapy is the need some therapists have to be liked, to feel that they are appreciated and that their efforts are warmly received" (p. 139). The need to be liked gives rise to powerful countertransference resistance in a case of schizophrenia.

When a great deal of transference hatred is being vented, the analyst feels unhappy because the patient is so hostile. The patient's total unawareness of the great effort being made to help him also hurts and offends the analyst who has a strong need to be liked. The lack of appreciation is resented. Instead of a few drops of the milk of human kindness that may be anticipated, the patient reciprocates with rage. The practitioner may eventually become resigned to dealing with an ingrate. When he is told, "I am not coming again," he may hope that the patient really means it.

The patient may say, "You don't understand me. You are

not helping me. I am getting nowhere." The therapist who is wounded by such accusations tends to get lost in narcissistic preoccupations and doubts—a prey to countertransference resistance. One who is not under pressure to be appreciated has no difficulty saying to the patient, "Let us assume, for the purposes of treatment, that you are correct. Why have I gotten nowhere?"

The need to be right.   Another powerful—and prominent—source of counter-resistance is the need to be right. Under its pressure, the therapist becomes aware of a strong desire always to give scientifically correct and complete interpretations instead of responding to the patient's immediate need for a communication that will have a specific maturational effect.

The beginning analyst is often afraid of saying the "wrong thing" to the patient. One student was convinced that she had done so when the patient complained that she talked like his "horrible" mother. Her reluctance to asking him how he thought she should have talked was resolved when she recognized that the patient's impressions of what she said were more significant than the correctness of her communications. She then felt more at ease when talking to him and was able to do so more spontaneously.

An allied problem arises when there is a strong need to demonstrate competence and earn the patient's respect. The therapist in whom this need is strong finds it humiliating to work with a patient who attacks him repeatedly and on all levels. Since it is antitherapeutic to register disagreement, the criticism has to be accepted and simply investigated with the patient. Hence, there is no opportunity to build up one's self-esteem.

Minor needs.   Another problem brought up by the student-analyst in supervisory sessions centers around the desire to be "good" to the patient and respond to his yearnings for affection. Early in the relationship, a need to be "nicer" than the original object, to soothe, appease, and console, is often experienced—anaclitic (nurturing) countertransference reactions. (If intervening in terms of these feelings shuts off communication, countertransference resistance is operating.)

More than one supervisee has said that when he limited

himself to working on resistance, he felt like a psychopath. The therapist's guilt feelings intensify when the patient asks, "What are you doing to earn your money?" Like the budding obstetrician performing a normal delivery, the student-analyst working with the schizophrenic patient in a state of evolving narcissistic transference usually feels that he has practically nothing to do and wants to intervene much more actively than the situation calls for.

A young therapist consulting me reported difficulties in dealing with an adolescent schizophrenic patient's infantile demands for love. It was the patient's impression that the therapist was silent because he had no interest in the patient. The young man reproached the therapist for not caring, and went on to say that he couldn't talk about anything because he was being kept "in a shell." The therapist admitted that he felt very timid about dealing with the "you-don't-care" resistance. He had lost track of what was going on in the relationship.

In the supervisory session, he became aware that his timidity in responding to the patient's accusations was connected with a fear of "smashing him to bits," as the therapist put it. The patient's demands for assurance that the therapist loved him had aroused a powerful reaction-formation connected with the therapist's own pattern of adjustment to a domineering father.

Awareness of this tendency helped the therapist master his timidity about engaging in emotional communication. Eventually the patient also developed strongly positive transference feelings for him.

When the therapist remains open to the patient's disagreeable feelings and retains the capacity to understand and communicate, the patient experiences a relationship he did not have in the past. Recognition that the analyst can experience the induced emotions and nevertheless behave appropriately unconsciously stimulates desires in the schizophrenic patient to prove to the analyst, and to himself, that he can tolerate disagreeable feelings and still behave appropriately. Refusing to sustain the patient's affects or acting on them in some way to influence the patient to withdraw from treatment are common forms of countertransference resistance in the treatment of severely disturbed patients.

A student-analyst reporting that a patient felt hopeless and miserable added that she felt miserable too. She recognized that she was experiencing what he felt and objected to doing so. "When I feel as he does, I lose sight of what is going on between us. I don't want to be understanding. I just want to kick him out of the office."

After she came to understand that the patient was inducing in her feelings he had experienced from his own mother and that their re-creation in the relationship was a curative mechanism, she accepted the "re-experiencing" as a requisite of successful treatment.

Inexperienced analysts often report that they become enraged with the schizophrenic patient for not functioning as they would like him to in the sessions. They may not recognize that it is their responsibility to find out precisely what is preventing the patient from cooperating and to address themselves to these obstacles.

By and large, the schizophrenic patient arouses a great deal of feeling that one is either not doing enough for him or that one cannot do anything for him. There are periods when the therapist feels that the case is getting nowhere and that it should not have been undertaken. Accepting the validity of these feelings and developing the capacity to sustain them comfortably, neither acting on them nor verbalizing them to the patient except to deal with a current resistance, are often difficult principles to master.

These are the problems that I focus on with therapists who are beginning to work with schizophrenic patients. Such work requires a special kind of supervision and training. Countertransference resistance is analyzed and the fledgling is helped to resolve it in the supervisory session (Spotnitz, 1976b, 1982). The active participation of the supervisee in this process often contributes significantly to his professional development.

SUPPLEMENTARY OBSERVATIONS

Health Hazards

Working with schizophrenic patients and other severely disturbed persons is hazardous for a therapist who is unable to analyze the severe neurotic or psychotic reactions they induce. The therapist may court the development of psychotic or psychosomatic reactions unless he secures immediate help (Spotnitz, 1963). For example, a student-analyst who was treating a patient suffering from Hodgkins disease said that he was experiencing the very feelings the patient complained about.

Whether or not exposure to the intense and disagreeable countertransference experience can produce actual mental or organic illness in the therapist is still an area for research. But it is undoubtedly hazardous for a therapist who has not undergone analysis himself to treat schizophrenic individuals.

Years ago an associate of mine (who withheld the fact that he had not been analyzed) developed intense resistance to experiencing rage and other intense emotions; he consistently repressed them in working with severely disturbed patients. Blocked against verbal expression, the induced feelings found release in paroxysmal attacks of tachycardia, a heart condition from which he eventually died. In order to work with these patients productively without endangering one's own health, one must be able to feel, recognize, and put into words the induced feelings.

Nonverbal Processes of Communication

It is usually assumed that the primary communications are from patient to analyst. In treating an extremely narcissistic individual, it is helpful to operate on the assumption that two-way nonverbal communication goes on from the initial contact without either party necessarily being aware of it.

Since the origin of a feeling immediately experienced is often unclear and may not be established for a long time, it is desirable to remain alert to two possibilities. One is that the patient may be inducing the feeling. During a session when a therapist became aware of strong feelings of irritation that he could not account for, he asked the patient if she found him particularly irritating that day. She replied, "How did you know? You must be a mind reader. I was just thinking on my way to the office that my husband was terribly irritating this morning." It is also possible that what appears to be a transference reaction of the patient may be a counter-reaction to the therapist's unverbalized feelings. At a time when the therapist is experiencing a personal grief, for example, the patient may ascribe the feeling to himself and—perhaps for the first time—begin to mourn the death of someone who was very significant to him.

Character problems may develop if the patient egotizes his perceptions of the analyst's feelings as a defense against feeling his own. Such emotional identifications may lead to transient improvement, but they make it more difficult for the patient to develop full awareness of his own true feelings and to act in terms of them. He is unable to become a fully integrated personality, and continues to feel that he is a stranger to himself.

Problems of this nature are avoided when the analyst helps the patient to discriminate between his self-feelings and the object feelings he egotized early in life. Techniques of resistance joining (illustrated in Chapter 10) facilitate the arousal first of the egotized object feelings. After these are de-egotized, the patient is helped to articulate the self-feelings.

Freedom to Function

Considerable ego strength is required to function comfortably and undefensively while sustaining the murderous feelings of the schizophrenic patient and utilizing them for his benefit. If the feelings are denied, it is impossible to get to understand how they are aroused in the relationship and how the patient defends himself against them. If, on the other hand, awareness of the induced feelings leads the practitioner into states of paralyzing anxiety, the patient is denied the relatively secure atmosphere he requires to mature emotionally.

What is primarily required of the analyst is a high degree of self-command, wedded to emotional responsiveness. By emotional responsiveness, I mean openness to the patient's transference feelings and the induced feelings *without* being swept up in them and thus swayed away from goal-oriented functioning (Epstein, 1982).

The analyst *does not reveal his emotional responsiveness in his manner of conducting the treatment.* (This operational principle is stressed because I have observed that it is often violated.) The amenities of the professional relationship are consistently observed. He greets the patient courteously on arrival, gives explanations in a polite manner, and does not show offense at insulting or provocative remarks. He conveys the attitude: My feelings are not important. What is important is getting to know you.

Self-command entails the ability to tolerate the mistakes one makes without being unduly disturbed by them. It is often easier to absolve a sense of guilt by confessing or denying them. But to admit or deny one's errors to a schizophrenic patient before he is able to verbalize his resentment freely is rarely desirable. If a patient accuses me of making an error, I may ask him, "Assuming that you are right about my making a mistake, where does that lead us?"

Usually the patient wants to know if the analyst, over and above his professional commitment, is really interested in helping him. There is always some testing-out on that score. Instead of either denying or admitting personal interest directly, it is often a good idea to investigate with the patient the therapeutic implications of granting or refusing the special requests he makes or the favors he seeks. The analyst presents himself, in effect, like the gruff parent doing his duty. Eventually the patient recognizes that the analyst is genuinely interested in him and has been permitting him to make that discovery for himself.

Chapter 10

INTERVENTIONS:
RANGE AND SEQUENCE

The basic "psychosomatic" function of speech (the central ve-hicle of psychoanalysis) I regard as the original bridge over sepa-ration between mother and infant, continuing in adult relationships, largely replacing the original bodily intimacies.
—Leo Stone (1981a, p. 97)

Voluntary communication with a patient in the analytic sessions is of two types: one can be silent or one can talk. Silence is mentioned first because, measured in time, it is the more important—and more difficult—activity. As the matrix for effective nonverbal communication, the analyst's silence also catalyzes or permits growth in the preoedipal personality. Nonverbal communication goes on even though voluntary silence is maintained.

Early in treatment, for instance, when the patient developing a narcissistic transference requires a virtually inanimate presence—preferably someone who does not even breathe—*motionless silence* communicates the message: I do not want to disturb you in any way. *Shared silence*, characterized by unobtru-

sive changes in position, tells a person who in one way or another has been expressing a wish to be silent that the practitioner
is not waiting impatiently for him to talk. Fidgeting, coughing,
and jerky movements create a *restless silence*, which may tactfully
convey the contrary message.

The decision to intervene—that is, to communicate voluntarily—is a matter of theoretical significance. In order to max-
imize the patient's own capacity for successful functioning in life,
the psychoanalyst, as a practitioner of indirect psychotherapy,
observes the principle of parsimony in communication. Since it
is desirable that the patient's personality should be the product
of his own input, the therapist exerts no more influence than
necessary to facilitate the sought-for changes in the patient's
behavior. Interventions are made primarily to resolve resistance.

That was the purpose Freud had in mind when he reported on his psychotherapeutic activity in Chapter IV of the
Studies on Hysteria. His first formulation on technique also suggests both the broad range of resources at the practitioner's disposal for removing the "continual resistance" and what he strives
to accomplish by doing so.

These resources, Freud states, "include almost all those by
which one man can ordinarily exert a psychical influence on
another." Patience is advocated because resistance "can only be
resolved slowly and by degrees" (emphasis added). Reckoning on the
patient's development of intellectual interest, one may, by "explaining things" and giving information about psychical processes, turn the patient into a collaborator, and "push back his
resistance" by inducing him to regard himself with "objective
interest."[1] Once the motives for the patient's defense have been
discovered, the "strongest lever" is to "deprive them of their
value or even to replace them by more powerful ones."

To the best of one's power, Freud continues, one works as

[1]Rather than bank on the development of intellectual interest, I recommend that explanations be withheld until the patient displays a
genuine interest in obtaining them. The schizophrenic patient rarely
demonstrates a hunger for intellectual information before completing
several years of treatment.

elucidator, teacher, and father confessor, giving absolution with sympathy and respect. One gives, too, as much human assistance as one's personal capacity and sympathy for the patient permit. An "essential precondition" for this activity is to divine the nature of the case and the motives for the defense, for the patient frees himself from his hysterical symptom by "reproducing the pathogenic impressions that caused it and by giving utterance to them with an expression of affect, and thus the therapeutic task *consists solely in inducing him to do so*[2] (Breuer & Freud, 1893–1895, pp. 282–283).

But disappointments ensue if one banks on arousing the schizophrenic patient's intellectual interest or tries to woo him into collaboration with human assistance and sympathy. Even today, some analysts recommend a warm and outgoing manner to establish a relationship with a schizophrenic patient. In my experience this is *contraindicated*. Instead, it is desirable to maintain an attitude of reserve, to be cool, *until* the patient has developed the capacity to release hate tensions comfortably in emotional language and, in addition, displays a strong intellectual interest in cooperating in the treatment and in understanding it. Otherwise, the information may be utilized destructively.

Nevertheless, Freud's earliest account of his technique, unencumbered as it is of strictures against noninterpretive communications, conveys admirably the purpose and spirit of interventions in a case of schizophrenia. The reference to patience is eminently pertinent. It applies not only to silence but also to saying one thing over and over again with all the verbal dexterity at one's command. The repetition is essential. Like a young child, the schizophrenic individual has to be *induced* to master the obstacles to intrapsychic growth, without being exposed to undue pressure. This is, inevitably, a gradual process.

The principle of intervening only when and as much as necessary to resolve resistance transcends unrealistic dichotomies in technique, such as that between the so-called passive and

[2]An important precondition, as viewed by the modern psychoanalyst, is that the patient's resistance to reproducing the pathogenic impression be resolved with the help of the analyst.

active approaches. In recent years the need for *specificity* has received growing emphasis—varying degrees of activity and inactivity and the precise types, or series, of interventions that would effectively resolve the resistance being worked on at the moment. With some schizophrenic patients, it is possible to function silently for long intervals; other patients require a great deal of activity immediately. Moreover, as patterns of resistance change in the course of the treatment, so too do the types of interventions to which the patient responds. Indications and contraindications for dealing with these patterns constitute the basis for a comprehensive and logical system of interventions.

Competently trained practitioners, regardless of their theoretical orientation, are usually well versed in the various techniques needed; however, guides to administering them with maximum psychological effectiveness are lacking. The beginner in the field tends to base his interventions on a priori notions that certain types are necessary, rather than giving consideration to what each might, or might not, accomplish in a given situation—the important factor.

An intervention is of value only when it helps the patient move out of a pattern of resistant behavior that is being engaged in "right *now*." He may express attitudes that are immature or irrational, but as long as he is verbalizing these spontaneously and with affect, nothing is gained by interrupting him to conceptualize the attitudes. The value of an interpretation of content is determined by its immediate impact on the here-and-now resistance. When a patient is not functioning cooperatively, it is a good rule of thumb not to intervene until one understands the current resistance and has decided what to do about it.

The beginner may have difficulty, too, in grasping the principle of sequence in interventions. This applies not only in dealing with a single manifestation of resistance, which usually entails a series of communications, but also in responding to its myriad manifestations throughout the case. As the general character of resistance changes, any one type of intervention may become more or less necessary than it was at earlier stages of treatment. The sequence itself is not invariable; it has to be *discovered* for each patient.

By and large, however, effective interventions in a case of schizophrenia move in the direction of more complex levels of communication, ranging from commands and brief questions to explanations and interpretations. The unconscious communication in the order in which they are introduced is that the analyst understands the patient's need to assimilate simple communications before tackling more complex ones. The psychology of verbal feeding parallels the principle of infant feeding—no solid food on a regular basis until it is psychologically digestible.

Any type of intervention that helps the patient say what he really feels, thinks, and remembers without causing narcissistic injury (Lucas, 1983) is designated as a *maturational communication*. Early in the case, a brief question that helps the patient articulate impressions of external realities (an aid in managing the fragmentation resistances that usually develop when interest is shown in his symptoms, dreams, and fantasies) is a maturational communication.At the other end of the continuum is the interpretation that is given when requested, and when it will help the patient articulate his own thoughts and feelings. (Interpretations given in the line of duty to share an insight with the patient without regard for the immediate consequences may have the contrary effect.) The therapeutic intent underlying the maturational interpretation is to help the patient talk progressively, rather than repetitively.

Many communications that have a maturational effect reflect the old adage: If you can't lick 'em, join 'em. The analyst often responds to a "stonewall" resistance in that spirit, whether to bring the resistance into focus, to manage it, or to help the patient outgrow the need for it. The term "joining" denotes the use of one or more ego-modifying techniques to help the patient move out of a repetitive pattern.

Indirectly, by reducing the pressure for impulse discharge, the joining of resistance has the effect of reinforcing the preoedipal personality. Conceptualized in different ways, this approach figures in various systems of psychotherapy—e.g., Viktor Frankl's technique of paradoxical intention (1960)—although its value and indications for its use are not always specified. Resistance-joining, in my view, should be employed in indirect psychotherapy only to help the patient function cooperatively in the treatment relationship by removing an immediate obstacle to communication. The resistance is joined, positively or negatively, for the express purpose of helping the patient give it up.

The patient's words may be repeated, with or without feeling, in a question or declaratory statement. As has been pointed out (Eissler, 1958), the effect of such repetition may be equivalent to an interpretation. An unverbalized attitude may be joined. But resistant *behavior* in the sessions (acting in) is outside the realm of resistance patterns that are supported. The therapist frustrates it by a calm and contemplative attitude, or discourages it more actively when the behavior is clearly destructive to the treatment.

In presenting the innumerable emotional confrontations engaged in to manage a "stonewall" resistance, monotony is avoided. Genuineness of feelings, based on the objective countertransference, and freshness of encounter make important contributions to the effectiveness of these communications (Davis, 1978).

Some are experienced by the patient as pleasant, others as unpleasant; the difference often depends on the tone of voice in which the intervention is made. When the effect is ego-dystonic, negative feelings are mobilized and defenses against verbalizing them are activated. When the patient talks disagreeably, agreeable joining may mitigate the strength of the resistance to being disagreeable. (I have observed that initially supervisees tend to feel that they "said something wrong" when a patient verbalizes a negative reaction to an intervention, but eventually they learn that helping the patient develop the ability to express negative as well as positive feelings is one of the aims of the treatment.) Agreeable joining may result in the patient feeling comfortable and understood. When ego-syntonic communications mobilize positive feelings, the therapist works to reduce the patient's resistance to verbalizing them.

In the section that follows, types of interventions that are frequently and productively employed with the schizophrenic patients are illustrated. These characteristic communications are discussed in the sequence in which they are usually presented in the course of the treatment. The interventions include commands, questions, explanations, joining, mirroring, and reflective procedures, and maturational interpretations.

Sequence in interventions is then discussed in the context of transference resistance. Successive approaches to the dominant resistance—the pattern of bottling up destructive aggression in its myriad forms—are illustrated.

COMMANDS (ORDERS)

The preferred intervention when the treatment gets under way is the command. Commands are not issued to secure obedience. The therapist's intent, rather, is to find out whether the patient wants to obey or defy and to help him communicate why he wants to do so—in other words, to mobilize resistance and, eventually, to resolve it.

"Lie on the couch and talk" is a typical formulation of the fundamental rule for the schizophrenic patient. Instead, he may be ordered to "tell your life story" or "talk." (As already pointed out, the patient is *not* asked to engage in free association.) Pertinent reminders of the rule are phrased in similar terms.

Commands that are formulated in terms of the patient's resistive attitudes are often effective. The patient may say, for example, that he is not going to talk any more. A reminder that he is supposed to talk tends to intensify the resistance of a negatively suggestible person, but if he is told, "You've talked too much. Keep quiet for the rest of the session," he may reply, "I will not"—and continue talking.

To give another example: commanding a patient who is out of control to cry has the effect of restoring his control so that he continues to talk. One may speculate that as a young child the patient was told by a parent: "Don't cry." Instructing him to cry reverses the pattern. This is an example of positive versus negative mirroring, based on paradoxical intention.

An explanation of the realistic basis of the command is more likely to resolve the resistance of a positively suggestible person. For example, in reflecting the resistive attitude of a woman who "really didn't want to" remain on the couch, the therapist said that this was not mandatory but preferable. He then helped her to verbalize all of her objections and these were discussed. Some of them had some validity and this was readily conceded. The therapist said, "I am not trying to make you as comfortable as possible, but to do what is best for the treatment." The woman raised no further objection; the explanation also helped her to recognize that she had the right to assert herself in the relationship.

Countercommands may be issued. When ordered to do something by the patient, the therapist may say, "You do it." A patient who commands the therapist to "Keep quiet, " may be told, "You keep quiet too." "Tell me," "Say it," and other brief statements in the imperative mood are often made.

Marshall (1982) illustrates a number of joining techniques "oriented toward supporting *and* resolving narcissistic resistances" (p. 62), which he regards as the interventions of choice in dealing with preverbal patterns. On the use of a similar technique with a negatively suggestible nine-year-old boy who engaged in assaultive behavior in treatment sessions, Marshall reports:

> As I became more aware of his extremely contrary nature while I tried to set limits, I ordered him to act in a destructive manner. Behind a barrage of "Who says so?" "Who's gonna make me?" etc., he behaved in a pleasant manner, but lapsed into silence. I then ordered him to maintain his silence, at which point he launched into a series of reproaches, arguments, etc., which revealed important material and provided grounds for discussion. Later, when I ordered him to speak unpleasantly to me and not about nice things, he spoke of the fun of his vacation. (p. 69)

Because the therapist in this instance orders the patient to engage in resistance, Marshall refers to the technique as "prescribing the resistance" (p. 69).

For patients who do not respond to questions, commands may serve as effective alternatives. I became aware of this many years ago when a young woman indicated that she could not tolerate being questioned. When I asked her why, she could not give an immediate explanation. Eventually she recognized that her distress at being questioned reminded her of a very painful period when, following an appendectomy, she developed an abscess. She continued, "My doctor came in every day and put a probe into the wound. And every time you ask me a question, you put that probe in again. I can't stand it." When I inquired whether she could stand being given orders, she said, "Order me all you want to." Eventually that solved the problem.

On the other hand, one occasionally encounters a patient who responds angrily when commanded to do something or feels that he is being attacked. Apparently, what matters is not whether one questions or issues an order to a patient, but precisely what that communication suggests to that patient—how it is being perceived (Spotnitz, 1981b). One needs to begin employing an intervention tentatively while studying its effectiveness and adapting it to the needs of each patient.

QUESTIONS

Commands are usually followed by questions. These may be positive (expressing interest) or negative (expressing depreciation, or meeting dissatisfaction with dissatisfaction). In addition to initiating questions, the therapist usually counters the patient's questions with questions.

At the beginning of treatment, the therapist usually asks only factual or object-oriented questions. It is preferable that these be posed when the patient addresses the therapist. As Meadow has pointed out, "Contact functioning replaces the subjectively determined timing of classical interpretation with what might be called "demand feeding," in which the timing and type of communication are what the subject asks for" (1974, p. 92).

Factual Questions

Because of the patient's characteristically vague manner of reporting an external event, it may be opportune to query him about such elementary details as when and where it occurred. The patient may also be asked for the names of people he has mentioned, or to identify books, theatrical productions, and the like by title. To reassure a patient who becomes anxious about doing so, the analyst may let him know that he (the analyst) is interested in obtaining the facts.

Questions may also be asked to clarify or highlight the repetitive nature of the patient's communications. A patient bogged down in fulsome praise of his parents may be asked, "Are your parents really wonderful people?"

Grilling for Evidence

Without in any way challenging the validity of a delusionary idea, the analyst may investigate it with the patient. Investigations of that nature are appropriately carried on late in treatment.

For example, after at least a year of treatment, a patient who attributes some feeling of his own to the analyst may be asked to provide the evidence. A series of questions (condensed) that helped a patient recognize that he was projecting his own anger is presented below.

[P (shortly after entering the office): You are angry at me.

A: What makes you think so?

[P: When you opened the door you had an angry expression on your face.]

A: Did I look angry when you left here yesterday?

[P: No. You smiled in a rather friendly way.]

A: Then why should I be angry with you today?

[P I don't know why. Come to think of it, as I was coming here today, I began to feel angry at you because you didn't answer that question I asked you in the last session.]

A: Why should I be angry at you because you are angry at me for not answering that question?

[P: Maybe you aren't. But I thought you were because I was angry at you.]

A: How are we going to settle this question?

[P: It's settled. You aren't angry at me. I'm angry at you.]

The analyst may also ask one question after another when the patient "egotizes" (introjects) feelings. When, for example, a woman said she was very fatigued 15 minutes after entering the office looking fresh and vigorous, the analyst asked, "You've been coming here so often at this hour, and this is the first time you've complained of fatigue. How do you account for it?" She tried to do so on a realistic basis. After each explanation she advanced was investigated with her, she began to suspect that the feeling of fatigue might not be connected solely with her own experience. Further questioning led her to conclude that she had detected signs of weariness on the analyst's face when he opened the door to the consulting room. And she had not wanted to say so, she explained, out of fear of displeasing him.

Object-Oriented Questions

The second series of questions, countering the patient's introspective tendencies, draws attention to external objects as a factor in the patient's repetitive communications. Margolis (1983b), in a detailed discussion elucidating the significance of the object-oriented question, emphasizes that its basic function is to resolve resistance to communication. Its uses for that purpose, Margolis adds, "embrace a range of occasions extending from the solely protective to the most complex analyst-patient transactions" (p. 37).

At a time when the patient has been complaining repetitiously, for example, the therapist may inquire, "Have I been disturbing you?" or whether someone has been disturbing the patient at home. A patient who has been crying may be asked such questions as "Did I do something to upset you?"; "Am I causing you unhappiness?"; "What can I do to make you more comfortable?"

By verbally assuming some degree of responsibility for the distress, the therapist draws attention to what others might have done to cause it or might do to alleviate it. The questions often suggest that the therapist is a person of unlimited power. (Examples of this "egomaniacal" approach are given later.)

Ego-Oriented Questions

Questions that direct the patient's attention to his own functioning are rarely asked in early stages of the relationship.

Eventually, the schizophrenic patient becomes capable of talking about himself in an emotionally significant way, and when he demonstrates that he can do so without becoming more self-absorbed, the analyst begins to pose a third type of question. Three series of ego-oriented questions that are often asked late in treatment are illustrated below.

The key to analytic cure. A person who has been complaining about his own inadequate functioning may be asked what he expects to accomplish through the complaint. An investigation of his wishes and expectations often leads to a discussion of his ideas about how the treatment should be conducted. The drift of the questioning is suggested by the interchanges that follow.

A: Suppose you convince me that you are as inadequate as you say you are, where does that lead us?

[P: That will help you treat me.]

A: How will it help me?

[P: Then you will understand me.]

A: How will my understanding help you?

[P: It will help me get well.]

A: Understanding alone doesn't help anyone get well. I have been demonstrating understanding and you are not getting better.

[P: Then how am I going to be cured?]

A: What cures you is dealing successfully with whatever interferes with your talking out your feelings, thoughts, and memories as they occur to you here.

Investigations of the patient's theories of analytic cure continue until the initial resistances to progressive communication are given up. This may take weeks or months.

The patient's expectations. Rather than pointing out directly that a pattern of resistant behavior is motivated, consciously or unconsciously, by an unrealistic expectation, the analyst may insinuate as much in the course of tactful questioning.

A severely disturbed young man who was asked how he thought the treatment should be conducted said he would like

the therapist to "behave differently." In response to further
questioning, he said that he would like the therapist to suffer as
much as he did, to say things that would help him feel better,
and not to charge for the treatment.

The therapist replied that he would consider suffering with
the patient, giving him free treatment, and communicating what
he would like to hear. "But I would like you to explain to me
how such behavior would help you get well."

When the patient's ideas are repeatedly explored with him,
he usually gets to recognize that they will not further treatment. He may then be willing to consider the therapist's plan of
operation and stop working at cross-purposes.

The analyst's shortcomings.   During the transitional phase
(oscillating transference states) the patient may be asked for his
impressions of the analyst and his problems. The usual reaction
is surprise or indifference. He doesn't really know the analyst;
hence his views would be of no value. Such questions should be
put to someone more competent to answer. It is frequently suggested, "Return to your own analyst if you need help."

But the practitioner conveys the idea that what he wants to
hear are the patient's impressions. "You are sensitive to people.
If you will tell me what you think of me and help me with my
problems, perhaps I can be more helpful to you and other patients."

EXPLANATIONS

When the treatment is undertaken, explanations of its requirements are brief, and given primarily in response to direct
questions from the patient. It is repeatedly stated that whatever
the analyst says in the sessions is said just to help the patient talk
out the feelings, thoughts, and memories that occur to him at
the moment—not to influence his behavior outside the relationship.

Occasionally, as a means of facilitating rapport, the analyst
volunteers information on subjects raised by the patient—the
news of the day, social and cultural events, and the like. In such

discussions, the analyst does not voice personal opinions. He presents different points of view on controversial topics and consistently parries the question, "What do *you* think?" Explanations of behavior follow the same pattern. The patient is helped to verbalize impulses to engage in destructive behavior as well as constructive behavior, and the possible consequences of each course are delineated. Alternative solutions to a problem are explored, and their respective advantages and disadvantages are pointed out.

After the first year of treatment, explanations of unconscious mechanisms are provided at the patient's request. While the narcissistic transference is evolving, however, such explanations are communicated mainly to control the frustration level rather than to promote understanding.

During the transition from the preoedipal to oedipal phases of the treatment, information is given when it would facilitate communication and withheld when it would have the contrary effect. Asked, for example, if he has read a book mentioned by the patient, the analyst may say, "Why do you ask?" If the patient replies that he would like to discuss it, he may be told, "It is better to discuss the book without knowing whether I have or have not read it." The patient, if cooperative, will then verbalize his impressions of the book. The analyst may then say, "I have (have not) read the book."

Although he does not answer questions that would make it easier for the patient to report his own experiences and perceptions, the analyst usually confirms an accurate perception of himself as a person after it has been adequately explained. Asked, for instance, if he was taking a walk in Central Park Sunday afternoon, he may say, "Why do you want to know?" The patient who replies, "I thought I saw you there," is asked for concrete details. After he reports the exact time and place, the analyst may say, "You are correct."

As the patient reveals more and more about himself, the therapist is justified in revealing some information about himself. In the process of helping the patient to undress psychologically—to reveal his impulses, feelings, thoughts, and memories—it is usually desirable for the therapist gradually to shed the anonymity that necessarily cloaks him, as a transference object, at the beginning of treatment. From the point of view of developing a more equal relationship, the more emotionally mature the patient becomes, the more the patient is entitled to know about the analyst; eventually, the stage is reached in which the patient gets to know a great deal about the analyst as a real person. In other words, as the patient improves, the welcome process referred to as "dissolving the transference" goes on. After the transference resistance has been resolved, there is no justification for the therapist remaining a phantom figure.

Hiding behind one's professionalism is an attitude that patients resent—justifiably. To be treated as an inferior by their partner in a prolonged, intimate, and deeply human relationship is an example of irrational deprivation (Stone, 1981b), as well as a humiliating experience. I emphasize this fact after encountering a goodly number of beginning therapists who labor under the impression that they are not supposed to reveal any information about themselves no matter how many years they work with a patient.

JOINING TECHNIQUES

Preoedipal resistance patterns are rarely responsive to objective understanding. The term "joining techniques" is loosely applied to a number of basically similar interventions to manage these patterns, particularly those reflecting preverbal functioning. In making the interventions, the therapist supports and may even reinforce continued operation of the resistance until the patient "develops the awareness and ego strength to replace it with a more adaptive and controlled behavior pattern" (Marshall, 1982, p. 87).

Examples of various joining techniques follow. By and large, all of these interventions communicate the same message to the patient: I am like you. Which strategy is employed to convey this idea depends on what the therapist has to do to appear like the patient.

Joining and mirroring are both ego-modifying techniques. They are employed to deal with preverbal resistance patterns, usually those containing aggressive impulses that were stultified. In joining a resistance, the therapist agrees with the patient's words or his conscious or unconscious attitudes. In mirroring, the therapist operates as a twin image. The patient wants to make contact with agreeable, similar objects, and will attack a dissimilar, disagreeable object if he feels it is safe enough to do so. The formula seems to be as follows: If you are enough like me and like me enough, it will be safe to attack you if I am convinced I will not be injured in the process.

Ego-Dystonic Joining

Ego-dystonic joining is employed primarily to facilitate the discharge of negative affects. Various examples of this approach are illustrated below.

Weather.   When a patient complaining monotonously about the weather asks, "Isn't it pretty nasty?" the therapist may say, "Do you think it could have something to do with the barometric pressure?" On another occasion he might respond to the same question by asking, "Do you think the weather is hexing you?" or "Do you think it reflects your nasty disposition?"

Falling apart.   In working on a compulsive repetition the practitioner may question the patient for some time and then make statements that reflect the pattern, whether faithfully or in a somewhat exaggerated manner.

A patient who repeats that he is becoming confused, feels unreal, is losing his bearings—"falling apart," as he often puts it—may first be asked some factual questions. For example, when had he first experienced such feelings; were they troubling him that very moment; could they be connected with something happening in the session? Should he continue to complain, he may be asked if the analyst might be arousing the feelings. The patient may then be asked, "What reason might you have for making yourself fall apart?"

Instead of asking a question, the analyst may say that he feels unreal and confused too. As he repetitively reflects the pattern blocking emotional release, he may indicate different degrees of confusion—"somewhat confused, but not as much as you," "much more confused," and so forth.

Saturating with suggestions.   If the patient seeks advice, the practitioner may ask, "What makes you think that I will advise you?" The frequent retort, "I'm paying for it!" may meet with the reminder, "You are paying me to analyze you, not to advise you."

Often the analyst saturates the advice-seeker with suggestions or recommendations. Many possible courses of action are objectively outlined, and the patient is helped to verbalize freely his reactions to each alternative.

But this approach rarely satisfies him. Usually he wants to know "what you would do in my place." The therapist may then inquire, "What difference would it make to you if I tell you what I would do?" If the patient answers that the information would influence him in making his own decision, the analyst may say, "Why should you permit me to influence you in any way?"

Meeting threats with threats.   "No action, just talking please," the analyst may say. His reminders that all force is to be turned into language may be gentle, pleading, persuasive, or phrased more sternly.

A person who threatens to leave "if you don't talk to me" may be told, "If you don't talk the way I want you to, I may terminate this session now." Obscenities and insults may be countered in similar vein.

When a college student stubbornly maneuvering for control hinted that his father might not let him come any more, the analyst said, "Unless you get your father to agree, I may stop the treatment." Another young man, trying to force the analyst to talk to him, shouted that he would "get off the couch and bash your head in." The analyst responded, "I'll bash yours in before you can get off the couch."[3]

Echoing the ego.   In illustrating this ego-strengthening

---

[3]Repetition of the threats serves to assuage the patient's guilt about them.

266 MODERN PSYCHOANALYSIS OF THE SCHIZOPHRENIC PATIENT

procedure for highlighting a pattern of self-attack, Nagelberg and Spotnitz (1958) hypothesized that it might have the effect of reversing the "original process of ego formation, when the infantile mental apparatus failed to release hostile feelings toward its earliest object since the latter was experienced as being too distant. . . . contribut[ing] to the formation of a pattern of directing these impulses back upon the mental apparatus" (p. 796). Of interest in this connection is the observation that schizophrenic patients use echopraxia (repetition of actions seen) to get close to another person (Day & Semrad, 1978).

In employing the echoing procedure, the analyst may say, "I agree with you" to a person who has been low-rating himself, or repeat his statement with some degree of exaggeration. A patient harping on the idea that he is the "worst person alive" may be told that he is the worst "who ever lived." Usually he indicates that, though he is really as worthless as he presents himself, he would rather not hear the analyst say so. Convincing echoing of this nature thus has the effect of eventually shifting the target of the attack from ego to object.

Repetitive evaluations of the superior or mediocre "I" may also be greeted with a "yes you are."

Overevaluating the object. Instead of echoing the ego, the therapist may present himself as its psychological twin. In the process of reflecting the patient's repetitive evaluations of himself as the "greatest," the therapist talks at times like an egomaniac. Highlighting the vainglorious attitudes of an extremely self-centered person, he may say, in effect: I am all-powerful, omniscient, the only person in the world who can help you. This series of interventions usually fosters the development of the "idealizing" aspect of the narcissistic transference.

Devaluating the object. At other times, in mirroring the patient's sticky references to himself as the most inadequate or contemptible of human beings, the analyst chimes in with a "me, too!" He presents himself as depressed and humble, proclaiming, in effect: I'm a failure too. The patient's attitude may be reflected faithfully or in a somewhat exaggerated manner.

Powered with the emotional charge of the objective countertransference, this series of interventions is presented *after* the patient has acquired some feeling for the analyst as an external object. The characteristic aspect of the narcissistic defense—the lowly ego prostrating itself before the wonderful object in order not to risk the loss of its valuable services—is worked on in this way for the purpose of facilitating the discharge of aggressive impulses.

Almost inevitably, the time comes when both parties feel that the treatment has failed. The analyst's interventions (summarized here)[4] genuinely reflected his feelings at the time the interchange reported below took place. In that session, his efforts to reverse the flow of mobilized aggression from ego to object proved successsful. The mirroring procedure resolved the patient's resistance to "letting go" (relaxing defenses).

A young woman complained that she felt like a "lifeless shadow." She couldn't assert herself in social situations; besides, she was never asked out on dates.

A: Obviously I haven't helped you.

[P: I apologize for painting such a gloomy picture. It is I who have failed, not you.]

A: I have failed you.

[P: You make me uncomfortable when you say that. I prefer to think that I am at fault. I tell you I'm a failure to annoy you but I'm really not because I don't do or feel a thing.]

A: I'm responsible for that.

[P: You can show me how to walk but you can't walk for me. What's the point of blaming you if I don't want to move? In a way, though, you're right. I ought to be wanting a husband instead of always sitting alone and doing nothing. Now you're making me feel terrible. Why must you get me so worked up about things? I hate to say it, but you really should have helped more than you have. No, that isn't true. I haven't cooperated. I should have talked more freely.]

A: You have talked freely.

[P: Are you certain? You're right. I've told you everything

[4]The dialogue is reported more extensively elsewhere (Nagelberg & Spotnitz, 1958, pp. 799–800).

but it hasn't helped. What about all the time and money I've put into this treatment? If you get me to believe you, I'll be too mad to ever come again.]

A: Why can't you be mad and still come? Even if I have failed, all this can change. I can begin to understand you if you'll help me.

[P (shouting): That would be a cheap way out for you, but if you haven't helped me by now, you never will. Besides, since when is it *my* job to help *you*? If you need help, go and see an analyst yourself.]

A: You have spoken freely here, but you have not attempted to help me make you as popular as you want to be. We could work together to accomplish this if you would display more initiative.

[P: . . . I hate you too much to help you. My foot! I'll help you into the grave. If I let it sink in that you've botched up my treatment, I'd go crazy, scream, and cut my throat. No! It's you who ought to go to prison for getting me into such a state. I was too nice to tell you what I thought of you before, but now I'm so mad I don't care. I ought to report you and sue you for my money. If I tore you to pieces I could plead insanity and get off scot-free. . . . You've gotten me into a mess and now you'll have to get me out of it.]

A: Why don't you get *me* out of it?

[P: I wouldn't lift my little finger to help you. (laughing) You see how I hate you when you don't let me have my way. If you won't let me win, I won't let you either, even if my whole treatment goes up in smoke. Now you see how furious I can get when I let myself go. And there's still plenty of anger inside me.]

"Outcrazying" the patient. The therapist, talking in a serious manner, may carry to the point of absurdity a hare-brained scheme or unrealistic idea preoccupying the patient. [*Exaggerated mirroring*]

A man who harped on his intention to publish books on microcards was asked if he had also considered the possibility of publishing newspapers, bankchecks, and personal letters on microcards. It was suggested to another man, boasting incessantly of his ability to design a motion picture projector that would make him a fortune, that he ought to invent one that would flash pictures on a screen in a distant location. "You're a real crackpot," he exclaimed.

Through such interchanges, the notion emerges that if the analyst, with all his crazy ideas, can live in the real world, the patient too should be able to cope with it.

Suicide or patienticide.   When the patient verbalizes self-hatred and thoughts of suicide, the analyst may say, "I hate myself. I feel like committing suicide too." (An illustration of *egodystonic, negative mirroring* leading to verbal attack on the object.)

[P: You don't mean it. Why would *you* want to kill yourself?]

A: Do you think I like to sit in this dark room hour after hour listening to a hateful person like you?

[P: Go drown yourself!][5]

An ego-oriented approach (ego-dystonic joining) to the same repetitive pattern may eventually be employed when the practitioner can comfortably communicate murderous feelings for the patient who habitually talks of wanting to destroy himself. A series of interchanges (over many sessions) that led to the externalization of the patient's impulse to kill is outlined below.

[P: I hate myself. I feel like killing myself.]

A: Sometimes I hate you and would like to kill you.

[P: You wouldn't do it. You don't hate me.]

A: Why wouldn't I hate you? Why wouldn't I feel like killing you?

[P: Maybe you do feel like killing me, but I'd rather do it myself.]

A: If your life really isn't worth living, why deprive me of the pleasure of putting you out of your misery? You're entitled to a mercy killing.

[P: Do you really mean it?]

A: Why shouldn't I mean it? Some physicians recommend

[5] If the patient expresses sympathy, the intervention is unsuccessful, its purpose being to facilitate the verbal discharge of aggressive impulses.

euthanasia to relieve intolerable and interminable suffering. I might be glad to cooperate.

[P: How would you go about it?]

A: There are plenty of ways to do it. I'll describe them and you can take your pick. Would you like to leave a suicide note?

[P: I'm beginning to think you would really enjoy killing me off.]

A: Why shouldn't it give me immense pleasure?

[P: To hell with you! I'm not interested in giving you pleasure. I'd rather kill you first.]

Success! The aggressive impulse that was first attached to the patient's ego has been redirected toward the object; it becomes the target of a verbal attack.

The schizophrenic ego usually malfunctions because the primary object that influenced its formation failed to meet the infant's maturational needs. The analytic process may be viewed as one involving the removal of the defective internal object and replacing it with a good object.

The interpretation that the patient hated the parent at one time and now hates himself, however correct, would not remedy the situation. Correcting the defective functioning, and then understanding what caused it, is more constructive; it reduces the tendency to revert to the original pattern. The ego-modifying techniques just illustrated are directed toward that goal.

Ego-Syntonic Joining and Mirroring

Anna Freud's account (1926) of the initial phase of her treatment of a ten-year-old boy implicitly conveys the spirit of ego-syntonic joining:

> At first, for a long time, I did nothing but follow his moods and humours along all their paths and bypaths. Did he come to his appointment in a cheerful disposition, I was cheerful too; if he were serious or depressed, I was the same. . . . I followed his lead in every subject of talk, from tales of pirates and questions of geography to stamp-collections and love stories. (p. 9)

Illustrations of agreeable joining and mirroring procedures follow. In some instances, it will be noted that the analyst
gives positive directions by command or example.

Warm acquiescence.   The analyst may associate himself
verbally with a patient's negative views of members of his family, or mankind in general. For example, if the patients says that
his parents are "impossible people," the therapists may express
agreement. If the patient advances the opinion that analysts are
no good, the rejoinder may be, "I agree with you. Even I'm no
good at times." If he says again and again that the world is a
ghastly place filled with revolting people, the analyst may say,
"You're right. We're all going to hell!" [*Joining*]

The analyst may indulge in an emotional outburst against
someone the patient is talking about. A student, reporting a
mortifying experience, said that one of her instructors had rid-
iculed her before the whole class and denied her the opportunity to defend herself against his unfair criticism. The therapist
exclaimed, "What a terrible instructor! He had absolutely no
right to treat you that way." [*Joining*]

When a man leaving the office castigated himself for using
the session for relief rather than work, the therapist remarked,
"You have the right to waste an hour." "O.K. This is my wasted
hour," the man said. He was told, "And I'm the bad analyst who
permitted and helped you to waste it." [*Joining and mirroring*]

The analyst may respond with praise and encouragement
when the patient refers to a desirable course of conduct or says
that others are in the "same boat." If, for example, the patient
clings to the idea that he needs a "good night's sleep," he may
be told that the therapist also needs one. A student who reported attending a late party with his girlfriend was told, "She
probably wants one, too." Later, the response to the communication may be, "A good night's sleep would do you a world of
good." [*Ego-syntonic mirroring*]

Modeling new behavior.   In applying himself to help the
patient talk and act in harmony with his conscious wishes, the
analyst may, directly or indirectly, model an appropriate pattern of behavior.

He may say, while reflecting the emotional attitude of a patient, "You feel like a pretty worthless human being."

[P: That's what I've been telling you.]

A: You shouldn't agree with me. You should tell me to keep quiet.

[P: That's right! You talk too much. You shouldn't say such things to me.]

A young man who repeatedly verbalized fantasies of cutting off his testicles and melodramatically offering them to his mother was asked if he would castrate himself for the analyst. The idea terrified him; he could say nothing. The analyst asked, "Why aren't you furious with me for asking that question? Any person who makes such a demand on you should be told to go to hell." The young man laughed uproariously for 5 minutes. The intervention resolved his preoccupation with terrifying castration fantasies (Spotnitz, 1961b, p. 36).

Helping the ego.   Occasionally, when a patient repeatedly questions his ability to do something he feels would be in his best interests, the analyst may offer to help him or do it for him. (An intervention that would have the effect of silencing the patient, however, is out of order.) The analyst makes the kind of offer that will mobilize the patient to talk of making the effort himself.

A young man harboring misgivings about preparing for a career more or less mapped out for him felt unequal to discussing his own wishes in the matter with his father. The analyst asked, "Would you like me to talk to your father?" After the pros and cons of such an intercession were explored for several sessions, the patient decided to make the explanation himself.

MATURATIONAL INTERPRETATIONS

Obstacles to progressive communication are not conceptualized as ego defects. The analyst explains them in terms of cause and effect, as normal personality tendencies whose excessive development was inevitable in a special set of circumstances; no other alternative was possible. The patient who asks, for example, why he is so narcissistic may be told, "You were very deprived early in life and developed problems that are difficult to deal with. As a result, you frequently become self-absorbed." The situation is explained in this ego-syntonic manner when the patient wants an interpretation and when, in the analyst's judgment, it will help the patient respond with additional feelings, thoughts, and memories. Eventually, the patient receives total explanations of the significant patterns of transference resistance.

The potentially therapeutic responses that the patient can make are those that contain his concealed impulses, feelings, thoughts, and memories (listed in the general order of their hierarchical organization in the mind). When verbalized, they carry with them a feeling of genuineness; the analyst recognizes that the patient has, at that moment, been totally honest.

Like Strachey's notion of the mutative interpretation (1934), the maturational interpretation is formulated to produce change, and it is formulated to effect that change with a minimum of suffering. It is acceptable to the patient because he does not feel that he is being attacked (Spotnitz, 1963).

It should be borne in mind, however, that whether an interpretation is maturational or not depends not only on the way it is presented but also on the setting and circumstances. For example, an interpretation that is acceptable and proves helpful to a patient in the one-to-one relationship may provoke injury or rage if given at an early stage of the group therapeutic situation, when the patient does not want the other members of the group to have any derogatory information about him. (An interpretation made in the group setting appears to have a more profound effect on the patient and to involve much more of the personality structure than in the dyad.)

Interpretations are presented in the same sequence as questions. The repetitive pattern is described first in terms of general experience, far removed from the patient's ego. Later, utilizing the evidence at his disposal, the analyst couches his explanations in terms of the family, the patient's own objects. Later the interpretation may be made in terms of the internalized object, and then in terms of the ego. In short, interpretations are given when the patient wants them, can assimilate them, and can use them constructively.

If, for example, the patient asks why he hates himself, the

analyst may point out that many people do so because in their childhood they preferred hating themselves to hating their parents. The feelings of self-hatred are then interpreted in the context of the patient's earliest interchanges with his own parents and other significant objects. Interpretations presented late in treatment may be dominated by the theme: You hate yourself because you hate the way you behave.

A patient with strong guilt feelings about masturbation may repeatedly ask whether he should give it up. The analyst does not convey either approval or disapproval. He may say that masturbation does give people pleasure because it eases sexual tensions; on the other hand, it tends to isolate them. Hence, while it may be desirable to limit such indulgence when one wants to be sociable, it is a good idea to masturbate more when one does not want to be sociable.

If the patient continues to bring up the subject, the therapist may tell him what other patients have reported about their masturbatory activity and their experiences in giving it up. Standard interpretations are provided later if the patient is really interested in understanding his own masturbatory urges.

Crying and other preverbal resistance patterns may be interpreted to a schizophrenic individual after it has been demonstrated that they are temporarily reversible. Until then, questions about the patterns are responded to with counterquestions and reflective interventions.

SEQUENCE AND TRANSFERENCE STATES

Narcissistic Transference (Early Stage)

A well-conducted analytic session is usually characterized by mild deprivation (to facilitate the release of the schizophrenic patient's aggressive impulses and feelings) followed by mild gratification later in the session. The defensive methods the patient utilizes to avoid discharging aggressive affects are psychologically mirrored by the analyst early in the session. Ego-syntonic interventions preferably follow so that the patient may leave the office in a state of relative comfort. The interventions

should not be so positive as to discourage the patient from expressing negative feelings or from finding fault with the therapist. These are the general principles for conducting the
sessions although they are not implemented consistently
throughout the treatment.

Directions (usually issued as commands) and questions alternating with statements reflecting the patient's repetitive
statements are the dominant types of interventions throughout
this stage. The analyst, by asking a few questions of the patient
who does not attempt to make contact during the sessions, ed-
ucates him (by identification) to the idea that he may ask them;
in the process, the analyst provides a disguised form of verbal
feeding. The patient is told that talking freely on any subject is
cooperative behavior; he is helped to articulate his disagreeable
impulses, feelings, and thoughts.

Usually the patient becomes aware during this period of a
host of feelings he does not want to experience. He may solicit
help in changing those feelings so that he will constantly experience "good" feelings. Inasmuch as the therapist has the task
of influencing the patient to verbalize *all* of his feelings, and
preferably the unwanted ones first, there is apt to be a conflict early
in treatment over the patient's desire to "feel good all the time."

A patient who repeatedly says that he is miserable may be
told, "You have a right to be miserable." If he says he is very
disturbed, the analyst may say, "You may feel disturbed as long
as you are willing to report it. What is important is not the feeling itself but verbalizing it."

A patient who becomes restless and says he wants to get off
the couch may first be asked why he feels that way; but if he
becomes insistent, the analyst may inquire, "Why don't you get
off the couch if you're so uncomfortable?" A patient who says
he doesn't feel like talking may be told that he is supposed to
talk whether he feels like it or not. If he complains that he is not
being given any information, the therapist may ask, "Why
should I?" or "Why don't I give you any information?" Answers
to such questions are elicited and discussed to help the patient
release hostility in graduated doses, thus reducing the danger
that he will react explosively as his dissatisfaction with the treatment situation mounts. (Even when his objections are repeat-

edly explored, the patient may shout, "Damn you, I didn't expect just to lie here and talk.")

Questions focused on himself help the analyst recognize and understand any temptation to provide more verbal sustenance than is necessary to manage resistance. He usually becomes aware of strong desires to alleviate discomfort, which is appropriate, and to assuage hostility, which is undesirable. If the analyst maintains too positive an attitude—is excessively gratifying—the patient tends to regress into psychosis. In order to become emotionally healthy, the patient needs to be helped to operate consistently in terms of some verbalization of hostile feelings. The practitioner must therefore not behave in such a way as to discourage the expression of such feelings.

When, for example, a patient complains of feeling miserable outside the office, the therapist may feel like suggesting ways of alleviating that misery. His main task, however, is not to help the patient feel less miserable outside the office, but to help him say everything. A therapeutic art that needs to be exercised with some schizophrenic patients is to make suggestions in such a manner that the patient reacts negatively to them and feels justified in expressing his resentment.

Initially, the therapist limits himself to interventions that will facilitate the unfolding of the narcissistic transference. As long as it is needed for therapeutic purposes, he also refrains from asserting himself in any way that would dissolve it. He does *not*, for instance, tell a patient who jumps off the couch and threatens violence, "Calm down, I'm not your mother (or father)." When such incidents are reported in supervision, I usually point out two ways of dealing with them. One can explain to the patient quickly and firmly that he belongs on the couch; he can get up if necessary but it would be better to remain there. It is perfectly all right for him to feel as he does about it, but getting off the couch isn't entirely proper behavior. On the other hand, the analyst may make an interpretation pointing out the significance of his own behavior, such as "You jumped off the couch because I stirred up too much emotion." Such an interpretation tends to facilitate the verbalization of hostility by the patient.

In the process of investigating the patient's request for information without providing it, the analyst accepts distorted perceptions of himself. In responding to a suspicious patient who asked, "Are you an FBI agent?" the therapist indicated that the patient was permitted to verbalize his hostility and negative opinions of the analyst:

A: Why do you ask?

[P: If you are, I won't come here anymore. If you aren't, I'll consider coming.]

A: In that case, if I wanted to keep you as a patient, I would have to say that I am not an FBI agent. If I wanted to get rid of you, I would tell you that I am one.

[P: Do you really mean that?]

A: Do you think I would lie to you?

[P: Yes, I think you'd lie. I don't trust you. I guess there's no point asking the question.]

At other times when the patient verbalized the same suspicion, he was asked questions to the following effect: What if I do work for the FBI? Why do you think I do? What would I get out of working for the FBI? Assuming that you are correct, why do I work for the FBI? Why might I want to report you? What information about yourself do you want to hide?

Narcissistic Transference (Full Development)

In addition to continuing to facilitate the verbal expression of negative feelings by the patient to the therapist, interventions at this stage are designed to help the patient move from the narcissistic to the oedipal transference state.

The narcissistic-transference resistance, now very strong, is resolved primarily by joining or mirroring it. Whatever patterns the patient manifests are reflected.

If he says, for instance, that he feels horrible and is getting worse, the analyst may say, "You know, I am beginning to feel horrible. I think I am getting worse myself." [Mirroring]

A person who says he can no longer lie on the couch may be told, "It's about time you found the couch intolerable and wanted to leave it." [Joining]

When he says repeatedly that he is hopeless and incurable, the analyst may say, "You are doing fine. You are telling me just what you feel. The question is whether I am hopeless and cannot cure you. As long as you tell me what you feel, think, and remember, the only issue is whether I am able to deal with your feelings. Maybe I am hopeless, maybe I don't have the ability to cure you." [*Joining*]

Various joining techniques, such as those already illustrated, highlight the repetitive behavior. The same type of responses may be made repeatedly, or various series may be alternated until the unconscious emotional charge motivating the repetitive communication is released in language.

Oscillating Transference States

Preoccupation with the analyst becomes an increasingly significant theme in the patient's repetitive communications. For instance, after saying that he feels miserable, he may continue, "No, it's you who are miserable. You are making me feel this way." The analyst may say, "Assuming that I have a miserable effect on you, how am I producing it? What can I do to alleviate it?" Characteristically, the patient answers that he doesn't want to think about you; he just wants to tell you that he feels terrible. The analyst may then ask, "Why should I help you feel better if you won't help me? Why won't you tell me what I am doing or saying that makes you feel so miserable?"

As the analyst continues to focus more attention on himself, the patient becomes more aware and preoccupied with him. He communicates this awareness, and talks to an increasing extent of feelings for the analyst as a separate person. At such times, a repetitive pattern that was previously reflected may be explained. Instead of continuing to investigate the patient's distorted perceptions in a noncommittal manner, the analyst may now deal with them on a realistic basis. He may state, to return to an illustration given earlier, "It wouldn't make any sense to report you to the FBI."

Eventually, the patient gets tired of being joined in his immature attitudes. Sated with the confrontations of his old ways of thinking and feeling, he tends to communicate more progressively. As he turns to new ideas and experiences, he wants to hear something new. The analyst gives maturational interpretations with increasing frequency during this period.

In a state of object transference, the schizophrenic patient becomes increasingly aware of positive feelings. If he seems embarrassed about expressing them, the analyst may say, "Why am I not putting you at ease?" Such resistance usually responds to the standard approaches.

Hypocritical stage. In the process of moving out of old ego states and habituating himself to new modes of functioning, the schizophrenic patient characteristically reports that he is uncertain how he wants to behave. He feels like an actor offered a choice of roles, and may say that, in order to discover which is most natural for him, he has to try out all of them. He may equate genuineness with totally undisciplined and uncontrolled behavior, and cling to the idea that he is a hypocrite when he behaves otherwise.

In joining this resistance, the analyst may say, "You certainly should feel like a hypocrite if you behave properly when you don't feel like it." He may explain, "All people are hypocrites. One learns to be a good one by behaving properly in social situations whether one feels like it or not." Repetitive lamentations over the difficulty of becoming a genuine personality often yield to reminders that Shakespeare envisioned all the world as a stage and all men and women as "merely players."[6]

Conjoint (combined) treatment (Ormont & Strean, 1978) is especially helpful in resolving problems that surface during this difficult phase of oscillating transference states. For example, other members of the group provide models for desirable behavior.

Object Transference

Investigation is the keynote of the final phase of treatment. Many questions are asked to help the patient engage in self-analysis and verbalize his own ideas of his problems. As much

---

[6]The patient may report a new or stronger interest in dress and the social proprieties during this period. Some individuals enroll in acting courses or join amateur dramatic or dance groups; others avidly read books on etiquette.

additional understanding as he wants is communicated at the rate at which he can assimilate it. Responding to evidence of progress in this pursuit with praise and admiration, the analyst, in effect, presents a paradigm of the genuinely loving parent.

The patient is often keenly interested in exploring his life history and every aspect of his current behavior; he may even want to know how the treatment was conducted. Any explanations he may solicit about the initial therapeutic strategy or precisely how one or another hypothesis applied to his own case are in order after the frustration-aggression problem is solved.

But even when he understands himself, he manifests the old resistant attitudes at times. When they are recognized, the analyst employs the joining procedures to which the patient was most responsive in the early stages of the case. Explanations of the infantile patterns that crop up again are rarely helpful; the patient is usually aware of them and discouraged by his backsliding. He may say that, if the analyst isn't discouraged, he ought to be. "I haven't changed," one woman said. "Why are you working so hard to cure me?" Her own fantasy world, I told her, was far nicer than the one she was entering. Why then should she enter it, she wanted to know. I replied, "Because I want your company in this miserable world."

Toxoid response.   In the process of stablizing the more mature reaction patterns that the patient has formed in the relationship, the analyst also tries to immunize him against any tendencies to revert to the schizophrenic reaction should he encounter highly stressful situations in the future. On suitable occasions, the feelings realistically induced by the patient's transference behavior are fed back to him in graduated doses— toxoid responses (Spotnitz, 1963).

Among analysts who view themselves as recipients of the patient's projective identifications, this process is conceptualized in terms of containing and returning the feelings aroused by these projections. In the words of Ogden (1982), "the recipient psychologically processes the projection and makes a modified version of it available for reinternalization by the projector" (p. 36).

Toxoid responses, made with considerable caution to prevent undesirable reactions, are continued as long as the patient responds to injections of the induced feelings in an explosive way, clams up, or demonstrates some other regressive tendency. When he recognizes the therapeutic intent of these interventions and indicates that he has had enough of the "old stuff," this series of maneuvers has served its purpose.

A stubborn resistance in the case of a young man who entered treatment after a psychotic breakdown was what he called the "excruciating torture of torturing myself about torturing myself" (Spotnitz, 1961b, p. 36). The pattern was given up and other regressive tendencies were resolved after a long period of analysis. When it was nearing completion, at a time when the patient was happily married and beginning to enjoy life, he entered the office one day in a gloomy state. His persistent reports to persuade his employer to modernize his methods of doing business were getting nowhere, the young man reported. It was a great mistake for him not to have let well enough alone; it was his own fault that the boss was giving him such a "hard time." He berated himself again and again for trying to improve matters.

When the old pattern of self-torture was recognized, the patient was joined in this idea:

A: Why do you keep on tormenting yourself when your efforts are not appreciated?

[P: What gave you that idea?]

A: Didn't you say that you are unable to put your ideas across?

[P (after a pause): What are you up to?]

A: Don't you think your boss would have accepted your proposals if you had presented them in a convincing manner?

[P: Cut it out. You're torturing me again the way I used to torture myself. I've had enough of your accusations.]

A: Do you really mean that?

[P: Absolutely. I don't need any more lessons in self-torture because I don't intend to torture myself any more.]

A: Any time you want to start again, I'm ready to help you.

[P: Don't worry. I'll never give you the chance.]

INFLUENCING ONE RESISTANCE PATTERN

Different approaches to one repetitive pattern of communication facilitate the patient's shifts from destructive self-preoccupations to preoccupation with the analyst and, eventually, to a desire to understand how his personality developed. The thumbnail sketch that follows baldly suggests the general nature of the interventions at consecutive stages of treatment when the patient was bogged down in self-recrimination.[7]

Narcissistic Transference (Early Stage)

The patient says, over and over again, that he is very uncomfortable. He doesn't know what is wrong, but is irritated and annoyed with himself. He feels blue and complains of many other disturbing feelings. Nothing else matters.

The therapist studies the feelings the patient is inducing to secure some understanding of the latter's attempts to involve him emotionally. The induced feelings also guide the therapist, and may at times be expressed, in the object-oriented questions with which the therapist responds to questions the patient asks. For example, the therapist may ask: When did these feelings first occur? Who made you feel that way? Do your feelings have anything to do with me? (A few such questions may be asked in the session if the patient does not solicit information.)

Characteristic answers to these questions are that the patient doesn't know or that it "doesn't matter when these feelings developed." The patient just feels terrible. The feelings have nothing to do with the analyst. Why are you asking me such questions? They don't help me.

Narcissistic Transference (Full Development)

The patient complains that he is getting worse. He is continually annoyed and irritated with himself. He hates himself more than ever, and he couldn't feel more hopeless than he

---

[7]Interventions in terms of the treatment schema presented in Chapter 3 are illustrated elsewhere (Spotnitz, 1977, 1979b).

does. He goes around all day thinking that nothing can be done for him. He can't stand himself. Can't anything be done to help him?

A: What could I possibly do that would help you?

[P: I don't know. I only know that I'm feeling worse. I hate myself for it. Can't you do something for me?]

A: What do you want me to do?

[P: Say something to me?]

A: What would you like me to say?

[P: I don't know. But can't you say something to relieve me?]

A: Would it do any good if I told you that I feel miserable and hopeless, that I hate myself?

[P: No, that doesn't help. You don't help me at all. I just can't stand this. I hate myself so. I can't stand what I think and feel.]

A: I have to tell you I'm beginning to feel the same way. And do you know, I can't stand the way I am feeling.

[P: I don't believe you. You don't mean it. You are just talking and imitating me. This is a terrible state of affairs. I feel worse every time I come here. Nobody helps me. Nothing happens to relieve my terrible gloom and torture.]

A: I am getting gloomier, more miserable. I feel you are not helping me.

[P: Why should I bother about you? You can worry about your own problems.]

A: Then why should I worry about your problems?

[P (laughing): When you asked me that question, I felt better. Don't ask me why. I don't know.]

Psychological reflection of the repetitive complaints makes the patient feel that the object cares and accepts him as separate.

Oscillating Transference States

[P: I feel terrible. I wish I could get away from myself. I tell you how much I hate myself, but you just sit there like a mummy and don't do anything to help me. All you do is imitate, mock me, pontificate. You seem to have yourself on your mind all the time—how miserable you are. You aren't the least bit interested in me. Here I am in this miserable state and you don't even try to tell me why I feel so miserable.]

A: Why should I tell you that? What good will it do?

[P: You ought to do something to earn your fee. At least explain something to me.]

A: What good would that do? You won't feel any better than you do now.

[P: That may be true, but I want to know what is going on. You could satisfy my curiosity. If I have to wallow in this misery, I'd like to know at least what it's all about.]

A: Why should I give you information just to satisfy your curiosity?

[P: Stop being such a stingy bastard and tell me something! You really can't be as heartless as you appear. If you are, I ought to chop your head off. I just wish you were dead. You should drop dead this minute.]

A: You are trying to make me feel hopeless.

[P: I'll have to kill myself. Oh no, I will kill you first. I can't leave this world with a horrible person like you in it. If I have to die, you'll have to die first.] (*Vacillating between self-hatred and object-hatred.*)

Object Transference

[P: Gee, do I hate you! More than anyone I've ever known. I've gone through terrible suffering here, and you haven't raised a finger to help me. All you do is ask stupid questions and make flippant remarks. I never believed I could hate anyone this much. Do you think I could ever have hated my mother or father as much as I hate you?]

A: Did you ever hate your mother?

[P: What comes to my mind is hating her when she wouldn't let me go for a ride with father. Did I hate her then! And she hated me. She was so annoyed with me because I wanted to go with father. I didn't want to stay with her.]

A: How old were you at the time?

[P: I must have been two or three. I know I was about that age when father bought a new car. Mother wouldn't let me go out with him. She hated me so. Tell me, is that true? Could she really have hated me, and could I have hated her?]

A: What you have been telling me ever since this analysis began is that your mother hated you. She hated to take care of you; at times she found you a great nuisance. She was very busy with her writing and household chores, and wanted you to play quietly by yourself. She felt like murdering you when you wouldn't obey her.

[P: That is true, all of it. But are you saying that I've been hating myself all these years because she hated me? Is that what you mean?]

A: That's it.

As these discussions continue, the relationship between the patient and his parents is reconstructed and its emotional reenactment in the analysis is fully verbalized.

CONCLUDING OBSERVATIONS

In applying himself as a maturational agent in terms of communication function, the practitioner does not limit himself to the interventions to which I have given primary attention. The schizophrenic patient also requires the types of communications one usually makes to other patients. Those I have focused on, however, are the most necessary to deal successfully with narcissistic-transference resistance, as well as the most difficult to provide.

The student-analyst reading this chapter will undoubtedly find these interventions easy to grasp intellectually, and anticipate little difficulty in making them. Face to face with the patient, however, the story is quite different. Both his own feelings and those of the patient will interfere with full commitment to these emotional interchanges. Yet they are necessary, and need to be engaged in at the proper instant in terms of the actual transference-countertransference state of the moment.

What is most characteristic of such interventions is the attitudes of extremism they convey. In the early encounters with the schizophrenic patient, one perceives a strangeness, an uncanniness, an absence of something that makes one uneasy and anxious. As one gets to know him and accepts his verbal attempts at contact as cues to intervene, one recognizes that too much or too little in interpersonal relatedness apparently patterned the schizophrenic reaction. One is inclined not to talk for exceedingly long intervals or to talk too much at brief intervals. But actually to operate in that manner would expose the patient to extreme frustration alternating with inordinate gratification, both of which are undesirable. As Stone points out (1981a), in analytic work "overstimulation or excessive gratification as well as irrational deprivation" (p. 106) are to be avoided.

The therapist's initial posture is that of a student learning about the patient's functioning. What is learned will eventually be shared with the patient. Initially, however, the therapist presents himself as like the patient, in order to facilitate ego transference. In responding to the patient's contact functioning, rather than introducing anything "foreign" into the relationship, the therapist utilizes the induced feelings (objective countertransference) as much as necessary to help the patient engage in progressive communication. The therapist recognizes that he is being rewarded for dealing with a resistance successfully when he becomes the target of an emotional explosion or, preferably, a mild negative reaction. ("Blowouts" are undesirable.)

A study of the verbal mimicry engaged in suggests the nature of the subjective impressions that mobilized the hostile reactions that the patient failed to discharge fully. The mobilization and discharge of anger and rage free the patient to function cooperatively. When these outbursts are explored with him, he reports dreams, fantasies, or memories. The process of reconstructing his early impressions of the original situation and removing the "foreign" object impressions from the ego field of the mind is thus facilitated by the liberating force of the interventions.

When the interventions that proved most effective in resolving narcissistic-transference resistance are reviewed, the therapist recognizes why he was responded to more impressively when he presented himself as a nonentity or dictator than when he "came across" as an average human being. Apparently the patient experienced his early objects as extremists who provided either too rich a feast or a famine in human relations.

The patient's recovery requires an emotional relationship with an analyst who can at first appear to be like the extremists of the patient's childhood. Later the analyst presents himself as a moderating force. He demonstrates openness to the patient's suggestions for resolving any apparent counter transference resistance.

The Essence of Recovery

When narcissistic-transference resistance is at a maximum, the patient appears to be bogged down in an involuntary repetition of a few basic and essentially gross feeling-tones of early childhood. He sounds like an old-fashioned music box playing the same unappealing tunes over and over again. When the most powerful resistances to communication are resolved, he develops many nuances and refinements in feeling. Eventually he is able to experience the full range of human emotions. As he expresses them in the analytic relationship, one observes, in a sense, the emotional evolution of a human being. Eventually he acquires the rich "orchestration" of the mature personality.

The successfully treated individual commands an abundance of behavior patterns. Since he can express his feelings in socially appropriate ways, he does not have to go out of contact, however great the provocation, to prevent himself from behaving destructively. He is also able to accept and tolerate the emotions of other people. Emotional perceptiveness and easy responsiveness change his whole orientation to life. He can relate comfortably to people and face up to painful realities without resorting to the old narcissistic defense. No longer does the patient present evidence of his old pathological patterns except through careful diagnostic testing or skillful interviewing, which may reveal traces of his past limitations.

The recovered patient conveys the attitude that he has completed a voyage of self-discovery. "I'm just beginning to know what I'm really like," one woman said. Many patients feel that they have found a loyal and constant companion in the genuine self that can communicate in the language of feelings.

They experience this new awareness of feelings as an important asset in dealing with the contingencies of life.

Recovery does not mean that all difficulties have melted away or that new problems will not be encountered in the future. But the patient can now grapple with problems as a total personality and is thus in a position to resolve the primary fixations through re-educational methods (Glauber, 1982, p. xiii). There is a notable increase in the patient's capacity for self-fulfillment and happiness, and he can sustain the impact of traumatic events with considerable resiliency. He has developed the tolerance and understanding to entertain and resolve psychological conflicts of ordinary magnitude.

The fully recovered patient is able to recognize and describe the analyst's shortcomings, to criticize the treatment process constructively, and to suggest improvements in the analyst's approach. The patient, if called on to do so, can describe the factors that led to his illness and identify those that were essential for his progress.

The patient can understand other people; he knows what makes them tick. He can accept differences in perspectives and attitudes. He impresses his relatives and associates with his effective functioning at home, at work, and in social situations. He is a more sociocentric human being than when he entered treatment. He demonstrates that he can live among people with a sense of emotional integrity and self-respect, and that he prefers it to the isolation of living behind the stone wall of narcissism.

Obviously, modern psychoanalysis is dedicated to achieving far more than transforming a miserable human being into one suffering from common unhappiness—the therapeutic expectation stated by Freud (Breuer & Freud, 1893–1895) and repeated by Blum after nearly a century of clinical experience and expansion of psychoanalytic theory. Warning against overoptimism and high expectations in the treatment of the severe emotional disorders, Blum remarked that "classical analysis does not terminate with an ode to joy" (1982, p. 976).

The patient who has successfully undergone modern psychoanalysis emerges in a state of emotional maturity. With the full symphony of human emotions at his disposal, and abundantly equipped with psychic energy, he experiences the pleasure of performing at his full potential. When this state has been stabilized, modern psychoanalysis has achieved its ultimate goal.

REFERENCES

Abraham, K. 1908. The psychosexual differences between hysteria and dementia praecox. In *Selected papers of Karl Abraham, M.D.* New York: Basic Books, 1953.

Abraham, K. 1911. Notes on the psycho-analytical investigation and treatment of manic-depressive insanity and allied conditions. In *Selected papers of Karl Abraham, M.D.* New York: Basic Books, 1953.

Adler, G. 1967. Methods of treatment in analytical psychology. In B.B. Wolman (Ed.), *Psychoanalytic techniques.* New York: Basic Books.

Aichhorn, A. 1936. The narcissistic transference of the "juvenile impostor." In O. Fleischmann, P. Kramer, & H. Ross (Eds.) *Aichhorn A. Delinquency and child guidance: Selected papers.* New York: International Universities Press.

Almansi, R.J. 1960. The face-breast equation. *Journal of the American Psychoanalytic Association* 8:43–70.

Altshul, V.A. 1977. The so-called boring patient. *American Journal of Psychotherapy* 31:533–545.

Altshul, V.A. 1980. The hateful therapist and the countertransference psychosis. *Journal, The National Association of Private Psychiatric Hospitals* 11(4):15–23.

American Psychiatric Association 1952, 1968, 1980. *Diagnostic and Statistical Manual of Mental Disorders, I, II, & III*. Washington, D.C.: American Psychiatric Association.

Arieti, S. 1961. Introductory notes on the psychoanalytic therapy of schizophrenics. In A. Burton (Ed.), *Psychotherapy of the psychoses*. New York: Basic Books, 1961.

Arieti, S. 1962. Psychotherapy of schizophrenia. *Archives of General Psychiatry* 6:112–122.

Arieti, S. 1974. An overview of schizophrenia from a predominantly psychological approach. *American Journal of Psychiatry* 131:241–249.

Bak, R.C. 1952. Discussion of Dr. Wexler's paper. In E.B. Brody & F.C. Redlich (Eds.), *Psychotherapy with schizophrenics*. New York: International Universities Press.

Bak, R.C. 1954. The schizophrenic defense against aggression. *International Journal of Psycho-Analysis* 35:129–134.

Balint, M. 1952. New beginning and the paranoid and the depressive syndromes. *International Journal of Psycho-Analysis* 33:214–224.

Balint, M. 1959. Regression in the analytic situation. In *Thrills and regression*. New York: International Universities Press.

Balint, M. & A. 1939. On transference and countertransference. *International Journal of Psycho-Analysis* 20:223–230.

Beres, D. 1981. Self, identity and narcissism. *Psychoanalytic Quarterly* 50:515–534.

Berg, M.D. 1977. The externalizing transference. *International Journal of Psycho-Analysis* 58:235–244.

Binswanger, L. 1957. *Sigmund Freud: Reminiscences of a friendship*. New York: Grune & Stratton.

Birley, J.L.T., & Brown, G.W. 1970. Crises and life changes preceding the onset or relapse of acute schizophrenia. *British Journal of Psychiatry* 116:327–333.

Bleuler, E. 1950. *Dementia praecox and the group of schizophrenias*. New York: International Universities Press.

Bleuler, M. 1974. The long-term course of the schizophrenic psychoses. *Psychological Medicine* 4:244–254.

Bleuler, M. 1979. On schizophrenic psychoses. *American Journal of Psychiatry* 136:1403–1409.

Bloch, D. 1965. Feelings that kill; the effect of the wish for infanticide in neurotic depression. *Psychoanalytic Review* 52:51–66.

Bloch, D. 1976. Infantile autism and the inhibition of fantasy. *Modern Psychoanalysis* 1:231–242.

Bloch, D. 1978. *So the witch won't kill me*. Boston: Houghton Mifflin.

Blum, H.P. 1982. Theories of the self and psychoanalytic concepts: Discussion. *Journal of the American Psychoanalytic Association* 30:959–978.

Boyer, L.B. 1967. Office treatment of schizophrenic patients: The use of psychoanalytic therapy with few parameters. Introduction. In L.B. Boyer & P.L. Giovacchini, *Psychoanalytic treatment of schizophrenia and characterological disorders*. New York: Science House.

Braceland, F.J. 1978. Introduction. *Psychiatric Annals* 8:329–330.

Breuer, J., & Freud, S. (1893–1895). Studies on hysteria. *Standard Edition of the Complete Psychological Works of Sigmund Freud* (Vol. 2).

Brill, A.A. 1944. *Freud's contribution to psychiatry*. New York: W.W. Norton.

Brody, S. 1976. Somatization disorders: Diseases of communication. *Modern Psychoanalysis* 1:148–162.

Bullard, D. 1960. Psychotherapy of paranoid patients. *Archives of General Psychiatry* 2:137–141.

Bychowski, G. 1952. *Psychotherapy of psychosis*. New York: Grune & Stratton.

Bychowski, G. 1956. Release of internal images. *International Journal of Psycho-Analysis* 37:332–336.

Calne, D.B. 1984. The clinical relevance of dopamine receptor. In W.D. Horst (Ed.), *Roche Receptor* (Vol. 1) No. 3:6.

Cancro, R. 1979. The schizophrenic syndrome: Its dubious past and its certain future. *Hillside Journal of Clinical Psychiatry* 1:39–56.

Cancro, R. 1982. The schizophrenic disorders, Part II. In L. Grinspoon (Ed.), *Psychiatry 1982, The American Psychiatric Association Annual Review*. Washington: American Psychiatric Press.

Cancro, R. 1983. Individual psychotherapy in the treatment of chronic schizophrenic patients. *American Journal of Psychotherapy* 37:493–501.

Cancro, R., Fox, N., & Shapiro, L. 1974. *Strategic intervention in schizophrenia*. New York: Behavioral Publications.

Carpenter, W.T., Jr., Heinrichs, D.W., & Hanlon, T.E. 1981. Methodologic standards for treatment outcome research in schizophrenia. *American Journal of Psychiatry* 138:465–471.

Chasseguet-Smirgel, J. 1981. Loss of reality in perversions—with special reference to fetishism. *Journal of the American Psychoanalytic Association* 29:511–534.

Clark, L.P. 1926. The fantasy method of analyzing narcissistic neuroses. *Psychoanalytic Review* 13:225–239.

Cotman, C.W. & McGaugh, J.L. 1980. *Behavioral neuroscience: An introduction.* New York: Academic Press.

Cranefield, P.F. 1958. Josef Breuer's evaluation of his contribution to psychoanalysis. *International Journal of Psycho-Analysis* 39:319–322.

Crick, F.H.C. 1979. Thinking about the brain. *Scientific American* 24:219–232.

Davis, H.L. 1978. The use of countertransference feelings in resolving resistance. *Psychoanalytic Review* 65:557–578.

Davis, J.M. 1975 Overview: Maintenance therapy in psychiatry: Schizophrenia. *American Journal of Psychiatry* 132:1237–1245.

Davis, J.M., Janicak, P., Chang, S., & Klerman, K. 1982. Recent advances in the pharmacologic treatment of the schizophrenic disorders. In L. Grinspoon (Ed.), *Psychiatry 1982, The American Psychiatric Association Annual Review.* Washington: American Psychiatric Press.

Day, M., & Semrad, E.V. 1978. Schizophrenic reactions. In A.M. Nicholi, Jr., *The Harvard guide to modern psychiatry.* Cambridge, MA: Harvard University (Belknap) Press.

Dement, W.C. 1965. Dreaming: A biologic state. *Modern Medicine,* July 5, pp. 184–206.

Deutsch, H. 1926. Occult processes occurring during psychoanalysis. In G. Devereaux (Ed.), *Psychoanalysis and the occult.* New York: International Universities Press.

Eigen, M. 1977. On working with "unwanted" patients. *International Journal of Psycho-Analysis* 58:109–121.

Eissler, K. 1953. The effect of the structure of the ego on psychoanalytic technique. *Journal of the American Psychoanalytic Association* 1:104–143.

Eissler, K. 1958. Remarks on some variations in psychoanalytic technique. *International Journal of Psycho-Analysis* 39:222–229.

Epstein, L. 1982. Adapting to the patient's therapeutic need in the psychoanalytic situation. *Contemporary Psychoanalysis* 18:190–217.

Epstein, L., & Feiner, A.H. (Eds.) 1979. *Countertransference.* New York: Jason Aronson.

Ernsberger, C. 1979. The concept of countertransference as therapeutic instrument: Its early history. *Modern Psychoanalysis* 4:141–164.

Federn, P. 1952. *Ego psychology and the psychoses.* New York: Basic Books.

Fenichel, O. 1941. *Problems of psychoanalytic technique.* Albany, NY: *Psychoanalytic Quarterly.*

Fenichel, O. 1945. *The psychoanalytic theory of neurosis.* New York: W.W. Norton.

Ferenczi, S., & Rank, O. 1925. *The development of psychoanalysis.* New York: Nervous and Mental Disease Publishing Co.

Fincher, J. 1981. *The brain: Mystery of matter and mind.* Washington: U.S. News Books.

Flinn, D.E., Leon, R.L., & McKinley, R. 1981. Psychotherapy: The treatment of choice for all. *Psychiatric Annals* 11(10):13–23.

Fordham, M. 1979. Analytical psychology and countertransference. In L.E. Epstein & A.H. Feiner (Eds.), *Countertransference.* New York: Jason Aronson.

Frankl, V.E. 1960. Paradoxical intention: A logotherapeutic technique. *American Journal of Psychotherapy* 14:520–535.

Freeman, T. 1963. The concept of narcissism in schizophrenic states. *International Journal of Psycho-Analysis* 44:293–303.

Freeman, T. 1970. The psychopathology of the psychoses: A reply to Arlow & Brenner. *International Journal of Psycho-Analysis* 51:407–415.

Freeman, T. 1982. Schizophrenic delusions and their pre-psychotic antecedents. *International Journal of Psycho-Analysis* 63:445–448.

Freeman, T., Cameron, J.L., & McGhie, A. 1958. *Chronic schizophrenia.* New York: International Universities Press.

Freud, A. 1926. The methods of children's analysis. In *The psychoanalytical treatment of children.* New York: International Universities Press, 1959.

Freud, A. 1951. August Aichhorn: An obituary. *International Journal of Psycho-Analysis* 32:51–56.

Freud, S. 1892–1899. Extracts from the Fliess papers. *The Standard Edition*[1] *of the Complete Psychological Works of Sigmund Freud.* (Vol. 1). London: Hogarth Press.

Freud, S. 1894. The neuro-psychoses of defense. *S.E.*, 3.

Freud, S. 1900. The interpretation of dreams. *S.E.*, 4 & 5.

---

[1]*S.E.* in subsequent references denotes the *Standard Edition*, Vols. 1–24, 1953–1974.

Freud, S. 1905. Fragment of an analysis of a case of hysteria. *S.E.*, 7.

Freud, S. 1910. The future prospects of psychoanalytic therapy. *S.E.*, 11.

Freud, S. 1912a. The dynamics of transference. *S.E.*, 12.

Freud, S. 1912b. Recommendations to physicians practicing psycho-analysis. *S.E.*, 12.

Freud, S. 1913. On beginning the treatment. *S.E.*, 12.

Freud, S. 1914a. On narcissim: An introduction. *S.E.*, 14.

Freud, S. 1914b. On the history of the psycho-analytic movement. *S.E.*, 14.

Freud, S. 1914c. The Moses of Michelangelo. *S.E.*, 13.

Freud, S. 1915a. Instincts and their vicissitudes. *S.E.*, 14.

Freud, S. 1915b. Observations on transference love. *S.E.*, 12.

Freud, S. 1917. Introductory lectures on psycho-analysis, Part III. *S.E.*, 16.

Freud, S. 1920. Beyond the pleasure principle. *S.E.*, 18.

Freud, S. 1923a. Psycho-analysis. *S.E.*, 18.

Freud, S. 1923b. Remarks on the theory and practice of dream interpretation. *S.E.*, 19.

Freud, S. 1923c. The ego and the id. *S.E.*, 19.

Freud, S. 1924. Neurosis and psychosis. *S.E.*, 19.

Freud, S. 1925. An autobiographical study. *S.E.*, 20.

Freud, S. 1926. Inhibitions, symptoms and anxiety. *S.E.*, 20.

Freud, S. 1930. Civilization and its discontents. *S.E.*, 21.

Freud, S. 1933. New introductory lectures on psycho-analysis. *S.E.*, 22.

Freud, S. 1937. Analysis terminable and interminable. *S.E.*, 23.

Freud, S. 1940. An outline of psychoanalysis. *S.E.*, 23.

Freud, S. 1954. *The origins of psycho-analysis. Letters to Wilhelm Fliess. Drafts and notes: 1887–1902.* New York: Basic Books.

Freud, S. 1985. *The complete letters of Sigmund Freud to Wilhelm Fliess, 1887–1904.* J.M. Masson, (Ed.,Trans.). Cambridge, MA: Harvard University (Belknap) Press.

Fromm-Reichmann, F. 1952. Some aspects of psychoanalytic psychotherapy with schizophrenics. In E.B. Brody & F. Redlich (Eds.), *Psychotherapy with schizophrenics.* New York: International Universities Press.

Gedo, J.E., & Goldberg, A. 1973. *Models of the mind: A psychoanalytic theory.* Chicago: University of Chicago Press.

Gerard, R.W. 1960. Neurophysiology: An integration (molecules, neurons, and behavior). In *Handbook of Neurophysiology* (Vol. 3). Washington: American Physiological Society.

Giovacchini, P.I. 1979. Countertransference with primitive mental states. In L.E. Epstein & A.H. Feiner, *Countertransference*. New York: Jason Aronson.

Gitelson, M. 1952. The emotional position of the analyst in the psychoanalytic situation. *International Journal of Psycho-Analysis* 33:1–10.

Glauber, I.P. 1982. *Stuttering—A psychoanalytic understanding*. New York: Human Sciences Press.

Glover, E. 1949. *Psycho-Analysis* (2nd ed.). New York: Staples Press.

Gochfeld, L.G. 1978. Drug therapy and modern psychoanalysis. *Modern Psychoanalysis* 3(203–216).

Greenberg, J. 1978. The brain: Holding the secrets of behavior. *Science News* 114:362–366.

Greenson, R. 1965. The working alliance and the transference neurosis. *Psychoanalytic Quarterly* 34:155–181.

Greenson, R. 1967. *The technique and practice of psychoanalysis*. New York: International Universities Press.

Greenwald, H. 1973. *Decision therapy*. New York: Peter H. Wyden.

Grinker, R.R., Sr. 1969. An essay on schizophrenia and science. *Archives of General Psychiatry* 20:1–24.

Grotstein, J.S. 1977. The psychoanalytic concept of schizophrenia. *International Journal of Psycho-Analysis* 58:403–452.

Grotstein, J.S. 1980. A proposed revision of the psychoanalytic concept of primitive mental states. Part I. *Contemporary Psychoanalysis* 16:479–546.

Gunderson, J.G., reporter 1974. Panel: The influence of theoretical model of schizophrenia on treatment practice. *Journal of the American Psychoanalytic Association* 22:182–199.

Gunderson, J.G., Carpenter, W.T., & Strauss, J.S. 1975. Borderline and schizophrenic patients: A comparative study. *American Journal of Psychiatry* 132:1257–1264.

Hann-Kende, F. 1933. On the role of transference and countertransference. In G. Devereaux (Ed.), *Psychoanalysis and the occult*. New York: International Universities Press, 1953.

Hart, L.A. 1975. *How the brain works*. New York: Basic Books.

Hartmann, H. 1953. Contribution to the metapsychology of schizophrenia. *Psychoanalytic Study of the Child* 8:177–187.

Hayden, S. 1983. The toxic response in modern psychoanalysis. *Modern Psychoanalysis* 8:3–16.

Heimann, P. 1950. On countertransference. *International Journal of Psycho-Analysis* 31:81–84.

Heinrichs, D.W., & Carpenter, W.T., Jr. 1982. The psychotherapy of the schizophrenic disorders. In L. Grinspoon (Ed.), *Psychiatry 1982, The American Psychiatric Association Annual Review*. Washington: American Psychiatric Press.

Hendrick, I. 1931. Ego defense and the mechanism of oral rejection in schizophrenia: The psychoanalysis of a pre-psychotic case. *International Journal of Psycho-Analysis* 12:298–325.

Hill, L.B. 1955. *Psychotherapeutic intervention in schizophrenia*. Chicago: University of Chicago Press.

Hoffer, A., & Osmond, H. 1966. *How to live with schizophrenia*. New Hyde Park, NY: University Books.

Jaynes, J. 1976. *The origin of consciousness in the breakdown of the bicameral mind*. Boston: Houghton Mifflin.

Jenkins, R.L. 1950. Nature of the schizophrenic process. *Archives of Neurology and Psychiatry* 64:243–262.

Jones, E. 1953. *The life and work of Sigmund Freud*, (Vol. 1). New York: Basic Books.

Jones, E. 1955. *The life and work of Sigmund Freud*, (Vol. 2). New York: Basic Books.

Joseph, E.D. 1982. Normal in psychoanalysis. *International Journal of Psycho-Analysis* 63:3–13.

Jung, C.G. 1935. Principles of practical psychotherapy. In *Collected works of C.G. Jung*, (Vol. 16). Princeton: Princeton University Press.

Jung, C.G. 1936, *The psychology of dementia praecox*. New York: Nervous and Mental Disease Publishing Co.

Karasu, T.B. 1982. Psychotherapy and pharmacotherapy: Toward an integrative model. *American Journal of Psychiatry* 139:1102–1113.

Kardiner, A. 1959. Traumatic neuroses of war. In S. Arieti (Ed.), *American handbook of psychiatry*, (Vol. 1). 245–247.

Karon, B.P., & Vandenbos, G.R. 1981. *Psychotherapy of schizophrenia: The treatment of choice*. New York: Jason Aronson.

Katan, M. 1950. Structural aspects of a case of schizophrenia. *Psychoanalytic Study of the Child* 5:175–179.

Kavka, J. 1980. Michelangelo's Moses: "Madonna Androgyna" (A meaning of the artist's use of forefingers). In Chicago Institute for Psychoanalysis (Ed.), *The Annual of Psychoanalysis*, 8:291–315. New York: International Universities Press, 1981.

Kernberg, O.F. 1975. *Borderline conditions and pathological narcissism.* New York: Jason Aronson.

Kernberg, O.F. 1976. *Object-relations theory and clinical psychoanalysis.* New York: Jason Aronson.

Kernberg, O.F. 1982a. An ego psychology and object relations approach to the narcissistic personality. In L. Grinspoon (Ed.), *Psychiatry 1982, The American Psychiatric Association Annual Review.* Washington: American Psychiatric Press.

Kernberg, O.F. 1982b. Self, ego, affects and drives. *Journal of the American Psychoanalytic Association* 30:893–917.

Kesten, J. 1955. Learning for spite. *Psychoanalysis* 4:63–67.

Kety, S.S. 1979. Disorders of the human brain, *Scientific American,* 24(3):202–221.

Kety, S.S. 1980. Biological substrates of mental illness. *Journal, The National Association of Private Psychiatric Hospitals* 11(3).

Kety, S.S. 1981. Neuroscience in the future of psychiatry: Promise and limitations. *Psychiatric News*, July 3, 1981.

Kirman, W.J. 1980. Countertransference in facilitating intimacy and communication. *Modern Psychoanalysis* 5:131–145.

Klein, M. 1930. The importance of symbol-formation in the development of the ego. *International Journal of Psycho-Analysis* 11:24–39. Reprinted in *Contributions to psychoanalysis: 1921–1945.* New York: McGraw-Hill, 1964.

Klein, M. 1946. Notes on some schizoid mechanisms. In M. Klein, P. Heimann, S. Isaacs & J. Riviere (Eds.), *Developments in psychoanalysis.* London: Hogarth Press, 1952.

Klein, M. 1952. The origins of transference. *International Journal of Psycho-Analysis* 33:433–438.

Kohut, H. 1968. The psychoanalytic treatment of narcissistic personality disorders: Outline of a systematic approach. *Psychoanalytic Study of the Child* 23:86–113.

Kohut, H. 1971. *The analysis of the self.* New York: International Universities Press.

Kohut, H. 1972. Thoughts on narcissism and narcissistic rage. *Psychoanalytic Study of the Child* 27:360–400.

Kohut, H. 1977. *The restoration of the self.* New York: International Universities Press.

Kohut, H., & Wolf, E.S. 1978. The disorders of the self and their treatment: An outline. *International Journal of Psycho-Analysis* 59:413–425.

Krohn, A., & Krohn, J. 1982. The nature of the oedipus complex in the Dora case. *Journal of the American Psychoanalytic Association* 30:555–578.

Lagache, D. 1953. Some aspects of transference. *International Journal of Psycho-Analysis* 34:1–10.

Langs, R., 1984. Freud's Irma dream and the origins of psychoanalysis. *Psychoanalytic Review* 71:591–617.

LeBoit, J., & Capponi, A. (Eds.) 1979. *Advances in psychotherapy of the borderline patient.* New York: Jason Aronson.

Liberman, R.P. 1982. Social factors in the etiology of the schizophrenic disorders. In L. Grinspoon (Ed.), *Psychiatry 1982, The American Psychiatric Association Annual Review.* Washington: American Psychiatric Press.

Lichtenberg, J.D. 1963. Untreating—its necessity in the therapy of certain schizophrenic patients. *British Journal of Medical Psychology* 36:311–317.

Liegner, E. J. 1974. The silent patient. *Psychoanalytic Review* 61:229–245.

Liegner, E. J. 1979. Solving a problem in a case of psychosis. *Modern Psychoanalysis* 4:5–17.

Liegner, E.J. 1980. The hate that cures: The psychological reversibility of schizophrenia. *Modern Psychoanalysis* 5:5–95.

Lishman, W.A. 1983. The apparatus of mind: Brain structure and function in mental disorder. *Psychosomatics* 24:699–720.

Little, M. 1958. On delusional transference (transference psychosis). *International Journal of Psycho-Analysis* 39:134–138.

Little, M. 1966. Transference in borderline states. *International Journal of Psycho-Analysis* 47:476–485.

Loewenstein, R.M. 1956. Some remarks on the role of speech in psychoanalytic technique. *International Journal of Psycho-Analysis* 37:460–467.

London, N. 1973. An essay on psychoanalytic theory: Two theories of schizophrenia. *International Journal of Psycho-Analysis* 54:169–193.

Lucas, M.R. 1982. An historical study of narcissistic injury. Final paper. Unpublished.

Mahler, M.S. 1981. Aggression in the service of separation-individuation: Case study of a mother-daughter relationship. *Psychoanalytic Quarterly* 50:625–638.

Mahler, M.S., & McDevitt, J.B. 1982. Thoughts on the emergence of the sense of self, with particular emphasis on the body self. *Journal of the American Psychoanalytic Association* 30:827–848.

Mahler, M.S., Pine, F., & Bergman, A. 1975. *The psychological birth of the human infant.* New York: Basic Books.

Margolis, B.D. 1978. Narcissistic countertransference: Emotional availability and case management. *Modern Psychoanalysis* 3:133–151.

Margolis, B.D. 1979. Narcissistic transference: The product of overlapping self and object fields. *Modern Psychoanalysis* 4:131–140.

Margolis, B.D. 1981. Narcissistic transference: Further considerations. *Modern Psychoanalysis* 6:171–192.

Margolis, B.D. 1983a. The contact function of the ego: Its role in the therapy of the narcissistic patient. *Psychoanalytic Review* 70:69–81.

Margolis, B.D. 1983b. The object-oriented question: A contribution to treatment technique. *Modern Psychoanalysis* 8:35–46.

Marmer, S.S. 1980. Psychoanalysis of multiple personality. *International Journal of Psycho-Analysis* 61:439–459.

Marsella, A.J., & Snyder, K.K. 1981. Stress, social supports, and schizophrenic disorders: Toward an interactional model. *Schizophrenia Bulletin* 7:152–163.

Marshall, R.J. 1982. *Resistant interactions: Child and psychotherapist.* New York: Human Sciences Press.

McGlashan, T.H. 1983. The we-self in borderline patients: Manifestations of the symbiotic self-object in psychotherapy. *Psychiatry* 46:351–361.

McLaughlin, J.T. 1982. Issues stimulated by the 32nd Congress. *International Journal of Psycho-Analysis* 63: 229–240.

Meadow, P.W. 1974. A research method for investigating the effectiveness of psychoanalytic techniques. *Psychoanalytic Review* 61:79–94.

Meerloo, J.A.M. & Nelson, M.C. 1965. *Transference and trial adaptation.* Springfield, IL: Charles C. Thomas.

Menninger, K.A. 1938. *Man against himself.* New York: Harcourt Brace.

Menninger, K.A. 1945. *The human mind* (3rd ed). New York: Alfred Knopf.

Menninger, K.A. 1958. *Theory of psychoanalytic technique.* New York: Basic Books.

Menninger, K.A., & Holzman, P.S. 1973. *Theory of psychoanalytic technique* (2nd ed). New York: Basic Books.

Modell, A.H. 1976. "The holding environment" and the therapeutic action of psychoanalysis. *Journal of the American Psychoanalytic Association* 24:285–307.

Moeller, M.L. 1977. Self and object in countertransference. *International Journal of Psycho-Analysis* 58:365–374.

Molina, J.A. 1982. Psychobiosocial "maps"; A useful tool in milieu therapy and psychiatric education. *Journal of Clinical Psychiatry* 43(5):182–186.

Money-Kyrle, R. 1956. Normal countertransference and some of its deviations. *International Journal of Psycho-Analysis* 37: 360–366.

Mosher, L.R., & Keith, S.J. 1979. Research on the psychosocial treatment of schizophrenia: A summary report. *American Journal of Psychiatry* 136:623–631.

Nadelson, T. 1977. Borderline rage and the therapist's response. *American Journal of Psychiatry* 134:748–751.

Nagelberg, L., & Spotnitz, H. 1958. Strengthening the ego through the release of frustration-aggression. *American Journal of Orthopsychiatry* 28:794–801. Reprinted in Spotnitz 1976a.

Nelson, M.C. 1956. Externalization of the toxic introject. *Psychoanalytic Review* 43:235–242.

Nelson, M.C. 1981. The paradigmatic approach: A parallel development. *Modern Psychoanalysis* 6:9–26.

Nunberg, H. 1921. The course of the libidinal conflict in a case of schizophrenia. *Practice and Theory of Psychoanalysis*. New York: Nervous and Mental Disease Monographs, No. 74, 1948.

Nunberg, H., & Federn, E. (Eds.) 1962. *Minutes of the Vienna Psychoanalytic Society* (Vol. 1). New York: International Universities Press.

Oakes, E.S. 1982. Object relations theory and the supervisor/supervisee relationship: The trouble is the objective case. *Smith College School for Social Work Journal*, Spring 1982, pp. 2–6.

Ogden, T.H. 1982. *Projective identification and psychotherapeutic technique*. New York: Jason Aronson.

Oremland, J.D. 1980. Mourning and its effect on Michelangelo's art. In Chicago Institute for Psychoanalysis (Ed.), *The Annual of Psychoanalysis* (Vol. 8), 1980. New York: International Universities Press.

Ormont, L.R. 1981. Principles and practice of conjoint psychoanalytic treatment. *American Journal of Psychiatry* 138:69–73.

Ormont, L.R., & Strean, H. 1978. *The practice of conjoint therapy*. New York: Human Sciences Press.

Pao, Ping-Nie 1965. The role of hatred in the ego. *Psychoanalytic Quar-*

terly 34:257–264.

Penfield, W., & Perot, R. 1963. The brain's record of auditory and visual experience: A final summary and discussion. *Brain* 86:595–702.

Perri, B.M. 1982. A modern perspective on the negative therapeutic reaction. Unpublished doctoral dissertation. Manhattan Center for Modern Psychoanalytic Studies.

Perri, M.E., & Perri, B.M. 1978. The psychoanalytic contract: Therapeutic and legal aspects. Unpublished dissertation. Manhattan Center for Modern Psychoanalytic Studies.

Polatin, P., & Spotnitz, H. 1943. Ambulatory insulin shock technique in the treatment of schizophrenia. *Journal of Nervous and Mental Disease* 97:567–575.

Proceedings 1981. Symposium on Infant Psychiatry, 1979. *Journal of Preventive Psychiatry* 1:113–139.

Racker, H. 1957. The meaning and uses of countertransference. *Psychoanalytic Quarterly* 26:303–357. Reprinted in H. Racker, *Transference and countertransference*, 1968. London: Hogarth Press.

Rangell, L. 1982. The self in psychoanalytic theory. *Journal of the American Psychoanalytic Association* 30:863–891.

Ries, H. 1958. Analysis of a patient with a 'split' personality. *International Journal of Psycho-Analysis* 39:397–407.

Roazen, P. 1969. *Brother animal: The story of Freud and Tausk.* New York: Alfred Knopf.

Roazen, P. 1975. *Freud and his followers.* New York: Alfred Knopf.

Rosen, J.N. 1953. *Direct analysis: Selected papers.* New York: Grune & Stratton.

Rosen, J.N. 1962. *Direct psychoanalytic psychiatry.* New York: Grune & Stratton.

Rosen, J.N. 1963. The concept of early maternal environment in direct psychoanalysis. Doylestown, PA: Doylestown Foundation.

Rosenbaum, M., & Muroff, M. (Eds.) 1984. *Anna O.: Fourteen contemporary reinterpretations.* New York: Free Press.

Rosenfeld, H.A. 1947. Analysis of a schizophrenic state with depersonalization. *International Journal of Psycho-Analysis* 28:130–139.

Rosenfeld, H.A. 1952a. Notes on the psychoanalysis of a superego conflict in an acute schizophrenic patient. *International Journal of Psycho-Analysis* 33:111–131.

Rosenfeld, H.A. 1952b. Transference phenomena and transference-analysis in an acute catatonic schizophrenic patient. *International Journal of Psycho-Analysis* 33:457–464.

Rosenfeld, H.A. 1954. Considerations regarding the psychoanalytic approach to acute and chronic schizophrenia. *International Journal of Psycho-Analysis* 35:135–140.

Rosenfeld, H.A. 1964. On the psychopathology of narcissism: A clinical approach. *International Journal of Psycho-Analysis* 45:332–337.

Rosenfeld, H.A. 1965. *Psychotic states: A psychoanalytical approach.* New York: International Universities Press.

Rosenthal, L. 1979. The significance of the resolution of group resistance in group analysis. *Modern Psychoanalysis* 4:83–103.

Rosenthal, L. 1985. *The resolution of resistance in group psychotherapy.* New York: Jason Aronson. In press.

Rothstein, A. 1982. The implications of early psychopathology for the analysability of narcissistic personality disorders. *International Journal of Psycho-Analysis* 63:177–188.

Rudolph, J. 1981. Aggression in the service of the ego and the self. *Journal of the American Psychoanalytic Association* 29:559–579.

Schilder, P. 1938. *Psychotherapy.* New York: W.W. Norton.

Schlesinger, B. 1962. *Higher cerebral functions and their clinical disorders.* New York: Grune & Stratton.

Schulz, C., & Kilgalen, R.L. 1969. *Case studies in schizophrenia.* New York: Basic Books.

Schur, M. 1972. *Freud: Living and dying.* New York: International Universities Press.

Searles, H.F. 1959. The effort to drive the other person crazy—an element in the aetiology and psychotherapy of schizophrenia. *British Journal of Medical Psychology* 32:1–18. Reprinted in Searles, 1965.

Searles, H.F. 1963. Transference psychosis in the psychotherapy of schizophrenia. *International Journal of Psycho-analysis* 44:249–281.

Searles, H.F. 1965. *Collected papers on schizophrenia and related subjects.* New York: International Universities Press.

Searles, H.F. 1967. Concerning the development of an identity. *Psychoanalytic Review* 53:507–530.

Sechehaye, M. 1956. *A new psychotherapy in schizophrenia.* New York: Grune & Stratton.

Shakow, D. 1971. Some observations on the psychology (and some fewer, on the biology) of schizophrenia. *Journal of Nervous and Mental Disease* 153:300–330.

Spitz, R. 1965. *The first year of life*. New York: International Universities Press.

Spotnitz, H. 1957. The borderline schizophrenic in group psychotherapy. *International Journal of Group Psychotherapy* 7:155–174. Reprinted in Spotnitz, 1976a.

Spotnitz, H. 1961a. *The couch and the circle*. New York: Alfred Knopf; Lancer Books, 1972, 1973.

Spotnitz, H. 1961b. The narcissistic defense in schizophrenia. *Psychoanalysis and the Psychoanalytic Review* 48(4):24–42. Reprinted in Spotnitz, 1976a.

Spotnitz, H. 1962. The need for insulation in the schizophrenic personality. *Psychoanalysis and the Psychoanalytic Review* 49(3):3–25. Reprinted in Spotnitz, 1976a.

Spotnitz, H. 1963. The toxoid response. *Psychoanalytic Review* 50:612–624. Reprinted in Spotnitz, 1976a.

Spotnitz, H. 1966. The maturational interpretation. *Psychoanalytic Review* 53:490–495. Reprinted in Spotnitz, 1976a.

Spotnitz, H. 1967. Techniques for the resolution of the narcissistic defense. In B.B. Wolman (Ed.), *Psychoanalytic techniques*. New York: Basic Books. Reprinted in Spotnitz, 1976a.

Spotnitz, H. 1969. *Modern psychoanalysis of the schizophrenic patient* (1st ed.) New York: Grune & Stratton.

Spotnitz, H. 1974. Group psychotherapy with schizophrenics. In D.S. Milman & G.D. Goldman (Eds.), *Group process today: Evaluation and perspective*. Springfield, IL: Charles C. Thomas.

Spotnitz, H. 1975. Object-oriented approaches to severely disturbed adolescents. In M. Sugar (Ed.), *The adolescent in group and family therapy*. New York: Brunner/Mazel. Reprinted in Spotnitz, 1976a.

Spotnitz, H. 1976a. *Psychotherapy of preoedipal conditions: Schizophrenia and severe character disorders*. New York: Jason Aronson.

Spotnitz, H. 1976b. Trends in modern psychoanalytic supervision. *Modern Psychoanalysis* 1:201–217.

Spotnitz, H. 1977. Narcissus as myth, Narcissus as patient. In M.C. Nelson (Ed.), *The narcissistic condition: A fact of our lives and times*. New York: Human Sciences Press.

Spotnitz, H. 1978. Aggression and schizophrenia. In G.D. Goldman & D.S. Milman (Eds.), *Psychoanalytic perspectives on aggression*. Dubuque, IA: Kendall/Hunt.

Spotnitz, H. 1979a. Narcissistic countertransference. In L.E. Epstein &

A.H. Feiner (Eds.), *Countertransference*. New York: Jason Aronson. Reprinted in *Contemporary Psychoanalysis* 15:545–549.

Spotnitz, H. 1979b. Psychoanalytic technique with the borderline patient. In J. LeBoit & A. Capponi (Eds.), *Advances in psychotherapy of the borderline patient*. New York: Jason Aronson.

Spotnitz, H. 1979c. Modern psychoanalysis: An operational theory. In G.D. Goldman & D.S. Milman (Eds.), *Therapists at work*. Dubuque, IA: Kendall/Hunt Publishing Co.

Spotnitz, H. 1981a. Aggression in the therapy of schizophrenia. *Modern Psychoanalysis* 6:131–140.

Spotnitz, H. 1981b. Ethical issues in the treatment of psychotics and borderline psychotics. In M. Rosenbaum (Ed.), *Ethics and values in psychotherapy*. New York: Free Press.

Spotnitz, H. 1982. Supervision of psychoanalysts treating borderline patients. *Modern Psychoanalysis* 7:185–213.

Spotnitz, H. 1983. Countertransference with the schizophrenic patient: Value of the positive anaclitic countertransference. *Modern Psychoanalysis* 8:169–172.

Spotnitz, H. 1984. The case of Anna O.: Aggression and the narcissistic countertransference. In M. Rosenbaum & M. Muroff (Eds.), *Anna O.: One hundred years of psychoanalysis*. New York: Free Press.

Spotnitz, H., & Meadow, P.W. 1976. *Treatment of the narcissistic neuroses*. New York: Manhattan Center for Advanced Psychoanalytic Studies.

Spotnitz, H., & Nagelberg, L. 1960. A preanalytic technique for resolving the narcissistic defense. *Psychiatry* 23:193–197.

Spunt, A.R. 1979. Written communications in modern psychoanalytic treatment: Their use and psychotherapeutic value. Unpublished thesis, Manhattan Center for Modern Psychoanalytic Studies.

Steiner, J. 1982. Perverse relationships between parts of the self: A clinical illustration. *International Journal of Psycho-Analysis* 63:241–251.

Stern, H. 1978. *The couch: Its use and meaning in psychotherapy*. New York: Human Sciences Press.

Stone, L. 1954. The widening scope of indications for psychoanalysis. *Journal of the American Psychoanalytic Association* 2:567–594.

Stone, L. 1967. The psychoanalytic situation and transference: Postscript to an earlier communication. *Journal of the American Psychoanalytic Association* 15:3–58.

Stone, L. 1981a. Notes on the noninterpretive elements in the psychoanalytic situation and process. *Journal of the American Psychoanalytic Association* 29:89–118.

Stone, L. 1981b. Notes on the noninterpretive elements in the psychoanalytic situation and process. In Panel Report. *Journal of the American Psychoanalytic Association* 29:648–651.

Strachey, J. 1934. The nature of the therapeutic action of psychoanalysis. *International Journal of Psycho-Analysis* 15:127–159.

Strauss, J.S. 1982. The clinical pictures and diagnosis of the schizophrenic disorders. In L. Grinspoon (Ed.), *Psychiatry 1982, The American Psychiatric Association Annual Review*. Washington: American Psychiatric Press.

Strauss, J.S. 1983. The diagnosis of schizophrenia: Past, present, and future. *Psychiatry Letter*, Fair Oaks Hospital, Summit, NJ.

Strauss, J.S., & Carpenter, W.T. 1981. In S.M. Woods (Ed.), *Schizophrenia*. New York: Plenum Publishing Corp.

Sulloway, F.J. 1979. *Freud, biologist of the mind: Beyond the psychoanalytic legend*. New York: Basic Books.

Tausk, V. 1918. On the origin of the influencing machine in schizophrenia. *Psychoanalytic Quarterly* 2:519–556, 1933. Also in R. Fliess (Ed.), *The Psychoanalytic Reader*, Vol. 1, 1948. New York: International Universities Press.

Tower, L.E. 1956. Countertransference. *Journal of the American Psychoanalytic Association* 4:224–255.

Volkan, V.D. 1976. *Primitive internalized object relations: A clinical study of schizophrenic, borderline, and narcissistic patients*. New York: International Universities Press.

Volkan, V.D. 1979. The "glass bubble" of the narcissistic patient. In J. LeBoit & A. Capponi (Eds.), *Advances in psychotherapy of the borderline patient*. New York: Jason Aronson.

Waelder, R. 1925. The psychoses: Their mechanisms and accessibility to influence. *International Journal of Psycho-Analysis* 6:259–281.

Wallerstein, R. 1967. Reconstruction and mastery in the transference psychosis. *Journal of the American Psychoanalytic Association* 15:551–583.

Weiss, E. 1957. The phenomenon of "ego passage." *Journal of the American Psychoanalytic Association* 5:267–281.

Wexler, M. 1971. Schizophrenia: conflict and deficiency *Psychoanalytic Quarterly* 40:83–99.

Will, O.A., Jr. 1965. The beginning of psychotherapeutic experience. In A. Burton (Ed.), *Modern psychotherapeutic practice*. Palo Alto, CA: Science and Behavior Books.

Will, O.A., Jr. 1974. Individual psychotherapy of schizophrenia. In R. Cancro, N. Fox, & L. Shapiro (Eds.), *Strategic intervention in schizophrenia*. New York: Behavioral Publications.

Wilson, C. 1981. *The quest for Wilhelm Reich*. Garden City, NY: Anchor Press/Doubleday.

Winnicott, D.W. 1949. Hate in the countertransference. *International Journal of Psycho-Analysis* 30:69–75. Reprinted in *Through paediatrics to psycho-analysis*. New York: Basic Books, 1958.

Wolf, E. 1979. Countertransference in disorders of the self. In L.E. Epstein & A.H. Feiner (Eds.), *Countertransference*. New York: Jason Aronson.

Wyatt, R.J., Cutler, N.R., DeLisi, L.E., Jeste, D.V., Kleinman, J.E., Luchins, D.J., Potkin, S.G., & Weinberger, D.R. 1982. Biochemical and morphological factors in the etiology of the schizophrenic disorders. In L. Grinspoon (Ed.), *Psychiatry 1982, The American Psychiatric Association Annual Review*. Washington: American Psychiatric Press.

Zilboorg, G. 1931. The deeper layers of schizophrenic psychoses. *American Journal of Psychiatry* 88:493–511.

Zimmerman, D. 1983. Analysability in relation to early psychopathology. *International Journal of Psycho-Analysis* 63:189–200.

Zipf, C. 1949. *Human behavior and the principle of least effort: An introduction to human ecology*. Cambridge, MA: Addison-Wesley Press.

Zubin, J. 1974. Foreword. In R. Cancro, N. Fox, & L. Shapiro (Eds.), *Strategic intervention in schizophrenia*. New York: Behavioral Publications.

Zubin, J., & Spring, B. 1977. Vulnerability: A new view of schizophrenia. *Journal of Abnormal Psychology* 86:103–126.

SUGGESTED READING

Introduction (Chapter 1)

[General Perspectives]

Bellak, L. (Ed.) 1979. *Disorders of the schizophrenic syndrome.* New York: Basic Books.

Borowitz, E. 1976. Modern psychoanalysis in the state mental hospital: A series of interviews. *Modern Psychoanalysis* 1:75–96.

Boyer, L.B., & Giovacchini, P.I. 1967. *Psychoanalytic treatment of characterological and schizophrenic disorders.* New York: Science House.

Dawson, D., Blum, H.M., & Bartolucci, G. 1983. *Schizophrenia in focus: Guidelines for treatment and rehabilitation.* New York: Human Sciences Press.

Feldman, Y. 1978. The early history of modern psychoanalysis. *Modern Psychoanalysis* 3:15–27.

Gunderson, J.G., & Mosher, L.R. 1975. *Psychotherapy of schizophrenia.* New York: Jason Aronson.

Kemali, D., Bartholini, G., & Richter, D. (Eds.) 1976. *Schizophrenia today.* Oxford, New York: Pergamon Press.

Menninger, K.A. 1921–1922. Reversible schizophrenia. *American Journal of Psychiatry* 1:573–588.

Pao, P.N. 1980. *Schizophrenic disorders: Theory and treatment from a psychodynamic point of view.* New York: International Universities Press.

Polatin, P. 1966. *A guide to treatment in psychiatry.* Philadelphia: J.B. Lippincott.

Stone, M.H., Albert, H.D., Forrest, D.V., & Arieti, S. 1983. *Treating schizophrenic patients: A clinico-analytical approach.* New York: McGraw-Hill.

Usdin, G. 1977. *Schizophrenia: Biological and psychological perspectives.* New York: Brunner/Mazel.

Conceptualization of the Illness (Chapter 2)

Arieti, S. 1975. *Interpretation of schizophrenia* (2nd ed). New York: Basic Books.

Bateson, G., Jackson, D.D., Haley, J., & Weakland, J.H. 1956. Toward a theory of schizophrenia. *Behavioral Science* 1:251–264.

Bergman, P., & Escalona, S. 1949. Unusual sensitivities in very young children. *The Psychoanalytic Study of the Child* 3/4:333–352. New York: International Universities Press.

Bettelheim, B. 1967. *The empty fortress: Infantile autism and the birth of the self.* New York: Free Press.

Burnham, D.L., Gladstone, A.I., & Gibson, R.W. 1969. *Schizophrenia and the need-fear dilemma.* New York: International Universities Press.

Gibson, R.W. 1966. The ego defect in schizophrenia. In G.L. Usdin (Ed.), *Psychoneurosis and schizophrenia.* Philadelphia: J.B. Lippincott.

Laing, R.D. 1966. *The divided self.* London: Penguin.

Lipton, S.D. 1961. Aggression and symptom-formation. (Discussion). *Journal of the American Psychoanalytic Association* 9:585–592.

Lorenz, K. 1966. *On aggression.* New York: Harcourt, Brace & World.

Mahler, M.S., Pine, F., & Bergman, A. 1975. *The psychological birth of the human infant.* New York: Basic Books.

Ogden, T.H. 1982. *Projective identification and psychotherapeutic technique.* New York: Jason Aronson.

Scott, J.P. 1958. *Aggression.* Chicago: University of Chicago Press.

Silverberg, W.V. 1947. The schizoid maneuver. *Psychiatry* 10:383–393.

Sluckin, W. 1967. *Imprinting and early learning.* Chicago: Aldine Publishing Co.

Spitz, R. 1965. *The first year of life.* New York: International Universities Press.

Spotnitz, H. 1976. *Psychotherapy of preoedipal conditions: Schizophrenia and severe character disorders.* New York: Jason Aronson.

Stuart, G. 1955. *Narcissus: A psychological study of self-love.* New York: Macmillan.

Amplification of the Basic Theory of Technique (Chapter 3)

Arlow, J.A., & Brenner, C. 1964. *Psychoanalytic concepts and the structural theory.* New York: International Universities Press.

Ferenczi, S. 1938. *Thalassa, a theory of genitality.* Albany, NY: Psychoanalytic Quarterly.

Guntrip, H. 1961. *Personality structure and human interaction.* New York: International Universities Press.

Kanzer, M., & Blum, H.P. 1967. Classical psychoanalysis since 1939. In B.B. Wolman (Ed.), *Psychoanalytic techniques.* New York: Basic Books.

Lampl-de Groot, J. 1967. On obstacles standing in the way of psychoanalytic therapy. In *Psychoanalytic Study of the Child* 22. New York: International Universities Press.

Lewin, B.D. 1950. *The psychoanalysis of elation.* New York: W.W. Norton.

A Neurobiological Approach to Communication (Chapter 4)

Amacher, P. 1965. Freud's neurological education and its influence on psychoanalytic theory. In *Psychological Issues,* Vol. IV (No. 4). New York: International Universities Press.

Greenfield, N.S., & Lewis, W.C. (Eds.) 1965 *Psychoanalysis and current biological thought.* Madison and Milwaukee, WI: University of Wisconsin Press.

Lennard, H., & Bernstein, A. 1960. *The anatomy of psychotherapy: Systems of communications and expectations.* New York: Columbia University Press.

Pribam, K.H., & Gill, M.M. 1974. *Freud's "Project" reassessed.* New York: Basic Books.

Rapaport, D. 1950. *Emotions and memory* (2nd ed). New York: International Universities Press.

Whyte, L. 1960. *The unconscious before Freud.* New York: Basic Books.

From Rudimentary to Cooperative Relationship (Chapter 5)

Brody, E.B. 1958. What do schizophrenics learn during psychotherapy and how do they learn it? *Journal of Nervous and Mental Disease* 127 (No. 1).

Brody, S. 1964. Syndrome of the treatment rejecting patient. *Psychoanalytic Review* 51:243–252.

Davis, H.L. 1965–1966. Short-term psychoanalytic therapy with hospitalized schizophrenics. *Psychoanalytic Review* 52:421–448.

Ekstein, R., & Wallerstein, R.S. 1957. *The teaching and learning of psychotherapy.* New York: Basic Books.

Kanzer, M. 1981. Freud's "analytic pact": The standard therapeutic alliance. *Journal of the American Psychoanalytic Association* 29:69–87.

Kubie, L.S. 1950. *Practical and theoretical aspects of psychoanalysis.* New York: International Universities Press.

Spotnitz, H. 1981. Ethical issues in the treatment of psychotics and borderline psychotics. In M. Rosenbaum (Ed.), *Ethics and values in psychotherapy.* New York: Free Press.

[Group Psychotherapy]

Bernstein, V.F. 1981. Toward a developmental model for group affects. In T. Saretsky, *Resolving treatment impasses: The difficult patient.* New York: Human Sciences Press.

Day, M., & Semrad, E. 1967. Psychoanalytically oriented group psychotherapy. In B.B. Wolman (Ed.), *Psychoanalytic techniques.* New York: Basic Books.

Ormont, L.R. 1970–1971. The use of the objective countertransference to resolve group resistance. *Group Process* 3:95–110.

Ormont, L.R., & Strean, H. 1978. *The practice of conjoint psychotherapy.* New York: Human Sciences Press.

Rosenthal, L. 1963. A study of resistances in a member of a therapy group. *International Journal of Group Psychotherapy* 13:315–327.

Slavson, S.R. 1964. *A textbook in analytic group psychotherapy.* New York: International Universities Press.

Spotnitz, H. 1968. The management and mastery of resistance in group psychotherapy. *Journal of Group Psychoanalysis and Process* 1:5–22.

Spotnitz, H. 1980. Constructive emotional interchange in group psychotherapy. In L.R. Wolberg & M.L. Aronson (Eds.), *Group and family therapy 1980: An overview.* New York: Brunner/Mazel.

Recognition and Understanding of Resistance (Chapter 6)

Artiss, K.L. (Ed.) 1959. *The symptom as communication in schizophrenia.* New York: Grune & Stratton.

Clevans, E. 1957. The fear of a schizophrenic man. *Psychoanalysis* 5 (No. 4):58–67.

Dahl, H. 1965. Observations on a "natural experiment"; Helen Keller. *Journal of the American Psychoanalytic Association* 13:533–550.

Freud, A. 1946. *The ego and the mechanisms of defense.* New York: International Universities Press.

Kavka, J.S. 1980. The dream in schizophrenia. In J.M. Natterson (Ed.), *The dream in clinical practice.* New York: Jason Aronson.

Miner, W.R. 1982. "Resistances to Treatment" in patients at a modern psychoanalytic training clinic: An exploratory study. Final project, Center for Modern Psychoanalytic Studies. Unpublished.

Reich, W. 1945. *Character-analysis.* New York: Orgone Institute Press.

Weiss, E. 1960. *The structure and dynamics of the human mind.* New York: Grune & Stratton.

Management and Mastery of Resistance (Chapter 7)

Bibring, E. 1954. Psychoanalysis and the dynamic psychotherapies. *Journal of the American Psychoanalytic Association* 2:745–770.

Ekstein, R. 1965. Historical notes concerning psychoanalysis and early language development. *Journal of the American Psychoanalytic Association* 13:717–731.

Glover, E. 1955. *The technique of psycho-analysis,* Chapters IV, V. New York: International Universities Press.

Greenson, R.R. 1965. The problem of working through. In M. Schur (Ed.), *Drives, affects, behavior,* (Vol. 2). New York: International Universities Press.

Morris, J. 1985. *The dream workbook.* Boston, MA: Little Brown.

Nacht, S. 1959. *Psychoanalysis of today.* New York: Grune & Stratton.

Novey, S. 1962. The principle of "working through" in psychoanalysis. *Journal of the American Psychoanalytic Association* 10:658–676.

Narcissistic Transference (Chapter 8)

Abrams, E.K. 1976. The narcissistic transference as a resistance. *Modern Psychoanalysis* 1:218–230.

Bion, W.R. 1955. Language and the schizophrenic. In M. Klein, P. Heimann, & R. Money-Kyrle (Eds.), *New directions in psychoanalysis.* New York: Basic Books.

Ekstein, R., & Friedman, S. 1967. Object constancy and psychotic reconstruction. *Psychoanalytic Study of the Child* 22. New York: International Universities Press.

Glover, E. 1955. *The technique of psycho-analysis* (Chapters VII, VIII). New York: International Universities Press.

Greenacre, P. 1954. The role of transference: Practical considerations in relation to psychoanalytic therapy. *Journal of the American Psychoanalytic Association* 2:671–684.

Orr, D.W. 1954. Transference and countertransference: A historical survey. *Journal of the American Psychoanalytic Association* 2:621–670.

Schecter, D.E. 1968. Identification and individuation. *Journal of the American Psychoanalytic Association* 16:48–80.

Countertransference: Resistance and Therapeutic Leverage (Chapter 9)

Borowitz, E., & Calmas, W.E. (Eds.) 1977–1978. Emotional communication and countertransference in the narcissistic and borderline disorders: A symposium. T. Lidz, J. Masterson, H. Spotnitz, V. Volkan. *Modern Psychoanalysis* 2:149–179.

Epstein, L., & Feiner, A.H. (Eds.) 1979. *Countertransference.* New York: Jason Aronson.

Fleming, J., & Benedek, T. 1966. *Psychoanalytic supervision*. New York: Grune & Stratton.

Fliess, R. 1953. Countertransference and counteridentification. *Journal of the American Psychoanalytic Association* 1:268–284.

Fromm-Reichmann, F. 1950. *Principles of intensive psychotherapy*. Chicago: University of Chicago Press.

Glover, E. 1955. *The technique of psycho-analysis* (Chapters I, VI). New York: International Universities Press.

Grinberg, L. 1962. On a specific aspect of countertransference due to the patient's projective identification. *International Journal of Psycho-Analysis* 43:436–440.

Little, M.I. 1981. *Transference neurosis and transference psychosis*. New York: Jason Aronson.

Masterson, J.F. 1983. *Countertransference and psychotherapeutic technique: Teaching seminars on psychotherapy of the borderline adult*. New York: Brunner/Mazel.

Meadow, P.W., & Clevans, E. 1978. A new approach to psychoanalytic teaching. *Modern Psychoanalysis* 7:185–213.

Meerloo, J.A.M. 1964. *Hidden communion: Studies in the communication theory of telepathy*. New York: Garret Publications.

Nacht, S. 1965. Interference between transference and countertransference. In M. Schur (Ed.), *Drives, affects, behavior* (Vol. 2). New York: International Universities Press.

Roazen, P. 1985. *Helene Deutsch: A psychoanalyst's life*. Garden City, New York: Anchor Press/Doubleday.

Saretsky, T. 1981. *Resolving treatment impasses: The difficult patient*. New York: Human Sciences Press.

Searles, H.F. 1979. *Countertransference and related subjects*. New York: International Universities Press.

Spotnitz, H. 1982. Supervision of psychoanalysts treating borderline patients. Discussant: O. Sternbach. *Modern Psychoanalysis* 7:185–213.

Interventions: Range and Sequence (Chapter 10)

Aull, G., & Strean, H. 1967. The analyst's silence. *Psychoanalytic Forum* 2:72–87.

Eissler, K.R. 1953. Notes upon the emotionality of a schizophrenic patient and its relation to problems of technique. *Psychoanalytic Study of the Child* 8:199–250.

Freud, A. 1965. *Normality and pathology in childhood,* pp. 227–235. New York: International Universities Press.

Grossman, D. 1964. Ego-activating approaches to psychotherapy. *Psychoanalytic Review* 51:401–423.

Hayden, S. 1983. The toxic response in modern psychoanalysis. *Modern Psychoanalysis* 8:3–16.

Lorand, S. 1946. *Technique of psychoanalytic therapy.* New York: International Universities Press.

Love, S. 1979. Maturational interventions with two boys in modern psychoanalytic psychotherapy. *Modern Psychoanalysis* 4:165–182.

Nelson, M.C., Nelson, B., Sherman, M.H., & Strean, H.S. 1968. *Roles and paradigms in psychotherapy.* New York: Grune & Stratton.

Sherman, M.H. 1961–1962. Siding with the resistance in paradigmatic psychotherapy. *Psychoanalytic Review* 48(No. 4):43–59.

Strean, H.S. 1959. The use of the patient as consultant. *Psychoanalytic Review* 46 (No. 2):35–44.

Weeks, G.R., & L'Abate, L.L. 1982. *Paradoxical psychotherapy: Theory and practice with individuals, couples and families.* New York: Brunner/Mazel.

NAME INDEX

316

SUBJECT INDEX